# MOLIÈRE

# MOLIÈRE

## The Theory and Practice of Comedy

ANDREW CALDER

THE ATHLONE PRESS
London & Atlantic Highlands

*First published 1993 by*
THE ATHLONE PRESS
1 Park Drive, London NW11 7SG
and 165 First Avenue,
Atlantic Highlands, NJ 07716


© Andrew Calder 1993
British Library Cataloguing in Publication Data
*A catalogue record for this book is available*
*from the British Library*


ISBN 0 485 11427 5


Library of Congress Cataloguing in Publication Data

Calder, Andrew, 1942–
    Molière: the theory and practice of comedy / Andrew Calder
        p.      cm.
    Includes bibliographical references and index.
    ISBN 0–485–11427–5
    1. Molière. 1622–1673 – Criticism and interpretation. 2. French
drama – 17th century – History and criticism – Theory, etc. 3. French
drama (Comedy) – History and criticism – Theory, etc. I. Title.
    PQ1860.C3    1993
    842'.4 – dc20                                        92–30595
                                                              CIP

*Typeset by*
Datix International Limited, Bungay, Suffolk
Printed and bound in Great Britain by
Bookcraft (Bath) Limited

For Ruth,
Ellen and Barnabas

# Contents

# *Preface*

Oh for a breath of Aristophanes, Rabelais, Voltaire, Cervantes, Fielding,
Molière! These are spirits that, if you know them well, will come when
you do call.

Meredith, 'An Essay on Comedy'

Good comic writers are always fresh and lively company because
they invite us to forget about the timeless and solemn questions
of who we are, where we came from and what should be the
long-term goals of the human race, and to focus instead upon
the glorious absurdities of what we and all around us are getting
up to now in our day-to-day lives. They encourage us to share
with them in seeking out and enjoying the ridiculous in ourselves
and in others. La Rochefoucauld wrote that, when we do know
someone who seems to us to be entirely free from the ridiculous,
we are simply not looking hard enough.

The comic literature of seventeenth-century France – the
plays of Molière, the *Maximes* of La Rochefoucauld, the *Fables*
of La Fontaine and the *Caractères* of La Bruyère – glories in the
limitations and absurdities of human beings. The laughter of
these witty observers of men, however, though always agreeable,
was rarely gratuitous. For them, laughter was the sensible man's
response to the spectacle of life, including – and especially –
one's own part in it. It was axiomatic that good laughter was an
aid to self-knowledge, helping men and women to see themselves
as others saw them; Molière and contemporary comic writers
believed that the shock of sudden laughter could break men free
from the slack habit of seeing themselves as special cases, as
interesting individuals who, when viewed in the right light,
were never – or hardly ever – ridiculous at all.

Molière's world is full of pictures in which we can easily
recognize our own behaviour and the behaviour of our families,
friends and colleagues: pictures of bickering couples, tyrant

husbands, tetchy fathers, would-be-learned wives, mothers and sisters bullying their families and friends with new ideologies, affected aesthetes, pedants, professional men who are quite sure that, without them, the world will cease to turn upon its axis – and many more.

The apparently timeless quality of Molière's comedies, however, can be misleading. We often read, perform and even study his plays as if they were written for a twentieth-century public. As a result, the satirical content of his work is either ignored or seen as peripheral to his achievement.[1] In fact, a moment's reflection will persuade us that Molière wrote his comedies to please and amuse the audiences and the people he knew, and that when he turned to satire, he portrayed behaviour which would be instantly recognizable to the theatre-going public of seventeenth-century France. Molière was famed in his own age for the biting power of his laughter. He himself wrote that though he aimed to portray the follies of mankind in general, his special concern was to highlight the follies of the men and women of his own generation.[2] Rapin wrote in his *Réflexions sur la Poétique d'Aristote* (Paris, 1674) that the ridiculous was the key to Molière's comedies; for John Dennis, too, one of the earliest Englishmen to proclaim Molière's genius, the soul of comedy for Molière was the *ridiculum*.[3] If, then, Molière laughed at human folly in its seventeenth-century forms, we should try to see what these were. Only by doing so can we see how he shaped his comedies, enter into the perspective from which he viewed human nature, and discover what kind of laughter he sought to inspire.

First, however, before turning to satire in the later chapters, I look at the mechanisms of Molière's comedies as a whole. In Chapters 1 to 3 the concepts of character, plot and action, and the nature and purpose of drama in general, are examined in order to see what Molière and his contemporaries expected of a comedy. There was a wealth of theoretical writing on tragedy and comedy available to Molière; Renaissance and seventeenth-century critics had set themselves the task of defining as precisely as possible all the parts of drama.[4] Molière did not allow himself to be constrained by the demands of theorists or the conventions of earlier playwrights, but their work gave him a deeper understanding of his craft.

In Chapters 4 to 8 I discuss the question of what Molière found funny, and why. At a simple level, a child can understand and share Molière's sense of the ridiculous; when we look more closely at his comic perspective, however, the issues become more complex. Molière found ridiculous everything which departed from common sense, and common sense, for the well-educated men and women of Molière's age, was quite unlike the heteroclite assumptions of homespun wisdom which are improperly termed 'common' sense in the twentieth century. I have no wish to paint an idealized picture of seventeenth-century polite society – Molière's portraits in *La Critique de l'École des femmes*, *Le Misanthrope* and *Les Femmes savantes* make it clear that his society contained a normal share of fools, hypocrites, rogues and pedants – but this was an age in which the educated were obsessively interested in defining and practising what they considered to be the right code of social behaviour. Aware of the rich cultural heritage of the Renaissance, polished and often erudite men and women sought to extract from the unwieldy corpus of written texts on wisdom a practical 'honest' code for day-to-day living. The question of what constituted *honnêteté* was a topic for endless discussion, and even those who could not understand the finer points of the arguments, still less translate true *honnêteté* into their own social performance, at least knew the terms and the general context of the debate. Molière's plays reveal his easy mastery of the issues behind this whole question; they reflect the taste, measure, refinement and sound judgement which embodied the highest ideals of *honnêteté*. These qualities could be appreciated only by audiences which, in some degree, shared them; if we are to appreciate his comic portraits, we, too, should share something of Molière's taste and judgement.

Having looked at the classical and Renaissance sources – especially the *Essais* of Montaigne – which helped to shape Molière's understanding of himself and the human condition, I focus in Chapters 9 and 10 on two of the commonest themes in his work: social relationships in general, and family relationships in particular. It is in these domains that we find expressed most clearly Molière's comic vision of a world in which men and women live together in a state of almost perpetual blindness and injustice.

Finally, in Chapters 11 to 15, I look more closely at Molière as satirist. Good satires are shaped by the particular characteristics of the follies or abuses under fire. We need to understand something of scholasticism and seventeenth-century medicine in order to appreciate Molière's portraits of pedants and doctors, and to be aware of the *précieux* movement as we read or watch *Les Précieuses ridicules* and *Les Femmes savantes*. The religious background to *Le Tartuffe* and *Dom Juan*, so remote from today's world, presented issues of burning topicality to Molière and his public; we must, at least in imagination, share their involvement if we are to join with the clear-sighted members of Molière's audiences in 1664 and 1665 in feeling to the full the satirical aptness and power of these plays.

My approach to Molière and his comedies is neither biographical nor chronological. For readers who may wish to remind themselves of the order of composition and performance of his plays, or to situate the plays against the main phases of Molière's life, I have added a brief chronology after the last chapter.

This book is addressed to all who are interested in Molière, in seventeenth-century France, or in comedy; to sixth-formers and undergraduates reading Molière for the first time; to general readers and theatre-goers who wish to know more about one of the world's great comic writers; and to scholars with a special interest in seventeenth-century French theatre who may wish to compare their own findings with mine. In order to make the text accessible to all, passages in French, Latin or Italian are translated into English.[5] Equally, I assume that not all will wish to read every chapter. There is a central thread running through the book for those who wish to follow it, but each chapter is self-contained, and those who prefer to pick and choose, or to read chapters out of order, should be able to make sense of them.

I cannot thank all those who have helped me directly or indirectly to write this book. My most copious supply of helpers has been the successive generations of students of University College London whose intelligent laughter at Molière's comic portraits I have enjoyed sharing. The editors of Molière's plays, the scholars who have worked on them and the historians of ideas who have written on Renaissance and seventeenth-century theories of criticism are acknowledged in the notes and the Bibliography. I have profited, in the earlier stages of my work on Molière, from the friendship and wisdom of the late Frances Yates, D.P. Walker and W.G. Moore. In writing the book, I have often sought the advice of J.S. Cummins, Ruth Calder, Robert McBride and, in particular, M.A. Screech, with whom I read Molière and Rabelais as a student and who showed me by example the richness and variety of the pleasures to be found in the study of literature. Robert McBride and M.A. Screech have also read the typescript; while thanking them for their invaluable advice, I freely absolve them from any of the blame for what follows.

I am also very grateful to the University of London Publications Fund for its financial support.

To conclude on the proper satirical note, remembering that folly begins at home, I leave the last word to Erasmus. From *Praise of Folly*, it is addressed to those 'who court immortal fame by writing books':

> They add, change, remove, lay aside, take up, rephrase, show to their friends, keep for nine years and are never satisfied. And their futile reward, a word of praise from a handful of people, they win at such a cost – so many late nights, such loss of sleep, sweetest of all things, and so much sweat and anguish.[6]

# 1
# *Character*

## 1. Aristotle's *Poetics* and New Comedy

A particularly rich vein of humanist culture, and of special interest to Molière as playwright, was the study of poetics. Literary criticism, as a field of scholarly enquiry and theoretical speculation, passed through an extraordinary period of growth in the century before Molière began to act and to write for the theatre. Classical theories of comedy had been current throughout the Middle Ages, through texts of Donatus and Cicero, the *Ars poetica* of Horace, through commentaries on the comedies of Terence and as an element in the study of rhetoric.[1] The renewal of interest in the theory of comedy was part of the wider re-examination of all literary genres which came with the rediscovery and translation into Latin of Aristotle's *Poetics*; this brief text, not widely disseminated until the translation of Paccius (Alessandro de' Pazzi) published in 1536, was to inspire long, speculative commentaries whose purpose was to explain the whole nature and purpose of literature. The commentaries in turn were widely scrutinized. Rapin, a contemporary of Molière, in his *Réflexions sur la Poétique d'Aristote* (Paris, 1674), listed among the more important commentators Vettori, Maggi, Robortello, Castelvetro, Piccolomini, Beni, Riccoboni, Minturno, Vida, Patrizi and Vossius.

The prestige of the *Poetics* in the eyes of most poets and commentators would be hard to exaggerate. They culled from it not only the laws of tragedy and epic poetry but also the laws of comedy – even though Aristotle's remarks on comedy were few and it was assumed that his intended treatise on comedy had either remained unwritten or, if written, had been lost. The gaps in Aristotle's theory of comedy were filled largely by applying his views on tragedy to comedy.[2] Commentators further enriched their theories by comparing Horace's *Ars poetica* with the *Poetics*, by drawing on Aristotle's remarks on character in his

*Rhetoric*, and by quoting Cicero's views on laughter in *De Oratore*. To illustrate their theories, critics and commentators turned to the comedies of Plautus and Terence.

The consensus of theoretical opinion was that the highest form of comedy was New Comedy. The Old Comedy, represented by Aristophanes, was considered too rough and low in its language and too free in its use of invective against living public figures. New Comedy, associated with Menander and the golden age of Greek comedy, and then with its Roman imitators, Plautus and – above all – Terence, portrayed only invented characters against a background of an ordinary family; its language was polished, its plots were complex and elegantly arranged and its dénouements were surprising, tidy and wholly happy. Middle Comedy, about which critics had little to say, retained some of the polemical features of Old Comedy, while introducing the more complicated plots and humbler characters which were to become the rule in New Comedy.

Molière, well educated, a man of the theatre, counting scholars and men of letters among his friends, could not have remained unaware of this mass of theory and instruction on the functions of character, action, plot and the whole shape and purpose of drama.

## 2. Molière's distrust of theorists

The question of the relevance of the theory of comedy to the practical business of writing and performing comedies was raised by Molière in *La Critique de l'École des femmes* (1663). His portrait of Lysidas, the pedant who watches and appraises comedy strictly through the rules of Aristotle and Horace, would seem to suggest that he had no time for theorists. Speaking of *L'École des femmes*, Lysidas asserts: 'Those who know their Aristotle and Horace see immediately, Madame, that this comedy sins against all the rules of the art.' Through his *porte-parole*, Dorante, Molière ridicules such enslavement to rules. These so-called rules, he points out, are no more than a few common-sense observations on the things which can spoil the pleasure audiences derive from seeing plays; simple common sense, without the help of Aristotle and Horace, can reach the same conclusions any day it chooses. Pleasing the audience is the only rule that cannot be broken. Turning to Aristotle to check whether or not one is right to enjoy a play is like consulting a cookery-book to find out if the sauce one has just tasted is as delicious as it seemed (Sc. 6).

However, if Molière has nothing but contempt for the pedant who used his knowledge of classical and Renaissance poetics to attack his opponents, he showed no disrespect for Aristotle and Horace themselves. Dorante tells Lysidas that *L'École des femmes* 'does not break any of the rules', and adds: 'I have read them, thank God, as well as any man; and I can show you easily that there is perhaps no play more regular than this one.' Though Molière would recognize only one inviolable rule, to please the audience, he takes pleasure in pointing out that in doing so he has also written a play which conforms to the observations on the theatre of Aristotle and Horace. Lysidas is a fool for substituting rules learned by rote for common sense. Molière, however, guided in the writing of his comedy by the authority of common sense, had no quarrel with Aristotle and Horace, whose observations on drama, he considered, were also born of common sense; their theory and his practice, he argued, were in harmony.

Molière stated quite clearly – through Dorante – that he had read the *Poetics* of Aristotle and the *Ars poetica* of Horace. Confirmation that he knew at least some of the commentaries appears in his *Préface* (1660) to *Les Précieuses ridicules*. Listing the steps he might have taken to guarantee the success of his play, if only he had had more time, he says:

> I would have tried to write a beautiful and learned preface; and I am not short of books which would have furnished me with everything erudite there is to be said about tragedy and comedy, about the etymology of both, their origins, their definitions and everything else. (*O.C.*, I, p. 264)

The books which would have provided him with such erudite ammunition were the commentaries on Aristotle's *Poetics*. The implication is that Molière was familiar with the commentators' arguments, but thought it a waste of time to repeat them or add to them.

In another *Préface* (1662) to *Les Fâcheux*, Molière returned to this theme: 'the time will come for me to publish my remarks on the plays I have written, and I do not despair of showing one day that I, too, like a great author, can quote Aristotle and Horace' (*O.C.*, I, p. 483). The tone, again, is ironical, and he adds that he will probably never get round to it. His irony, however, is directed against those authors who believe that quoting from classical authorities guarantees their stature; there is no suggestion that he held the arguments of Aristotle and Horace in contempt. Later, in his *Préface* to *Le Tartuffe*, he was to allude to the trouble Aristotle had taken to formulate the precepts of drama as evidence that comedy had a useful role to play in a healthy society.

It is unlikely that it will ever be clear which, or how many, commentaries Molière read. His own contributions to comic theory, in *La Critique de l'École des femmes*, *L'Impromptu de Versailles*, the *Préface* to *Le Tartuffe* and (if he wrote it) the *Lettre sur l'Imposteur*, are expressed with the directness and authority of a practical man of the theatre. He repeats many of the arguments found in the great commentaries, but always presents them as common-sense observations. On present evidence, it is possible to conclude only that he had a thorough knowledge of the major classical source texts and that he had at least a general acquaintance with the main commentaries, whose contents tended to be repeated from one to another.

If we can only speculate as to how well Molière knew the theoretical writings on New Comedy, we know for certain that he was familiar with its practice in the plays of Plautus and Terence. It is common knowledge that *L'Avare* and *Amphitryon* are adaptations of Plautus's *Aulularia* and *Amphitryo*, while *L'École des maris* and *Les Fourberies de Scapin* owe much to the *Adelphi* and *Phormio* of Terence. Many other comic devices, dialogues, scenes and elements of plots have been traced to the comedies of the Latin playwrights. Molière was as ready to profit from Plautus and Terence and their Italian and Spanish imitators as the Latin playwrights had been to exploit the comedies of Menander and other Greek sources.

The practice of ancient comedy and the theory of classical and Renaissance critics furnish a rich store of material on the way drama functions – on character, plot, action, subject, the ridiculous and the didactic. This material provides the terms and framework within which Molière and his contemporaries thought about the theatre. Theories and sources cannot account for Molière's originality, but they provide an obvious starting point for a modern reader wishing to see how his comedies worked.

## 3. Character: moral and social status

It was generally agreed among theorists of drama that tragedy painted people as better than they are in real life, while comedy painted them as worse. The most important source for this view was Aristotle's remark that, as all poetry is imitation, the poet must of necessity paint men exactly as they are, better than they are, or worse than they are (*Poetics*, II, 1–7).

There was general agreement, too, though Aristotle did not say this, that comedy should portray lower levels of society. Kings, queens and great men, it was felt, did not offer fit targets for ridicule. The natural domain of comedy, as Robortello wrote, is 'low and trifling affairs such as take place in the private actions of people'.[3] This view found support in the practice of Plautus and Terence, who portrayed conflicts within families, the misunderstandings and quarrels of lovers, mistresses, parents and children and, at a lower level still, of slaves, pimps and courtesans. The social boundaries for the world of New Comedy were, in fact, quite wide, ranging from the wealthy landowning brothers Demea and Micio in Terence's *Adelphi*, to rough-tongued slaves such as Plautus's Grumio (*Mostellaria*). Renaissance commentators, however, tended to believe that the types at the bottom of this scale were better suited to comedy. Maggi, for example, lists 'viles, moriones, servos, ancillas, scurras' ('common folk, fools, slaves, slave-girls, buffoons') as the proper characters for comedies (Weinberg, p. 416).

Many of Molière's characters, even in the plays which manifestly do not belong to the genre of New Comedy but to the more popular tradition of the medieval French farce, fall well within the social and moral categories recommended by the commentators. His schemers, young lovers and peevish fathers in such plays as *L'Étourdi*, *Dépit amoureux* and *Les Fourberies de Scapin* are traceable directly to the world of Plautus and Terence: the quick-thinking and inexhaustibly inventive *valets*, Mascarille and Scapin, are the descendants of such slaves as Plautus's Tranio (*Mostellaria*) and Palaestrio (*Miles gloriosus*) and Terence's

Phormio (in the play of that name) and Davos (*Andria*). The fathers and sons in these plays of Molière have the same comic functions as those of the Latin playwrights: the fathers are there to be deceived, outwitted, cajoled and appeased, while their love-struck sons, given to sudden bouts of despair, soon yield to surges of new hope, as their *valets* think up new stratagems to save them and their mistresses from all manner of catastrophes.

The low-born characters of popular French farce, churlish and rough-tongued men such as *le Barbouillé* and Gorgibus, the coquettes, Angélique, Cathos and Magdelon, in *La Jalousie du Barbouillé* and *Les Précieuses ridicules*, the Sganarelles of *Le Médecin volant*, *Sganarelle ou le Cocu imaginaire*, *L'École des maris*, *Le Mariage forcé*, *Dom Juan*, *L'Amour médecin* and *Le Médecin malgré lui* are all both socially low and markedly morally inferior. Other low characters crop up throughout Molière's career: the rich and cuckolded peasant in *George Dandin*, the ludicrous and unpolished provincial would-be gentleman in *Monsieur de Pourceaugnac*, the underbred social climber of *Le Bourgeois Gentilhomme* and the bowels-obsessed hypochondriac of his last play, *Le Malade imaginaire*.

Another group of Molière's characters fits this pattern less well. In Ariste ( *L'École des maris*), so much more urbane than his rough-hewn brother, Sganarelle, in Chrysalde (*L'École des femmes*), Clèante and Elmire (*Le Tartuffe*), Philinte and Éliante (*Le Misanthrope*), Ariste, Clitandre and Henriette (*Les Femmes savantes*) and Béralde (*Le Malade imaginaire*), Molière presents us with a group of characters who are socially well placed, fashionable and polished Parisians, many of them moving in court circles, and none of them in the least morally inferior.

Another, more remarkable group, Arnolphe (*L'École des femmes*), Orgon (*Le Tartuffe*), Alceste (*Le Misanthrope*) and Philaminte (*Les Femmes savantes*), though the main fools in the plays in which they appear, are just as well placed socially and, though morally flawed, are not without some of the qualities that go to make an *honnête homme* or an *honnête femme*. In one play, *Le Misanthrope*, all the main characters belong to court circles; in another, *Dom Juan*, the central figure is a high-born aristocrat. Rapin was struck by Molière's originality in this domain; in 1674 he observed that Molière had portrayed the ridiculous at much higher social levels than his predecessors: 'others have played in their comedies only life in the middle and lower orders, while Molière has played all Paris and the court' (*Réflexions*, p. 218).

However, if these characters do not fit readily into the comic categories prescribed by the commentators, they do conform for the most part to Aristotle's observation that the comic poet portrays his characters as worse than they are in real life. Aristotle had advised tragic poets to follow the example of good portrait-painters who, while painting a true likeness, present their subjects in the best light, emphasizing their good points and making them better than they are (*Poetics*, XV, 11-12). The comic poet follows precisely the opposite process. His subjects may share the same defects as tragic heroes, but in their case the painter portrays the whole man through the belittling perspective of his flaws.

Molière's respectable fools, Arnolphe, Orgon, Alceste and Philaminte, his less attractive but equally well-born fools, Arsinoé and Oronte, his foppish or evil aristocrats, the *marquis* and Dom Juan, are in varying degrees incarnations and exaggerations of human folly and vice. The comic perspective makes them more flawed, more ludicrous than people sharing their foibles or vices might appear in real life. They fit easily into the Aristotelian definition of a comic character.

Even Molière's reasonable characters who are both well-born and free from obvious flaws can be seen as belonging to a comic world in which human affairs are dominated by the ludicrous. It is part of their reasonableness that they recognize this and are flexible enough to compromise with fools and villains and even, at times, to adopt consciously and in a harmless form the very vices and follies which make Molière's fools ludicrous. Chrysalde, for example, is driven by Arnolphe's manic determination never to be cuckolded into the mildly absurd role of detailing some of the pleasures that a level-headed cuckold can derive from his state (*L'École des femmes*, IV, 8). Elmire is forced by circumstances to play the role of seductress and wrestle with Tartuffe's impatient lust in an effort to restore her husband to sense and sanity (*Le Tartuffe*, IV, 5). We see Philinte, in *Le Misanthrope*, as he manfully strives to keep the social wheels turning, scolded by his friend Alceste, obliged to play the hypocrite in praising Oronte's mediocre sonnet and constrained

by social convention to listen with every appearance of patience
to the malicious gossip of Célimène and the *marquis* (I, 1 and 2;
II, 4). Not even his love for Éliante can rescue Philinte from his
unheroic role: his modest but realistic proposal that Éliante
might consider turning to him if ever she should despair of
Alceste is soon drowned in the roar of his angry, injured rival
asking Éliante to marry him to avenge the wrongs he has
suffered at the hands of Célimène (IV, 1 and 2). Clitandre, in *Les
Femmes savantes*, is another unheroic but realistic lover who,
finding the older sister too cold, turns to the more responsive
younger one; the abandoned Armande is quick to point out that
he is breaking the code of all true lovers.

The difference between the comic and tragic perspectives is
very clear when we look at these blameless figures. Though they
are more innocent than most tragic heroes and heroines, they are
portrayed in a context which strips them of all grandeur. A
tragic heroine would not have to ward off the lustful attentions
of a low-born hypocrite, as Elmire does; a Don Rodrigue could
not be expected to accept second place in the affections of his
mistress with the calm resignation of Philinte; nor could we
imagine him following Clitandre in transferring his frustrated
passion from an older to a younger sister.

Molière's reasonable characters are unpretentious, practical
people holding on to their sanity in a mad world. For all their
good qualities, they are seen to be largely ineffectual in their
struggle against folly and vice. While fools and villains wreak
havoc, the sensible people are usually obliged to compromise or
retreat in the face of vice and folly. They rarely influence events:
the happy endings to the plays are usually the consequence of
providential intervention rather than the result of human effort.
Their ambitions are modest; they ask nothing more than that, in
their dealings with one another, friends and members of families
should behave considerately and sensibly.

Even in the case of his best characters (morally speaking), the
perspective through which Molière invites us to view them is
essentially comic.

4. Comic types and decorum

As most of Aristotle's remarks on characters concerned

tragedy, Renaissance theorists simply adapted them and applied them to the characters of comedy. One of his observations concerned decorum: 'characters should be appropriate' (*Poetics*, XV, 4). The comic poet should be able to assign the proper behaviour to each of his characters, according to age, sex, disposition, nationality, station, and so on. Further authority for this view was found in the other great source-book of poetic theory, Horace's *Ars poetica*. Audiences can take pleasure in a play only if they find the characters on stage convincing and their actions plausible. Horace advises the playwright to 'note the manners of each age, and give a befitting tone to shifting natures and their years' (ll. 156–7).

A second element essential to the observance of decorum in character portrayal is the necessity of choosing those emotions and passions which are suited to comic characters as opposed to the graver emotions and passions suited to tragic characters. Quintilian, the great Roman rhetorician, had drawn a distinction between these two classes of emotions:

> One is called *pathos* by the Greeks and is rightly and correctly expressed in Latin by *adfectus* (emotion); the other is called *ēthos*, a word for which in my opinion Latin has no equivalent; it is however rendered by *mores* (morals), and consequently the branch of philosophy known as *ethics* is styled *moral* philosophy by us.[4]

The stronger emotions belong to the domain of *pathos* and the gentler to the domain of *ethos*. Quintilian said:

> The *pathos* of the Greeks, which we correctly translate by *adfectus*, is different, and I cannot better indicate the nature of the difference than by saying that *ethos* rather resembles comedy and *pathos* tragedy.
>
> (Herrick, p. 134)

The English critic and playwright John Dennis was later to take up and develop this theme from Quintilian in an essay addressed to George Granville, in 1702. He used the terms 'passion' and 'humour' in place of Quintilian's '*pathos*' and '*ethos*'. Having argued that humour is the proper domain of the comic poet, he goes on to explain what he means by the term:

> For to every passion there is a humour which answers to it, which humour is nothing but a less degree of that passion. As for example,

anger is a passion, peevishness and moroseness are humours, joy
when it is great is a passion, jollity and gayety perhaps may be said
to be humours, so that if any man asks for a description of humour,
I answer that 'tis the expression of some subordinate passion.[5]

The human weaknesses which inspire tragedy and comedy are
the same; the differences are of degree and of perspective. The
irascibility, querulousness, petulance, self–pity, avarice, vanity
and strutting boastfulness common in Molière's fools are comic
versions of tragic anger, jealousy and hubris; they are lesser
passions belonging to the domain of *ethos*. Molière sometimes
came close to the borderline between what Dennis called passions
and humours, but took care always to keep his portraits on the
comic side of the dividing line. Alceste, a man of some stature,
enslaved by love and driven to jealous rage by a charming but
coquettish society beauty, can easily be cast as an unfortunate
victim of high passion and female treachery. However, Molière
drew attention to the humorous origins of Alceste's irrational
behaviour in one of his proposed titles for the play: *L'Atrabilaire
amoureux*, or *The Bilious Lover* (*O.C.*, II, p. 125). Alceste, removed
from the context of the play, is certainly no more of a fool than
many a tragic figure – such as King Lear – but, merely by placing
him in a comic context, Molière invites his audiences to see his folly
as belonging to the comic domain rather than the tragic.

5. Comic types and moral philosophy

For Quintilian, then, the arts of understanding and portraying
character belonged to the domain of ethics, or moral philosophy:
the study of right and wrong, of the rules of human conduct.
Every schoolboy, in the course of his training in rhetoric and
moral philosophy, was expected to study character. There were
scholastic exercises – *ethologiae* – in which schoolboys portrayed
such types as 'rustics, misers, cowards and superstitious persons'.
Declaimers, according to Quintilian, 'should consider what best
suits each character':

> As a rule they impersonate sons, parents, rich men, old men, gentle
> or harsh of temper, misers, superstitious persons, cowards, and
> mockers, so that hardly even comic actors have to assume more
> numerous roles in their performances on the stage than these in their
> declamations. (Herrick, p. 133)

Herrick has shown that Quintilian and, after him, Renaissance rhetoricians drew on Terence as the major source of illustrations for *ethopoeia* (the acting out of characters) and *prosopopoeia* (impersonation of characters).

It is easy to grasp how a knowledge of moral philosophy came to be seen as essential to the art of creating comic characters for the stage. As Dennis wrote, 'for the succeeding in comedy, there is required a generous education, which comprehends: 1. Learning. 2. A knowledge of mankind and the world' (I, p. 290). The playwright must know the nature of man in general, the variety of dispositions among particular men and the various possible changes of humour which accompany the different ages of man. This is the demand Horace made in a famous passage in his *Ars poetica*, where he calls upon playwrights to study the four ages of man:

> The child, who by now can utter words and set firm step upon the ground, delights to play with his mates, flies into a passion and as lightly puts it aside, and changes every hour. The beardless youth, freed at last from his tutor, finds joy in horses and hounds and the grass of the sunny Campus, soft as wax for moulding to evil, peevish with his counsellors, slow to make needful provision, lavish of money, spirited, of strong desires, but swift to change his fancies. With altered aims, the age and spirit of the man seeks wealth and friends, becomes a slave to ambition, and is fearful of having done what soon it will be eager to change. Many ills encompass an old man, whether because he seeks gain, and then miserably holds aloof from his store and fears to use it, or because, in all that he does, he lacks fire and courage, is dilatory and slow to form hopes, is sluggish and greedy of a longer life, peevish, surly, given to praising the days he spent as a boy, and to reproving and condemning the young. Many blessings do the advancing years bring with them; many, as they retire, they take away. So, lest haply we assign a youth the part of age, or a boy that of manhood, we shall ever linger over traits that are joined and fitted to the age. (ll. 158–78)

The student of *decorum* in character would have turned, too, to Aristotle's *Rhetoric* (II, 12–17), where the qualities and behaviour appropriate in turn to youth, old age, maturity, the nobly born, the rich and the powerful are listed.

It is not enough, however, to have a general grasp of *decorum*. The playwright must, above all, have a sound knowledge of the accepted sources of moral wisdom. Horace wrote:

Of good writing the source and fount is wisdom. Your matter the
Socratic pages can set forth, and when matter is in hand words will
not be loath to follow. He who has learned what he owes his
country and his friends, what love is due a parent, a brother, and a
guest, what is imposed on senator and judge, what is the function of
a general sent to war, he surely knows how to give each character
his fitting part. (ll. 309–16)

This advice is applicable equally to tragic and to comic poets.
Both must know how different characters might behave in
different situations. The task of the comic poet seeking to
understand and portray some of the infinite variations in the
duties and actions of ordinary people is certainly no easier than
the task of the tragic poet who must understand the duties and
actions of senators, judges and kings. Horace refers his writer to
the dialogues of Socrates as a sound source of wisdom; in
Molière's time, the most obvious sources of moral wisdom
would have been Aristotle, Cicero, Seneca and, in more recent
times, Erasmus, Montaigne and Charron.[6]

## 6. Humours

Most comic theorists, again following Aristotle, agreed that all
comic characters displayed some defect which, without being so
serious as to inflict pain, was prominent enough to make them
laughable. Aristotle wrote:

> the laughable is a species of the base or ugly. It consists in some
> blunder or ugliness that does not cause pain or disaster, an obvious
> example being the comic mask which is ugly and distorted but not
> painful. (*Poetics*, V, 1–2)

In Renaissance and seventeenth-century comedy the defect is
usually seen as being 'humorous' in origin: the individual temperament is regulated by the balance of the four humours,
sanguine, choleric, phlegmatic and melancholic, and any excessive imbalance in the humours was thought likely to result in
unbalanced reasoning and behaviour. Ben Jonson, in *Every Man
Out of His Humour*, explains how the humours came to be
applied 'by metaphor' to the human disposition in general:

> we do conclude
> That whatsoe'er hath fluxure and humidity,

As wanting power to contain itself,
Is humour. So in every human body,
The choler, melancholy, phlegm, and blood,
By reason that they flow continually
In some one part, and are not continent,
Receive the name of humours. Now thus far
It may, by metaphor, apply itself
Unto the general disposition:
As when some one peculiar quality
Doth so possess a man, that it doth draw
All his affects, his spirits, and his powers,
In their confluxions, all to run one way,
This may be truly said to be a humour.

Jonson's analysis fits the behaviour and make-up of Molière's monomaniacal characters: the melancholic, atrabilious misanthropy of Alceste (*Le Misanthrope*), the melancholic hypochondria of Argan (*Le Malade imaginaire*) and the bilious irascibility of the jealous Arnolphe (*L'École des femmes*) all act as central qualities around which the feelings, reasoning and behaviour of each of these characters revolve.

## 7. Consistency and poetic truth

For Aristotle, it was not enough that characters in drama should be given qualities appropriate to their condition; they should also be consistent. He adds: 'Even if the original be inconsistent and offers such a character to the poet for representation, still he must be consistently inconsistent' (XV, 6). Horace insists on the same point: 'if you boldly fashion a fresh character, have it kept to the end even as it came forth at the first, and have it self-consistent' (ll. 125–27).

This emphasis upon consistency should be seen in the context of Aristotle's belief that the function of the poet, tragic, comic or epic, is to portray general truth. He argues that the real difference between a historian and a poet is 'that one tells what happened and the other what might happen'.

> For this reason poetry is something more scientific and serious than history, because poetry tends to give general truths while history gives particular facts.
>
> By a 'general truth' I mean the sort of thing that a certain type of

man will do or say either probably or necessarily. . . . In the case of comedy this has now become obvious, for comedians construct their plots out of probable incidents and then put in any names that occur to them. They do not, like the iambic satirists, write about individuals. (IX, 3–5)

Aristotle's argument is that the particular facts of history and everyday life can often be improbable and arbitrary, whereas the truth of poetry must be probable or inevitable.

If the poet is to portray general truths about human nature through drama, his characters must not mirror the confusing, volatile moods and constantly changing faces and preoccupations of the individual; such multifaceted characters would confuse the action of the plays. The comic poet must choose a dominant trait of character and build a coherent stage figure around it so as to make him a hyperbolic expression of that trait. The word 'character', in Greek, means 'stamp', and at every appearance the particular stamp of each character should be in evidence. A character bearing a particular stamp is inevitably a type. The titles of Molière's plays reflect this: *Le Misanthrope*, *L'Avare*, *Le Bourgeois Gentilhomme* are all types; even *Le Tartuffe* and *George Dandin*, though proper names, are names which have come to designate types. Characters should be clear, consistent, easily identified and even predictable:

> In character-drawing just as much as in the arrangement of the incidents one should always seek what is inevitable or probable, so as to make it inevitable or probable that such and such a person should say or do such and such; and inevitable or probable that one thing should follow another. (*Poetics*, XV, 10)

The artist selects and invents incidents and characters in such a way as to offer a coherent, poetic, and therefore, Aristotle argues, true image of life. Each type is the embodiment of certain qualities, attitudes and humours, of a particular way of seeing, understanding and responding to events and to other people, of a particular way of reasoning. A drama follows the interaction between types and, therefore, between different dispositions and values, different notions of good and evil, sense and folly. If a character loses his or her consistency, they lose their representative function, and the action and argument of the play break down.

As John Dennis wrote: 'Characters in comedy, like the several parts in musick, make up the consort of the play, and as soon as one character says anything which does not belong to it, there is a string which is out of tune, and the harmony of the whole is destroyed' (I, p. 283). One of the distinctive features of Molière's plays is this sense of inner harmony and rhythm, an irresistible, continuous, ordered motion, which follows encounters between different characters through to a carefully prepared conclusion. *Le Misanthrope*, with its many distinctive voices, heard in a well-linked sequence of different combinations, is perhaps Molière's finest piece of ordered composition.

## 8. Making character visible

I have quoted Quintilian's remark that declaimers had to learn almost as many roles as comic actors. To do this they practised the rhetorical exercise of *ethopoeia* through which students learned how to make visible through gesture, facial expression and tone of voice the inner qualities of whatever character they wished to imitate. This was precisely the skill required of the comic actor who had to exhibit in his outward appearance the particular moral stamp or character given to him by the comic poet.

Molière, playwright, leading actor and director, invented his characters, perfected the arts of movement and expression which permitted him to make inner character visible in outward appearance, and taught these skills to his troupe.

In *L'Impromptu de Versailles* (1663) he portrays himself and his actors at work creating their roles. Molière first gives incisive character sketches of each role so that the actors will have a clear understanding of the parts they have to play, and then offers some suggestions as to how they should look, move or speak in order to represent them: Du Croisy, for example, should capture the general air of the pedant, his 'sententious tone of voice and that exactness in pronunciation which emphasizes each syllable and does not omit a single letter of the strictest orthography'; Mlle Béjart should keep the character of the prude constantly before her eyes so that her face might slip readily into the distorted expressions of hypocrisy (Sc. 1); the *marquis* should comb their wigs and whistle a little tune through their teeth; their

exaggerated gestures and affected voices should reveal their
inner emptiness (Sc. 3).

Molière, in *L'Impromptu*, is heir to an ancient tradition of
rhetorical training in matching gesture and facial expression
with character. At the same time his emphasis was quite modern;
he was encouraging in his troupe the perfecting of the miming
skills, the fluency of gesture and physiognomical mobility of the
*Commedia dell'arte* who were playing to Paris audiences with
great success when he returned to the city.

This ability to make the invisible visible, to turn abstract
clashes of ideas and often complex moral problems into tangible,
immediately recognizable living situations, is at the heart of
Molière's achievement. The theme will recur like a leitmotiv as I
look at different aspects of his work throughout this book.

## 9. Satirical functions of character

Characters in New Comedy have only general characteristics.
Molière's characters have both universal and particular characteristics: they represent both timeless human types and types belonging to his own age. 'It is the business of comedy', Molière wrote
in *L'Impromptu de Versailles*, 'to present a general picture of all
the defects of men, and especially of the men of our own age'
(Sc. 4). In this respect, Molière departs from the traditions of
New Comedy and reintroduces an element from Old Comedy,
the practice of mocking recognizable contemporary figures. His
use of satire places him also in the tradition of Lucian and
Juvenal and, more especially, in the tradition of France's own
great satirist and comic genius, Rabelais.

Molière's blend of satire with more general comedy varies
considerably from play to play and from one character to
another within each individual play. His comic portraits of
tyrant figures, for example, are largely timeless. In the cases of
Sganarelle (*L'École des maris*), Arnolphe and Alceste, however,
Molière combines general mockery of tyranny with particular
mockery of certain wrong-headed seventeenth-century attitudes
to women, marriage, education and society; in these plays,
particularly in *L'École des femmes* and *Le Misanthrope*, the balance
between the universal and the particular is even; Arnolphe and
Alceste, the members of the audience feel, could easily be real

individuals, who might turn up in their own circles. In the case of Philaminte, in *Les Femmes savantes*, the satirical element, mockery of a kind of pretentious and empty learning particularly widespread among the women of seventeenth-century French *salons*, is dominant; the audience is more interested in Philaminte's misuse of learning than in her habit of bullying her husband. Molière's precious women, his religious hypocrite, Tartuffe, the lawless aristocrat, Dom Juan, the two pedants, Trissotin and Vadius, are all very pointed satirical portraits taken from Molière's own time and milieu; all of them share the usual timeless faults of vanity, hypocrisy and dishonesty, but it is the particular seventeenth-century forms these vices take which provide the comedy and confer upon each of them a strongly individual character. Molière's portraits of pedants and doctors in general, on the other hand, would have appeared almost timeless to contemporaries, as audiences had laughed at such figures for centuries. Yet even with types as ageless as these, Molière sharpened the focus of his satire by introducing elements which had special relevance to his own time.

It is possible to enjoy Molière's comedies by closing one's eyes to the particular follies satirized in each of his portraits and appreciating only the universal qualities. However, we can understand the plays and share his laughter much more fully if we take the trouble to replace his comedies in their period and find out as precisely as possible what he was laughing at.

# 2
# Plot and Action I: The Plots of New Comedy

## 1. Unity of action

Using 'plot' in the sense of 'the arrangement of the incidents', Aristotle argues that the plot is the most important element in drama, even more important than character:

> The most important of these [the constituent parts of drama] is the arrangement of the incidents, for tragedy is not a representation of men but of a piece of action, of life, of happiness and unhappiness, which come under the head of action, and the end aimed at is the representation not of qualities of character but of some action; and while character makes men what they are, it is their actions and experiences that make them happy or the opposite. They do not therefore act to represent character, but character-study is included for the sake of the action. (*Poetics*, VI, 12–13)

He also argues that if plot, in the sense of action, is the most important part of drama, the most important requirement of plot is that it should have unity (VII, 1–7). Robortello, like other theorists of comedy, did not hesitate to apply Aristotle's definition of action in tragedy to comedy. He wrote in his treatise on comedy: 'All the parts of the plot, indeed, ought to be so joined together that no part can be taken away or transplanted without ruining or disjoining the whole plot' (Lauter, p. 54).

## 2. The plots of New Comedy

Aristotle's definition of the plot is rather bare. Renaissance theorists turned to Plautus and Terence for more detailed examples of how the ideal comic plot should function. In general, they concluded that a comedy should begin with problems on every side, be rich in complications, reversals, misunderstandings, recognitions and surprises, and end with an astonishing discovery which removes all obstacles to universal happiness. This happy ending, with a marriage, feasting and rejoicing, is crucial to the genre of New Comedy. Impressed by the number of sudden changes of fortune and miraculous coincidences in the plays of Plautus and Terence, Renaissance theorists tended to gauge the quality of comic plots by their capacity to surprise. Minturno wrote:

> it is typical of the comic poet to give a pleasing and gay ending to his fable, which would not be possible unless he were able to induce surprise; things happening outside of our expectation are considered surprising. I do not know how the plots whose ending is not such can amuse anyone.[1]

Maggi goes further and asserts that wonder, *admiratio*, is inspired at every comic moment in the play: 'It must be remembered that laughter is dependent on wonder. Accordingly, in ridiculous things wonder cannot be separated from laughter.'[2]

When the Aristotelian call for unity of action in drama and the theorists' expectation that plots will be rich in surprises are conflated, they make impossible demands of the comic poet. To comply with the Aristotelian view, every incident in the development of a comedy should be logical, inevitable and therefore, in some degree, expected, while the example of New Comedy should prompt the comic poet to fill his plots with surprises. As Goldoni was to complain two hundred years after Robortello's treatise, the theatre-going public of his day habitually made such demands of comedy: 'Our Italians demand . . . that the plot be fairly rich in surprises and novelties. . . . They want an unexpected ending, yet originating from the development of the play itself.'[3]

Plautus, Terence and Molière combined elements of surprise and continuity in their plots in quite different ways.


## 3. Plautine plots

Plautus and Terence wrote comedies for Roman audiences of the third and second centuries BC. Performed on public holidays, their plays were part of a whole range of games and entertainments devised to amuse crowds enjoying freedom from the routine and hard work of their normal lives. The plays of

Plautus, in particular, reflect the robust holiday mood of a mixed crowd determined to have a good time. His characters – fathers, sons, mistresses, slaves, courtesans, slave-dealers, and so on – are vociferous, articulate and gifted talkers who, in the most colourful and varied rhetoric, quarrel, abuse and threaten one another or deliver witty tirades rich in popular wisdom on such topics as women, love, old age and avarice. Each scene is in itself a virtuoso stage entertainment and, together, the scenes lead in a loosely-linked sequence, but with immense verve, to a dénouement in which lovers are united, fathers forgive their sons, and a slave is given his freedom. Such is the power of the prevailing good humour in Plautus's plays that even the villains are drawn into the celebration. The thieving, lying pimp and slave-dealer Labrax, the cause of all the unhappiness in *Rudens*, is absolved in the closing scene and his dishonestly acquired wealth, lost in a shipwreck, is restored to him.

The primary function of character in Plautus's plays is not to shape plot; a particular character does not provide a point of view which will be argued consistently and coherently through-out the play, giving unity and shape to the action. Character influences action only in the broad sense that fathers consistently behave like fathers, sons like sons and slaves like slaves; other characteristics are invented to give variety and verve to the comedy. Even those dominant traits of character which give their colouring to the whole play barely influence the develop-ment of the plot. The plot of *Miles gloriosus* would function just as effectively if Pyrgopolynices were just a rich and selfish old man and not a braggart-soldier; his boastfulness has no function other than to provoke laughter. The miserliness of Euclio in *Aulularia* is incidental to the main plot until the closing scene, when he recovers from his miserliness and gives his pot of gold as a dowry to his daughter.

Plautus's comedies are full of reminders of the hardships and vices of the real world, of unjust masters and dishonest slaves, of penniless and self-willed children with avaricious and short-tem-pered fathers, of villains and courtesans who will turn to any-thing for gain. Yet folly and vice, like character, enrich the action of his comedies without dictating the course of events. Inside the world of the play, the rules of real life are relaxed, evil loses its sting, suffering and bondage lose their bite and characters are freed from the consequences of their actions. Vice and folly have no power over a world dominated by happiness. Beautiful and compliant young women, handsome, love-struck young men and wily but loyal slaves create such a tide of exuberant humanity that the old, the mean-minded and the wicked are either swept aside by it or, more often, caught up in it so that they become more human themselves. For all the dangers that lurk in the background of Plautus's plays, the world he creates is essentially an eldorado, securely ruled by love, youth and smiling Providence.

In the comedies of Plautus, the plot has two functions: first, it must provide enough trouble, conflict, scheming and surprises to see us through the full length of the play; and secondly, it must produce an unexpected – almost miraculous – dénouement which removes all remaining obstacles to universal happiness. Aristotle's view of plot as a marrying of character and incident into a single and coherent action from which no element might be removed without destroying the whole is simply not relevant to the plays of Plautus.

## 4. Terentian plots

In Terence's comedies plot is kept under tighter control, characters are more consistent and dialogue is more restrained; his comedies have much greater unity and continuity. He exploits his extremely complex plots to the full, extracting from them a rich yield of dramatic encounters. His characters, victims of misunderstandings which result largely from the plot, argue their cases and explain their grievances eloquently, with humanity and, so far as their partial knowledge of events permits, with reason.

Perhaps the most striking example of his measured and inventive exploitation of plot is to be found in *Hecyra*. In itself, the plot of *Hecyra* is even more preposterous than most others in New Comedy. Pamphilus has married Philumena, the girl next door, without knowing that she was the girl whom he had earlier raped, after a bout of excessive drinking, and from whom he had stolen a ring. Once married, he discovers that she is pregnant, believes the child cannot be his and, though he has grown to love his new wife tenderly, decides he must repudiate her. Meanwhile Philumena, ashamed of her pregnant state, has left her mother-in-law's house and returned to the house of her own mother in the hope of keeping her pregnancy secret. Philumena's parents-in-law and her father are all unaware of her pregnancy and, in consequence, are puzzled and upset by her departure from the house of her husband's family.

Terence makes remarkably effective use of this improbable plot. Each member of the two families misinterprets the behaviour of the others because of his or her incomplete knowledge of the facts. Each is deeply hurt, angered or puzzled. The portrait of the mother-in-law, Sostrata, wrongly accused by her husband of driving her daughter-in-law out of the house and prepared to abandon her own home in order to save her son's marriage, is particularly touching. All characters express their fervent hopes that the young couple will be reconciled and the two families able to live together in mutual esteem and affection. All, even the son whose wild youth has now given way to mature and considerate gentleness, behave so pleasantly that they deserve to be happy. The audience, if it has followed the dialogue sympathetically and attentively, is longing for a happy outcome. When, finally, the ring which proves that Pamphilus is the father of his wife's child is produced, there is an immense feeling of relief, a sense that everyone's frustrated goodwill can melt into love and harmony. The dénouement is no mere convention but the climax of the play, a perfectly timed explosion of joy.

The source of the unity and continuity of action in *Hecyra* is to be found in the smooth handling of the plot. As in the plays of Plautus, the action does not grow out of character, still less out of a portrait of human folly. Unlike Plautus, however, Terence took great care to make his plots neat and orderly. In his comedies, action grows from the careful arrangement of a sequence of chance circumstances. Character has an important part to play; the main purpose for which Terence uses the tricks of fortune is to reveal character; it is in response to the external accidents of plot that each figure confides his or her feelings. However, events themselves are not determined by character; left to themselves, without the intervention of mischance, the two families in *Hecyra* would be model households; the moment their luck turns, and circumstances permit them to behave normally, this is precisely the happy state to which they return.

In spite of their weaknesses and, at times, because of them, we find Terence's characters deeply human and easy to forgive; old and young, slaves and courtesans are charming, often urbane and fundamentally decent; even his fools, like Thraso in *Eunuchus*, are redeemable. Chaerea's response to his family and those around him towards the end of *Eunuchus* could be extended to embrace the whole company of Terence's characters:

> Where shall I begin? Who deserves most praise? Parmeno who gave me the idea, or myself who dared to carry it out? Or should it be Fortune who guided me and brought so many vital matters to a happy conclusion in a single day? Or my father for his kindness and good humour? All I pray is that heaven's blessing will continue![4]

It is in the plays of Terence that the conventional plots and dénouements of New Comedy fit most comfortably. The plot performs the vital function of sowing conflict between people who are too good-natured and reasonable to quarrel seriously under ordinary circumstances, while the dénouement serves to remove the source of the conflict and restore the characters to the harmony and good fortune that their good-heartedness so manifestly deserves. His dénouements answer perfectly to Aristotle's requirement that the end of the play should be the natural and logical consequence of all that has gone before. His plots and surprises are intimately bound up with the main actions of his plays.

Terence's formula works well in his hands. As a general formula for comedy, however, it poses two considerable problems. In *Hecyra*, there is much to move the emotions and give pleasure, but nothing to inspire laughter. No one deserves to be mocked. The lack of visual humour in this elegant and controlled comedy explains, perhaps, why the first two performances of the play failed to keep the audience's attention and had to be abandoned. The second problem, intimately connected with the first, is that no one who is evil or even profoundly unattractive can be accommodated on the Terentian stage; his unreservedly happy dénouements would not fit the main action if some of the characters taking part in it were too obviously deserving of blame.

## 5. Molière and New Comedy

Molière's plots fall broadly within the conventions of New Comedy; he most often portrays young lovers overcoming a series of obstacles and then, with the help of timely providential intervention, marrying happily at the end of the play.

At times, he follows Terence in presenting an action which is tied to the mechanical unfolding of a plot full of surprises. *Les Fourberies de Scapin* (1671) – based on Terence's *Phormio* – a play with a complex, quick-moving and elegant plot, whose characters are wholly conventional, belongs to this category. His early play, *L'Étourdi*, probably performed first in Lyons in 1655, whose plot is borrowed largely from the Italian play *L'Inavvertito* by Beltrame, is squarely in the tradition of New Comedy: the lovesick young, their tight-fisted parents and a *valet* who is a master-schemer are involved in a circular plot in which a single mechanism is repeated with variations in the course of the five acts; ten times we witness the scatterbrained young Lélie frustrating the different schemes dreamt up by Mascarille to raise the money necessary to buy the freedom of his adored slave-girl Célie.[5] Molière's *Amphitryon* (1668), adapted from Plautus's play of the same name, exploits the comedy that arises from a rich confusion of identities. The action of *Dépit amoureux* (1658) is inseparable from the intrigue; a double plot which includes such complications as the substitution at birth of a boy for a girl and the bringing-up of a girl disguised as a boy is designed to astonish the audience at every turn.

In these plays, Molière appears to concur with the theorists' view – expressed most emphatically by Maggi – that surprise is the major weapon of the comic poet. The spectators have the double pleasure of watching the surprise acted out by the figures on stage and of being surprised themselves. In *Dépit amoureux*, Molière clearly expected his audience to share Valère's amazement when he discovers that the man he is about to fight in a duel is really the woman he loves: 'I feel myself seized at once by wonder, love and joy' (ll. 1764–5).

For modern audiences, at least, the technique has limited success. In *L'Étourdi*, the cumulative effect of the complications which follow from Mascarille's inventiveness and his master's slow-wittedness is to render the main action rather mechanical and dull. In *Dépit amoureux*, the plot is so complicated and the surprises are so laboured that the play, in spite of its many good comic moments, sinks under their weight. Only when he returned to the formula of New Comedy late in his career, in *Les Fourberies de Scapin*, did Molière achieve the elegance, speed and charm which the genre demanded.

The conventions of New Comedy plots were never to be abandoned completely by Molière, but in most of his major plays the pleasures of complexity, of confused identity and surprise, were to be replaced by pleasures of a different kind.

# 3
# *Plot and Action II: Comic Fate*

## 1. Plot, subject and character

The feature of the typical plot of New Comedy which survives most obviously in Molière's major comedies is the dénouement – the sudden, miraculous turn of events which makes it possible for the plays to end in happiness. In *L'École des femmes* (1662) and *L'Avare* (1668) especially, where long-lost relatives appear after long years of travel just in time to solve all remaining problems before the twenty-four hours allotted to the action elapse, the dénouements appear to be completely traditional. If we look at the way plot functions in the earlier acts of these two plays, however, we see Molière using his plots to quite different ends from Plautus and Terence. In such plays as Terence's *Hecyra* and Molière's own most accomplished play in the genre of New Comedy, *Les Fourberies de Scapin*, the terms plot and action are interchangeable: the rhythm of the plot determines the movement of the action. In *L'École des femmes* and *L'Avare*, in contrast, the plot has a much less important role.

In these plays – and in *Le Misanthrope*, *Le Tartuffe*, *Les Femmes savantes*, *Le Bourgeois Gentilhomme* and *Le Malade imaginaire* – the audience is not invited to revel in the sheer complexity of the intrigue or to sit back and be charmed by a sequence of almost miraculous surprises and coincidences. The focus of the drama is not the magic of theatrical illusion but the comic spectacle of well-defined characteristics of human behaviour portrayed in recognizable contexts. Molière's brand of comedy is distinguished by the use of caricature and the exploitation of the ridiculous – techniques which he shared with the popular traditions of French farce but which had little place in the more literary traditions of New Comedy.

*L'Avare* is typical of Molière's major plays in that characters, setting and plot are determined by the subject of the comedy. All the constituent elements in the play are designed to display the comic effects of avarice. Harpagon is the incarnation of avarice. His alienation from his son and daughter is not the routine misunderstanding between father and children so common in New Comedy but an unbridgeable gulf created by avarice. The setting of the play, a neglected household in which everyone, father, children and servants, suffers the miseries of poverty, is itself a portrait of the destructive effects of avarice. Even apparently external accidents of plot usually stem from the character of the miser. The theft of Harpagon's money, for example, is doubly his own fault: his avaricious and unmannerly behaviour has offended La Flèche so that he is looking for an opportunity to teach Harpagon a lesson, and his miser's compulsion to keep checking that his money is still there leads La Flèche to its hiding place. Whatever their cause, accidents of plot are tied to the systematic treatment of the play's central themes and to the progressive revelation of character.

*L'École des femmes* is the first major five-act play in which Molière builds the whole action around a central subject. However, it is the fourth time he treats the theme of cuckoldry and jealousy in his comedies. If we follow the changing functions of the plot in his different treatments of cuckoldry from *La Jalousie du Barbouillé* (date unknown), one of the earliest of his surviving works, through *Sganarelle ou le Cocu imaginaire* (1660) and *L'École des maris* (1661), to *L'École des femmes* (1662), it is possible to see the stages through which Molière's different combinations of plot, subject, character and action passed as he perfected the formula which he would use again and again, with such extraordinary success, in such plays as *Le Tartuffe*, *Le Misanthrope*, *L'Avare*, *Le Bourgeois Gentilhomme*, *Les Femmes savantes* and *Le Malade imaginaire*.

## 2. *La Jalousie du Barbouillé*[1]

In *La Jalousie du Barbouillé*, a traditional one-act farce in which a flirtatious young wife and a possessive would-be tyrant husband act out another episode in the eternal battle of the sexes, plot plays only a small part. The comic interest lies in their quarrels and in the arbitrarily introduced pedant who does not affect the action. The plot gathers momentum for a brief moment in the eleventh scene, when Le Barbouillé's wife returns home late at night to find that he has locked her out; she tricks him into changing places with her so that when her father arrives she can accuse Le Barbouillé of coming home drunk. The function of this scene is to add a little visual comedy, life and variety to what is otherwise a rather static farcical picture of family life.

Yet this simple farce contains elements outside the range of New Comedy, elements which Molière will incorporate into his major plays. The attention of the audience focuses not on the unfolding of the plot – we are barely aware of the plot's existence – but on the flaws in the central character; it is Le Barbouillé's blustering anger and colourful invective which interest us. Also, though there is a lot of action and fun in the closing scene in which the pedant reappears in his nightshirt, there is no happy ending to the play; at the end Le Barbouillé is still in a rage and refusing to be reconciled with his wife. The play does not proceed from chaos to order, from unhappiness to happiness, but ends exactly where it began, with a husband and wife at each other's throats.

When Molière returned to the portrayal of the same futile struggle between husband and wife in *George Dandin* (1668) he underlined the cyclical nature of such behaviour still more clearly, portraying tyrant and coquette fighting the same battle three times over, in three separate acts, and ending still more unhappily than they began.

These farces, if at a less profound level, inspire the same sense of the impossibility of correcting human weakness which we experience at the end of *Le Misanthrope*, Molière's most sophisticated picture of the battle of the sexes. Alceste and Célimène, like the mechanical figures of farce, are further from achieving happiness at the end of the play than they were at the beginning.

### 3. *Sganarelle ou le Cocu imaginaire* (1660)

*La Jalousie du Barbouillé* contains some lively and entertaining set pieces of farce, but it does not explore the issues of love and marriage. Nor does it offer any sustained character interest; we know all we need to know about Le Barbouillé before he has finished his opening soliloquy.

When Molière returned to the theme of jealousy in *Sganarelle ou le Cocu imaginaire*, the play which he performed more often than any other in his repertoire, his treatment of the effects and implications of jealousy was much more varied. *Sganarelle* is a strange and uneasy hybrid of a comedy: a mixture of a plot which functions like the plots of New Comedy, a farce centred around the virtuoso role of Sganarelle, a clear descendant of Le Barbouillé, and a more weighty comedy of dialectic in which the issues of love, jealousy and marriage are discussed. The three elements are never quite joined into a single coherent action.

The development and momentum of the play, in its single long act of twenty-four scenes, is maintained, as was generally the case in New Comedy, by a series of external accidents. Molière constructs a plot-within-a-plot. In the first, minor, plot a young lover and his mistress are prevented from marrying by a bilious, money-loving father. Then, in the main plot, the two young lovers, helped on by a lost portrait and two fainting fits, are caught up with Sganarelle and his wife in a series of increasingly involved misunderstandings which lead all four to become victims of jealous and resentful anger. At the end of the play, to solve their problems, a servant has to stand all four of them in a line and untangle their misconceptions, while the obstacle in the minor plot is removed with the discovery that the rich rival suitor preferred by the father is already married.

The complications of plot provide the comic poet with a variety of contexts in which to portray jealousy at work and, at the same time, to reveal character. However, events and actions are the consequences of chance and misunderstanding, not of character. The play would function just as plausibly with the same misunderstandings and a quite different set of characters. Equally, the issues discussed at various points could be moved from one scene to another, or even replaced by the discussion of different issues, without destroying the mechanism of the plot which controls the action.

If it is the plot which keeps the action of *Sganarelle* in motion, however, the audience's interest is held principally by character. Sganarelle, played by Molière himself, a richly comic *bourgeois* husband, self-loving, bullying, cowardly, yet given to bouts of vindictive and impotent rage in which he resembles the stock figure of the braggart-soldier, is undoubtedly the comic focus of the play.

The cast of characters exhibits the same strange mixture of

farce and New Comedy as the main action. Sganarelle and his sharp-tongued wife, the *bourgeois* father Gorgibus, Célie's servant and Lélie's *valet* are crude stock figures from French farce, while the stage lovers, Célie and Lélie, belong to the more elegant world of literary comedy. The farcical figures add variety to the comedy of character, while the charming young lovers provide a love story designed to engage the emotions of the audience. The blend, however, is an awkward one: the audience has to accept the implausibility of two handsome and polished young people so easily becoming jealous of such a humble comic pair as Sganarelle and his wife.

Molière enriches his treatment of cuckoldry in this play with speeches on education, love, marriage and jealousy. Gorgibus, the tyrant father, is made to express laughably narrow views on education, scolding his daughter for reading novels instead of concentrating on edifying books of religious instruction such as *La Guide des pécheurs*; he is the first of Molière's portraits of tyrants who believe that the purpose of education and religion is to bend the minds of the young to suit the wishes of their elders (ll. 27–40). Through Célie's servant, Molière offers us a practical servant's-eye view of marriage: as ivy needs a tree, a woman needs a man to cling to; he warms her at night and provides a consoling 'God bless you!' every time she sneezes (ll. 63–90). Sganarelle's wife delivers a tirade on the subject of husbands whose passion for their wives grows cold when the novelty of marriage wears off (ll. 123–40). Sganarelle himself, in a soliloquy, the longest and funniest speech in the play, reflects on the double injustice of the cuckold's state: first he must suffer the wretchedness and dishonour of being cuckolded and then, if he wishes to remedy the situation by challenging his rival, he suffers the still worse fate of being obliged to put his very life at risk (ll. 407–74).

These speeches, together with other, more fleeting reflections on love and jealousy, add a level of interest to the comedy which is missing from *La Jalousie du Barbouillé*; they constitute a discussion, at a modest but amusingly shrewd level, of the issues behind the play. However, the speeches are written to provoke laughter for its own sake. They present a collection of unlinked views which are not blended into a coherent dialectic which can be followed throughout the play.

Many of the characteristics of the mature Molière are evident in *Sganarelle* – the comic exploitation of a central flawed character, the accumulation around him of a gallery of supporting characters presenting different points of view, and the use of comic dialectic in which reason is reshaped to suit the whim of the speaker. These elements, however, merge into a pleasing sequence of scenes without ever forming part of a continuous, unified central action. Character and dialectic amuse, but lead nowhere.

## 4. *L'École des maris* (1661)

It was in *L'École des maris* that Molière first brought character, dialectic and plot together into a single coherent action. The play begins with a methodical exposition of its subject and main themes; we hear a quarrel which establishes the identities and moral attitudes of the main characters and lays the foundations for both the plot and the main action.

The argument, between two brothers, concerns the right and wrong ways to behave in society. Ariste, the older brother, argues in favour of measuring and modifying one's behaviour in the light of the prevailing views and practice of the society to which one belongs. Sganarelle, the younger, believes that one should consult only one's own inclinations. In the second scene the argument moves on to the more immediate problem facing both of them: how to treat two sisters, Léonor and Isabelle, whose father has entrusted them to their care and whom they hope to marry. Ariste believes that he should show confidence in Léonor and encourage her to enjoy the entertainments appropriate to a woman of her age and station, while Sganarelle believes he should keep Isabelle locked up, safe from the corrupting influences of the world.

From this clear exposition of two contrasting viewpoints, action and plot grow together. The action of the play is the sequence of arguments and incidents which show how good sense, moderation, trust and kindness lead to happiness, while blind self-love, boastfulness and cruel bullying fail – an action which demonstrates the soundness of Ariste's arguments and the weakness of Sganarelle's. The plot espouses this action in a complex intrigue which leads both to the humiliation of

Sganarelle, who is outwitted and abandoned by Isabelle, and the vindication of Ariste, when Léonor, tired of the vanities of society and its tiresome, pleasure-seeking young men, chooses to marry him.

In *L'École des maris* Molière makes a conscious and clearly signalled decision to raise his comedy on to a new and higher plane. For the first time, he uses his rare comic gifts and skills to please and entertain by appealing to understanding and judgement rather than by simply relying on the well-tried techniques of comedy.[2] From the opening lines the spectator is plunged into a serious moral argument and, throughout the play, he or she will be invited to follow, through words, deeds and events, the ramifications of this argument.

Molière takes seriously the commonplace view that comedy should be an image of truth. To make comedy into a faithful reflection of truth, he rejected some of the most hallowed assumptions behind New Comedy – assumptions which found support in the most authoritative classical texts and which were repeated by the major Renaissance theorists. His most significant change was to modify the traditional formula according to which a comedy begins with troubles and unhappiness and ends in universal happiness and harmony. Sganarelle, the fool of this play, begins full of confidence and happiness but, misled by his folly, loses his mistress and ends in rage and despair.

This ending recalls the partially happy endings of farce – of *La Jalousie du Barbouillé*, for example – but there, the central fool is such a figure of fun that the audience has no sense that he is being punished for his folly. In *L'École des maris*, at a much deeper level, Molière introduced into the central action a moral order which made it necessary to distinguish between the happy outcome likely to follow upon well-judged behaviour and the unhappiness likely to result from blindness and selfishness. I shall return to this question when I look at the role of folly and evil in Molière's comedies in the next chapter.

Molière set aside another common assumption – and here he was flouting the conventions of farce as well as those of New Comedy – when he portrayed an older man in love with and loved by a much younger woman, while his brother, twenty years younger, is rejected by his mistress. Molière takes care to draw our attention to the fact that he is breaking the rules of stage decorum and running counter to the expectations of the spectator: in the crude world of farce an old man in love with a young woman is always cuckolded, and this is the expectation of Sganarelle, who says: 'How well the two of them are formed for each other! What a fine family! A foolish old man playing the fop in a broken body; a young woman for a mistress who is a supreme coquette' (ll. 252–5). Under a moral order, however, as opposed to the crude order which obtains in the world of farce, it is quite reasonable that a young woman should prefer an older man who is gentle, considerate, devoted and generous to a young man who is selfish, unpolished and inconsiderate.

In *L'École des maris* Molière calls upon his audience to respond to his comedy with judgement and taste. We are invited to mock those who unthinkingly share the prejudices of the crowd, who think it appropriate to laugh at people whose behaviour, though unconventional, is well-judged, generous and human. Spectators who found the match between the elderly Ariste and the beautiful young Léonor comic would be no better than the fatuous young men whose tedious conversation has driven Léonor to leave the ball early:

> They believe that everything should give way before their blond wigs, and think they have said the wittiest thing in the world when, in sneering tones, they come and laugh at you stupidly because you are loved by an old man. (ll. 1047–50)

We are invited to applaud her judgement when she says: 'I value the love of such an old man as this more highly than all the fine outpourings of a young brain' (ll. 1051–52).

Yet in *L'École des maris* Molière still does not achieve the total synthesis of character, plot and action which is characteristic of his great plays. The main action does not develop evenly through the three acts. Almost all the thought, dialectic and character interest are concentrated in the first; in the second and third acts, Isabelle, who plays the role of the master-schemer, takes over the direction of events and the interest of the play transfers to the mechanisms of intrigue and plot. We learn nothing new about Sganarelle after the first act and see only a limited exploitation of his character; the blinding effects of his self-love are amply illustrated, but the threat that his behaviour poses to the happiness of others – and to Isabelle in particular – is mentioned but not developed. Isabelle is so much more quick-witted than Sganarelle that we never fear for her happiness.

In effect, the play begins as comedy of ideas and ends as New Comedy.

## 5. *L'École des femmes* (1662)

Within a year and a half of the first performance of *L'École des maris*, Molière had written and given the first performance of another play with a similar name, a similar plot, and on the same themes of love, jealousy, marriage, cuckoldry and education. In this play, *L'École des femmes*, Molière combines subject, characters, dialectic and plot in such a way that all work together to provide a coherent action which unfolds with regularity and a strong sense of inevitability from the beginning of the first act to the end of the fifth.

The subject of the play is embodied in Arnolphe, who is a more sophisticated version of Sganarelle in *L'École des maris*. His first concern in life has been to evolve a method of acquiring a wife who would pose no threat to his honour or to his authority in his own home. Such an ambition reveals a rich store of misjudgements; about the nature of men and women, marriage, honour, education and love. Through his portrait of Arnolphe, Molière invites his audience to recognize and laugh at these misjudgements; at the false reasoning, the wrong choices and ridiculous behaviour to which they lead. Arnolphe is the cocksure exponent of the view that honour and happiness consist in not being cuckolded. He has studied the subject for twenty years or more, assiduously gathering information about cuckolds, not hesitating to laugh them to scorn, and maniacally and joyfully using his knowledge to invent a system which, he is sure, will guarantee him wholly against the disgrace of being cuckolded.

Even more than in *L'École des maris*, Molière consciously presents his fool in such a way as to lift the sights of his audience above the traditional world of farce. Arnolphe sees himself as a spectator enjoying the countless farcical scenes played out around him in the real world, where wives and lovers make fools of husbands. His is precisely the blunt morality of crude farce; at the end of his long tirade on cuckolds, he adds: 'there are subjects for satire on all sides; and may I not, as spectator, laugh at them ?' (ll. 21–45). Most audiences, in Molière's time or our own, would be quick to join in with Arnolphe's laughter. Yet Molière invites us to laugh not at cuckolds, but at inappropriate mockery of cuckolds; we are expected to join with him in finding ridiculous an obsessive concern with marital infidelity. This wish to raise the level of comedy explains, too, why Molière took such care to present Arnolphe as an *honnête homme* in all matters not concerned with marriage and cuckoldry. Arnolphe is not the usual well-off tyrant of farce who is mean with his money; he generously offers a full purse to his young friend Horace (ll. 281–86). Molière is showing us that honest men and women (like ourselves) are prone to become victims of the follies he is mocking. Through the character, actions and arguments of Arnolphe, Molière will present us with comedy which, if we are to enjoy it to the full, will demand of us real subtlety and refined judgement.

## 6. The role of secondary characters

All the remaining characters in *L'École des femmes* are invented and introduced in order to create a living context within which to expose the follies of Arnolphe. The most important of these is Agnès, one of Molière's most interesting characters. Unlike Isabelle in *L'École des maris*, Agnès, when we meet her at the beginning of the play, is simple and naïve; she is the product of an education designed by Arnolphe and carried out in obedience to his instructions. His aim has been to isolate her in the country and leave her unschooled in order to preserve her innocence and keep her free from the corruptions likely to follow from a knowledge of the world. As a result, she is comically ignorant, hopelessly unprepared for life in society, and dangerously gullible – her honour survives only because the first young man to take an interest in her is a gentleman.

Soon Molière shows Agnès becoming aware of her innocence, so that from being merely comic she becomes vulnerable, touching and even charming; as a result, the audience feels with increasing poignancy the cruelty of Arnolphe's treatment of her as he relentlessly pursues his campaign to shape her life to suit his own designs. As Agnès begins to grow in self-knowledge and pursue an independent line of conduct, we see another aspect of

Arnolphe's folly. After so many years studying human nature, he remains ignorant of the simplest truths about people: he fails to foresee that an uneducated girl will have no defence against love and that, once in love, she will be beyond his influence; the simplest words from her lover will carry more weight than all the moralizing arguments he can muster.

It is through Agnès that the biggest of all Arnolphe's misjudgements is revealed: not only is he mistaken in thinking that he can direct her behaviour, he is wrong in thinking that he can control his own. His self-appointed God-like role as ruler of Agnès's life very rapidly gives way to the unplanned and unforeseen role of pleading slave when he is surprised by love and finds himself powerless to resist it.

The function of Chrysalde is to show in more precise terms the weaknesses in Arnolphe's dialectic and to illustrate one of the major causes of his inability to reason soundly: his deafness to the arguments of others.

Molière allots to Horace a much fuller dramatic role than that of 'l'étourdi de la pièce', the scatterbrained young lover who easily falls into the traps of his rival. It is through Horace that we learn that Arnolphe can be a good and generous friend in matters not relating to his obsession with cuckoldry. Through him, too, we learn how quickly Arnolphe's friendship changes into vengeful hostility when he learns that Horace is his rival. Most importantly, Horace's tender, considerate and respectful love for Agnès provides a foil for the odious blend of condescension, self-satisfaction and bullying which characterizes Arnolphe's treatment of her.

The two servants, Georgette and Alain, who – like Agnès herself – have been chosen by Arnolphe for their simplicity, illustrate the kind of rough, unpolished environment that Arnolphe, with all his fear of the world and its polish and sophistication, is creating around himself. He is reduced to turning to these bumpkins as to his only friends and allies, depending for the success of his schemes on what he calls their 'affection' (ll. 1325–7).

## 7. The role of plot

The plot of *L'École des femmes* also grows directly out of the folly around which the whole action of the comedy is constructed. There are four main elements in the plot: Arnolphe's plan to marry Agnès, Horace's and Agnès's love for each other, the coincidence which makes Horace choose his rival Arnolphe as his confidant, and the appearance of the fathers of Horace and Agnès just in time to approve of their marriage and save Agnès from being immured in a convent.

The evolution of this rather bitty plot is rarely in the foreground, but Molière makes most effective use of it to advance the main action of the play – the progressive exposition of Arnolphe's folly and its implications. The first element in the plot, Arnolphe's marriage plans, gives an amusing picture of the extent of his folly: Arnolphe felt the first stirrings of interest in Agnès when she was four; struck by how much calmer and more gentle she appeared than her little companions, he at once saw that she would make him a good wife, arranged to take over her education, had her brought up in perfect ignorance in an obscure country convent and then transferred her to a secret town house in preparation for marriage (ll. 123–46). Ignorant, simple-minded and infinitely malleable (he believes), she is to become the perfect wife.

The second element, the progress of the love between Horace and Agnès, is much more than a conventional stage love intrigue (like the love between Isabelle and Valère in *L'École des maris*, for example). It provides the picture of normal, healthy love against which to judge the possessive and selfish love of Arnolphe.

The third element, Horace's choice of Arnolphe to confide in, is crucial to the action and to the whole comic meaning of the play. With the help of Agnès's transparent honesty and Horace's keenness to confide all his problems and plans, Arnolphe is in the ideal all-knowing position from which to manipulate events. As Molière modestly points out through Uranie in *La Critique de l'École des femmes*:

> I find the whole beauty of the subject of *L'École des femmes* resides in this perpetual confidence; and it seems rather amusing to me that a man of intelligence, who is told everything by an innocent girl who is his mistress, and by a scatterbrain who is his rival, still cannot escape his fate. (Sc. 6)

Equally, as Molière again explains in the same scene – through

Dorante this time – this element in the plot makes it possible for the spectators to observe Arnolphe's discomposure each time he hears from Horace that his plans for Agnès are failing.

Even such a minor element in the plot as Arnolphe's being locked out of his own house by his hand-picked cloddish servants reflects the main action of the play; it shows how Arnolphe is 'everywhere punished by the things he believed would ensure the success of his precautions' (*La Critique*, Sc. 6).

Every step in the plot of *L'École des femmes* leads us to see more deeply into the absurdity of the world that Arnolphe's false reasoning has created for him. Plot and character work in harmony to present an action which follows the struggle between two opposing forces. On the one side is a man whose judgement has been destroyed by folly – who, exalted by self-love, believes he can control his own and another's destiny; while on the other the normal forces of human nature, particularly love, quietly but implacably block his every move and wreck his hubristic schemes. The coincidences of the plot and the simplicity of the innocents are both designed to show that, with all possible circumstances working in his favour, a fool who understands neither himself nor the world in which he lives will be defeated by his own machinations.

## 8. The dénouement

If there is a weakness in the plot, it is in the fourth element, the surprise ending. In itself, the dénouement, depending on Agnès's father's timely return from America, is conventional and cannot be faulted. The problem arises from the fact that the comedy itself is not conventional. Molière has developed this profoundly and thought-provokingly comic portrait of human folly with such compelling logic and unity that the traditional whimsical dénouement, where a chance external event dictates the conclusion of the action, seems both arbitrary and discordant. The real culmination of the action of *L'École des femmes* occurs in the long scene which precedes the dénouement (V, 4). In this scene Arnolphe is faced with the full consequences of his folly: now in love with Agnès, he forgets all his earlier demands and, like the blind and indulgent husbands for whom he has expressed such contempt, promises her that, once married, she will be free to behave as she wishes. In response, Agnès, deprived by her lack of education of the social skills which would enable her to reject his suit with tact, baldly points out that she finds Horace in every way more attractive and lovable than him. After thirteen years of controlling Agnès's destiny, Arnolphe suddenly finds that his own destiny, his own future happiness, is in her hands and she, with infuriating simplicity, spurns him. After the rich comedy and irony of this scene, the dénouement feels dramatically a little flat.

Even more than was the case with *L'École des maris*, the audience receives the dénouement of *L'École des femmes* with mixed feelings. The marriage of Horace and Agnès comes as a relief but inspires little real joy; Horace is no doubt a worthy young man, but there is nothing in his character to capture the audience's imagination; Agnès, we feel, could easily find another equally suitable admirer. Our strongest feelings are of pleasure that Arnolphe's hubristic and harmful domination of Agnès has come to an end; he deserved to be punished and we are pleased to see it occur. Mixed with this pleasure, however, is a feeling of waste which, following some performances, can almost amount to pity. Arnolphe may be unjust and unreasonable, but he is profoundly human and we cannot leave the theatre with a sense that all is well with the world when the life of the character who has interested us most is in ruins.

## 9. Aristotelian action

This close combination of subject, character and plot to form a single unified action, so successfully practised in *L'École des femmes*, is the structure one finds in all Molière's major plays. Molière's attention to the plot, in the sense of intrigue, appears fitful in all of them. In *Dom Juan* and *Le Misanthrope*, for example, snatches of intrigue appear and disappear, never holding the audience's attention for long. In *Dom Juan*, the scorned Elvire promises in the first act that her revenge on Dom Juan will be terrible; then, by the time she reappears in the fourth, she has forgiven him and the threats have no sequel; a complex double seduction scene occupies the second act and is then forgotten; in the third act, our interest is engaged in a prospective duel between Dom Juan and Dom Carlos which will never take

place. *Le Misanthrope*, though less episodic, has a weak and often
loosely connected overall plot: Alceste's quarrel with Oronte in
the first act is hushed up off stage and then, after a brief account
of their awkward and insincere reconciliation in the fourth, is
mentioned no more; Alceste's court case is discussed twice but
never connected to other elements in the intrigue; Arsinoé's
revenge on Célimène, which leads to the dénouement in the
letter scene, is not directly linked to either of these earlier events.
On the superficial level of intrigue, these plays are bitty; at a
deeper level, the episodic events and dialogues of *Dom Juan* and
the changing encounters and confrontations of *Le Misanthrope*
are tightly and coherently ordered.

Like *L'École des femmes*, all Molière's major plays trace two
diverging paths: one, followed by sensible people, leads to
success and happiness; while the second, followed by fools or
villains, leads to failure and unhappiness. All portray at least one
character who is harmed by his or her folly and none, not even
*Le Bourgeois Gentilhomme* and *Le Malade imaginaire*, ends with a
dénouement which is unequivocally happy for all the characters.

Paradoxically, given Molière's publicly proclaimed conviction
that simple common sense should take precedence over classical
authority in matters of poetic and dramatic theory, his great
plays come closer to satisfying the exorbitant demands of Renaissance comic theory than those of Plautus and Terence, so often
cited by the theorists themselves as models to be imitated. Even
the comedies of Terence, the touchstone of perfection for medieval and Renaissance commentators, came less close than those
of Molière to achieving the sense of inevitability demanded by
those who applied Aristotelian views on tragedy to comedy.

At the same time, by introducing real vice, folly and evil into
his comic world, Molière changed fundamentally the prevailing
concepts of what a comedy should be.

# 4
# Comedy and the Ridiculous

## 1. Comedy as 'an imitation of life, a mirror of custom and an image of truth'

Essentially, New Comedy had no great need of the ridiculous. There was much visual comedy in Plautus's plays, but the visual element consisted of the clowning of slaves and villains rather than the spectacle of folly and vice held up to ridicule. The ridiculous was almost absent from Terence's plays, where the slaves are lively and attractive and even the parasites and courtesans are sympathetically portrayed. The ridiculous was absent, too, from all but one of Corneille's comedies. It was Corneille's special boast that he made people laugh without having to resort to 'ridiculous characters such as clownish *valets*, parasites, braggart soldiers, pedants, etc.'.[1] Good humour, an inventive plot, a rich sequence of surprises and a happy ending could and did provide adequate material for successful comedies. However, it is immediately clear from Molière's gallery of flawed characters, and from the close relationship in his plays between the main action and the portrayal of folly and vice, that for him the ridiculous was at the heart of his comic world.

A common demand of Renaissance theorists was that comedy, according to the formula attributed to Cicero by Donatus, should be an 'imitatio vitae, speculum consuetudinis, imago veritatis' ('an imitation of life, a mirror of custom and an image of truth').[2] Aristotle's assertion that poetry stems from man's need to imitate was taken as confirmation of this view (*Poetics*, IV, 1–6). Theorists saw the purpose of imitation as primarily didactic: Minturno was typical in stating that 'the New Comic poets imitate the life of private persons, so as to induce everyone to correct the manners which he sees criticised in others, and to imitate those which he sees approved' (p. 78). For such didacticism to work, the imitations from life must be based on sound observation; they must, according to Cicero's formula, be an 'image of truth'.

When Molière took Paris and the court by storm with his early run of comedies from *Les Précieuses ridicules* (1659) to *L'École des Femmes* (1662), the aspect of his work which attracted most praise was the accuracy of his satirical portraits of contemporary society. Donneau de Visé, in his attack on *L'École des femmes* in *Nouvelles nouvelles* (1663), conceded that Molière deserved the praise heaped upon him by contemporaries for his extraordinary skill in painting the society of his time. He recorded the courtiers' delight at seeing portraits of themselves on stage: 'He [Molière] discovered that people of quality asked nothing more than to laugh at their own expense, they wanted their faults to be displayed in public.' The critic paints a picture of courtiers surrounding Molière, after a performance, feeding him with examples of their own and one another's follies, while Molière looked round for paper so that he could make a note of them. People agreed, according to Donneau de Visé, that 'there had never been a man so capable of describing and representing human actions so naturally'.[3]

When Molière responded to this and other attacks in *L'Impromptu de Versailles* (1663), he was happy to accept the tributes of his critics, merely adding: 'I had not thought till now that it was deserving of blame in an actor to depict men too well'. The fidelity of his representation formed the basis of his own defence of his plays. He put into the mouth of a *précieuse* in *L'Impromptu*, played by Mademoiselle de Molière, the remark: 'Why does he write bad plays which all Paris flocks to see, and where he depicts people so well that everybody recognizes himself?'. In the same play, Brécourt, playing an *honnête homme*, claims to know 'twelve *marquis*, six *précieuses*, twenty coquettes and thirty cuckolds' who would be only too pleased to have their revenge on Molière (Sc. 5).

In an earlier scene, Molière takes over the role of Brécourt for a moment to remind the audience that he has barely begun his portrait of the follies of the age:

> Without looking beyond the Court, has he not another twenty types which he has not yet drawn upon? Has he not, for example, those who express the greatest friendship in the world and who, once their backs are turned, gallantly tear one another to pieces? Has he not those outrageous adulators, those tasteless flatterers who do not season their praise and whose flattery has the insipid sweetness

which turns the stomachs of those who hear it? Has he not those
base servants of favour, those treacherous adorers of fortune who
praise you when prosperous and curse you in disgrace?. (Sc. 4)

In the same scene, Molière makes the observation that 'it is the
business of comedy to represent all the defects of men, and
above all of the men of our own time'. Having already made his
mark when he wrote these words with his telling portraits of
*marquis*, *précieuses*, pedants and cuckolds, Molière was to go on
to add to his gallery religious and social hypocrites, a libertine, a
misanthropist, social climbers, a miser, a hypochondriac, more
variants of the pedant and *précieuse*, more doctors, servants,
peasants, merchants, provincial gentry, and many more. His
collected works form an extraordinary portrait of his age.


## 2. Follies fit for laughter

Although it played such a small part in New Comedy, Renaissance critics repeatedly asserted that the ridiculous was the
proper matter for comedy. They followed Plato, Aristotle and
Cicero, however, in limiting carefully the categories of folly and
vice which were fit subjects for laughter. Socrates argued, in the
*Philebus*, that we judge someone ridiculous when, lacking self-
knowledge, he thinks himself in some way better than he really
is; he adds, however, that the person suffering from the folly of
lack of self-knowledge is ridiculous only when he does not have
the power to harm others (48–50). For Aristotle, in the *Poetics*,
the comic mask is the perfect symbol of the laughable; it can be
incongruous and ugly, but does no harm to its wearer and can
readily be taken off and put to one side (V, 2). For Cicero, in *De
Oratore*, it was important to be guided by good taste; the fool
held up to ridicule should not be one of those men whom we
hold in respect, nor should he be someone whose behaviour
deserves punishment or pity (II, lviii, 237–lix, 239).

The view derived from these sources by Renaissance commentators was that the laughable arose from some departure from
nature, from some incongruity, disproportion or ugliness in the
soul or in the outward appearance, but that the fault, whatever
it might be, should never be so serious as to cause harm.[4]
Castelvetro expressed a typical view when he wrote: 'Ugliness

of soul embraces the ugliness which proceeds from wickedness
and that which proceeds from stupidity', and then affirmed that
only the second of these, 'the ugliness of soul which proceeds
from stupidity, moves men to laughter'.[5] Even the fools themselves – again in Castelvetro's words – should be 'neither harmed
nor pained by their stupidity or ugliness'.

If fools are to be laughed at only for the follies and vices
which do them no harm, the domain of the ridiculous is likely
to be narrow.

## 3. Evil and the ridiculous in New Comedy

Evil has a number of characteristics which make it unsuitable as
subject matter for comedy. By its very nature, it is harmful and
tends to engender an atmosphere of danger and threat rather
than a mood of optimism and good humour. According to
natural justice – and the demands of most literary theorists – evil
should be seen to be punished; in fact, the carefree world of
comedy has little room for the meting out of punishments. A
further difficulty is that real evil makes happy endings almost
impossible; since evil is not susceptible to rapid cures, it is
difficult for comic poets to include villains in the universal
harmony and rejoicing with which it was felt comedies should
end.

In fact, Plautus and Terence did portray evil deeds, but they
preserved a festive mood in their comedies by making the evil
harmless. Plautus's pimp and slave-dealer Labrax, in *Rudens*,
despite a life of crime, does no real harm either to himself or to
others in the course of the play, and the audience is quite happy
to see him hang on to his dishonestly acquired fortune. The only
potentially serious crimes in Terence's comedies are the rapes in
*Eunuchus* and *Hecyra*, and the perpetrators of these are both to be
seen as hot-blooded young men driven by love in the case of
Chaerea and drink in the case of Pamphilus; their crime is
further diminished by the fact that both marry their victims and
show every sign of living out the rest of their lives as good and
devoted husbands.

Corneille solved the problem of making vice innocent in the
same way. The lying hero of *Le Menteur* is so quick-witted and
charming that the audience has no wish to see him punished,

and in the dénouement Corneille appears to reward him for his career of deception by marrying him to the woman he loves. Corneille saw the full implications of this ending and admitted freely that the action of his play was immoral: 'It is certain that the actions of Dorante are not morally good, as they consist only of dishonesty and lies; and yet he gets what he wants.' His main line of defence was that the writer of comedies had only one overriding duty: to please his audience; and if he achieved this, he was not obliged also to offer instruction by dealing justly with the characters in his plays. He supported his case by showing that Plautus and Terence followed the same practice, rewarding young hotheads who had squandered their fathers' money to finance their illicit loves with rich and happy marriages; at the same time, the young men's slaves, their accomplices and often the architects of their masters' misdeeds, were also rewarded by being given their freedom.[6]

Molière's English contemporary, Dryden, also saw the fundamental inconsistency in the theorists' demands that comedy should both castigate vice and render it harmless, funny and easy to forgive. His solution and the details of his defence of his own practice are very close to – and were probably influenced by – those of Corneille. In the Preface to *An Evening's Love* (1671) he wrote:

It is charged upon me that I make debauched persons ... my protagonists, or the chief persons of the drama; and that I make them happy in the conclusion of my play, against the law of Comedy, which is to reward virtue, and punish vice. I answer, first, that I know no such law to have been constantly observed in Comedy, either by the ancient or modern poets. Chaerea is made happy in the *Eunuch*, after having deflowered a virgin; and Terence generally does the same through all his plays, where you perpetually see, not only debauched young men enjoy their mistresses, but even the courtesans themselves rewarded and honoured in the catastrophe. The same may be observed in Plautus almost everywhere.

Dryden argued, too, that 'the first end of Comedy is delight, and instruction only the second'. He added a further argument, which Corneille could have used equally appropriately: he suggests that the faults of comic characters are 'the frailties of human nature and not premeditated crimes'; they are the kind

of faults which 'move pity and commiseration, not detestation
and horror: such, in short, as may be forgiven, not such as must
of necessity be punished'.[7]

In short, Plautus, Terence, Corneille and Dryden all solved
the problem of the presence of evil in their comic worlds by
playing it down and inviting audiences to turn a blind eye to it
or to view it with good-natured indulgence.

## 4. Evil and the ridiculous in the comedies of Molière

One of Molière's achievements was to restore real evil to the
world of comedy with all its destructive powers intact. In
offering us his portrait of the life and manners of his age,
Molière saw evil and folly, often inextricably linked, all around
him. His was not a kindly portrait of human frailties. His
description in *L'Impromptu de Versailles* of the servile court
flatterers and self-seeking hypocrites whom he saw as providing
such a rich field for comedy reveals the cool lucidity and even
contempt of a detached observer rather than the indulgent eye
of one who smiles sympathetically at human foibles. Molière's
villains Tartuffe, Dom Juan and Béline are all guilty of premeditated crimes; their behaviour is more likely to inspire 'detestation
and horror' than 'pity and commiseration', and each is made to
pay for his or her crimes; Béline is repudiated by her husband,
Tartuffe is jailed and Dom Juan is damned. Such malevolent
figures as Arsinoé, bent on destroying Célimène's reputation,
and Trissotin, coldly and cynically intent on marrying Henriette
for her fortune, are no less unattractive and they, too, suffer for
their hypocrisy: Arsinoé is humiliated by Célimène and rebuffed
by Alceste, while Trissotin is exposed as a fortune-hunter.

Even Molière's less malicious fools are rarely lovable; the
laughter inspired by his doctors and pedants, his *marquis* and his
scribblers (Oronte and Vadius), and by his coquettes in *Les
Précieuses ridicules* and *Les Femmes savantes*, contains a much
stronger element of mockery than of commiseration. Almost all
Molière's protagonists are more or less unattractive – not merely his
blinkered tyrants, such as Sganarelle in *L'École des Maris*, Arnolphe,
Harpagon, and Philaminte, and the weak self-absorbed fathers of
*Le Bourgeois Gentilhomme* and *Le Malade imaginaire*, but also, I
would argue, his more worthy fools, Orgon and even Alceste.

Molière went further than simply making his fools unattractive: he constructed his plays in such a way as to bring out the full implications of their folly and villainy. While Plautus, Terence and Corneille passed lightly over the crimes of their characters and relegated them to the background, Molière placed the follies of his in the foreground. At every turn, one finds him shaping events in his comedies so that folly and evil are centre stage. He surrounds his tyrants with innocent dependants to show how they suffer at their hands. Agnès is the most striking example: bullied and imprisoned by Arnolphe, she is presented as a defenceless girl, almost a child, with no family of her own – until the final act – to defend her. The character of Done Elvire – another victim – takes on saintly characteristics in the course of *Dom Juan*, and her goodness has the effect of deepening the audience's perceptions of the evil behaviour of her seducer.

The whole structure of *L'Avare* is designed to contrast inhumanity with humanity. The play opens with confessions of love intended to soften the hearts of the spectator and prepare him or her to feel in all its coldness the inhumanity of the miser – 'de tous les humains l'humain le moins humain' ('the human of all humans the least human') – whose miserliness is the source of all the lovers' problems. In the same play, father and son are cast as rivals in love in order to emphasize the aridity of the old man's love; when the stilted language and mean behaviour of the old miser are contrasted with the stylish and urbane manners of the young man, the audience can see all the more clearly how a life devoted to the love of money renders a man incapable of loving another human being.

Even in *Le Misanthrope*, where the protagonist has so many redeeming qualities when measured against the hypocritical society he so despises, Molière does not dispose his audience to overlook the faults of his comic hero. On the contrary, the focus of the play is not the vanity of the world – something that Molière and the *honnêtes hommes* in his audience would have taken for granted – but the special stamp of self-righteous vanity which dominates the misanthrope's behaviour. Molière provides Alceste with a patient and loyal friend in Philinte, so that the audience can appreciate the full injustice of the self-glorifying anger Alceste directs against him. To illustrate Alceste's lack of sense in his choice of the worldly Célimène as his mistress,

Molière has him reject her attractive and much more worthy
cousin Éliante. But the moment at which Molière brings Alceste's selfishness into sharpest focus occurs when, having just
seen proof of Célimène's infidelity to him, he turns to Éliante in
his jealous rage and asks her to help him avenge this wrong by
marrying him. The request in itself reveals the insensitivity and
blind self-absorption of a man suffering from wounded vanity,
but Molière makes it seem even more distasteful by having
Alceste deliver it in the middle of a gentle, modest and intimate
conversation between Éliante and Philinte, in which the latter is
tentatively declaring his love (IV, 2).

In comedies which are telling portraits of folly and evil,
Molière rejects the pattern in which the reversals in the fortunes
of his characters are mere hiccups in the otherwise smooth
performance of a cure-all Providence. He could not, while
remaining within the bounds of verisimilitude, reform so much
folly and vice on stage. Molière is portraying, not the transitory
malfunctioning of Providence, but the ineradicable malfunctioning of human nature. His domain, in Philinte's words, is those
'vices which are a part of human nature'. One should be no
more surprised at finding vice in people than at finding 'vultures
hungry for carnage, malevolent monkeys and raging wolves' (ll.
173–8).

Molière's greatest plays are battlegrounds on which more or
less malevolent fools and villains attempt to sweep aside the rules
of common decency, crush the legitimate hopes and expectations
of their fellow men and replace right reason with their own
private versions of reason. Events and dialogue in Molière's
comedies are part of a developing dialectic between one of the
myriad forms of unreason and reason. For reason to win the
argument, the forces of unreason – of vice, folly or melancholy
madness – must be defeated.

As I noted when discussing Molière's dénouements, the major
source of satisfaction at the end of his plays is less the happiness
of the normal and reasonable people – often rather pale figures
with whom we do not identify strongly – than the defeat of the
fools and villains whose crimes against reason and humanity
have aroused our strong disapproval. The sympathy we do feel
for Molière's innocents at the end of each play is inspired not by
the opening up of new perspectives of marital bliss but by a

sense of shared relief that they have escaped the dreadful future towards which the fools and villains were driving them. We rejoice because Agnès has at last broken free from her lifelong jailer, because Orgon's family is to escape the poverty and imprisonment which could so easily have resulted from Tartuffe's fraudulent machinations, or because Henriette will not have to marry the fatuous, fortune-hunting scribbler Trissotin.

## 5. Useful comedy

We have noted that critics saw the purpose of imitation in comedy as primarily didactic: good behaviour on stage was thought to inspire emulation, while bad behaviour showed the spectators what to avoid. As Herrick has shown (pp. 64–79), the early commentators on Terence's comedies were concerned primarily with questions of ethics and rhetoric. Terence was used in the teaching of Latin, rhetoric and moral philosophy. Schoolmasters and their pupils studied his plays as models of elegant Latin and, at the same time, as a repertoire of moral judgements and examples of good and bad behaviour. The great humanist Melanchthon wrote, among his remarks on Terence's *Andria*: 'Authors of comedies wish to show examples of familiar manners and events by which we may be admonished and so the more prudently judge of human affairs and enrich our manner of speaking' (Herrick, p. 73). Another scholar, Ambrosius, writing in 1537, affirmed the didactic value of Terence still more emphatically: 'Much that Aristotle, Xenophon, Plato, Cicero, and others have written at great length is wisely and usefully transmitted in the plays of Terence by means of brief sentiments and fictitious characters' (Herrick, p. 76).

Other critics argued that the didactic value of comedy was reinforced by the spectator's experience of catharsis. Following the view expressed in the *Coislinian Tractate*, thought by some to be the work of Aristotle, Giraldi argued that the purging effects of terror and pity in tragedy were matched in comedy by the effects of laughter and jokes.[8]

Renaissance critics and writers shared, almost without exception, the commonplace Horatian view that the morally useful should be combined with the amusing. We have seen, however, that Corneille and Dryden, in the seventeenth century, had no

hesitation in placing the playwright's duty to amuse above his
duty to instruct. This is not to say that they considered they
had no duty to instruct. Corneille's arguments on the usefulness
of his comedies, outlined in his dedicatory *Épître* to *La Suite du
Menteur*, resemble those used by early commentators on Terence's comedies. For Corneille, plays were useful in two ways:
the skilful playwright could enrich his text with instructive
moral opinions and reflections, and, through a 'naïve picture of
vices and virtues', could make vice detestable and virtue attractive. According to Corneille, even when the ruses of vice
succeed, they inspire detestation rather than a desire to imitate
them (*Writings on the Theatre*, pp. 183–6).

Molière's didacticism runs much more deeply; it is part of the
very structure of his comedies.[9] He, too, placed the duty to
please first. He has Dorante say, in *La Critique de l'École des
femmes*, that the first requirement of any play is that it should
please the audience (Sc. 6). However, he states with equal clarity
in the *Préface* to *Le Tartuffe* that the function of comedy is the
correction of men's vices, and that nothing is more likely to
have a salutary influence upon most men than a comic portrait
of their defects. In Molière's portraits of fools and villains, vice
and folly have consequences which are illustrated within the
plays themselves. Folly and vice are punished by laughter. When
we laugh in a Molière comedy we agree, whether consciously or
involuntarily, that the behaviour we are laughing at deserves to
be mocked.

Molière's didacticism, however, is neither hectoring nor naïve.
He no doubt shared Philinte's view that nothing could be sillier
than trying to correct other people. The salutary effects of a
good comedy could be achieved only indirectly. The comic
poet merely depicts folly. The spectator is free to respond to
satirical portraits in whatever way he or she wishes. A man or
woman of taste will no doubt share the urbane response of
Uranie in *La Critique de l'École des femmes*, when she argues that
the satirist portrays behaviour, not people, and that we may
choose to profit privately from his portraits, but should never be
seen to take them personally: 'They are mirrors held up to the
public, in which we should never admit to seeing ourselves'
(Sc. 6). The *honnête homme* or the *honnête femme* at a comedy will
know that the proper response to the action portrayed is laughter

and enjoyment. Only fools lacking in taste and judgement, like the two *marquis* in *L'Impromptu de Versailles*, will draw attention to their own folly by reacting like children who are being scolded in public.

At a more profound level, however, the spectator who is interested in recognizing and identifying the nuances of character and behaviour in Molière's portraits, and who wishes to follow the closely argued dialectic in his plays, is likely to find in Molière's collected work a wealth of moral wisdom. He or she will find well-observed and wittily portrayed examples of many kinds and degrees of human folly and vice. Like his contemporaries La Fontaine, La Rochefoucauld and La Bruyère, Molière offers through the prism of comedy a coherent account of the functioning of self-love, folly, vice, and reason in humankind in general and in the society of his own age in particular.

## 6. The ridiculous and self-love

Commentators agreed that, in general, the ridiculous arises from certain kinds of baseness or ugliness [*turpitudo*]. Some defined this defect in more specifically Socratic terms as a failure in self-knowledge. Maggi wrote in 'De ridiculis':

> In the *Sophist* Plato says that this baseness is a great and varied ignorance. And rightly so. For the knowledge of our mind is so natural that the mind seems to have been given as a gift from a very great and good God to man for the sake of knowledge; now in general to withdraw from what is natural to itself is to slip into baseness; certainly, then, ignorance, since it is nothing else than a withdrawal from knowledge, will be baseness of the mind. (Lauter, p. 67)

Maggi links folly and vice with an inability to reason well, 'the ignorance of a deformed disposition . . . which is born of deformed ratiocination' (p. 68). The ridiculous is a sign of the fool's loss of grip on that right reason which, in a healthy mind, brings knowledge, understanding and judgement.

Castelvetro, in the midst of an enumeration of the different ways in which laughter can be inspired, speaks of the comic ignorance which results from self-deception. He follows Socrates' argument in the *Philebus* according to which the ridiculous occurs when man fails to know himself; Socrates gives examples

which show how unself-knowing men tend to overestimate
their own qualities, thinking themselves richer, more handsome
or – still more commonly – wiser than they really are. Castelvetro wrote in his *Poetica d'Aristotele*:

> what is ridiculous is the pretence to greater intellectual and physical
> powers than one actually possesses and the failure of these powers
> when they are put to the test, with the consequent discovery by the
> boaster that he has been the victim of self-deception. (Lauter, p. 91)

Whether or not Molière knew these passages from Maggi and
Castelvetro, he would have been familiar with the views expressed in them. As an *honnête homme* with a lifelong interest in
comedy and in making people laugh, it is still more likely that
he knew Plato's views on the relationship between imperfect
self-knowledge and the ridiculous.

The figure most likely to have influenced Molière's understanding of the comedy of self-love, however, is Rabelais. We know
that Molière did in fact turn to Rabelais and, in particular, to
the *Tiers Livre*, before creating his first fully developed self-
loving comic hero, Arnolphe in *L'École des femmes*. In Rabelais's
Panurge he found a richly characterized and delightfully comic
figure who is blinded by self-love, ever ready to launch into
erudite but distorted reasoning, quick to magnify his own
imagined strengths and to turn the qualities of others into
defects. Arnolphe, though quite different in the detail of his
behaviour, is based on Panurge. Both figures are obsessed with
cuckoldry, and approach marriage with no other thought than
how to avoid this fate; both regard women as dangerous animals
who need to be kept in check; neither gives any thought to the
question of regulating his own behaviour in such a way as to
become a good and affectionate husband. Ignorant of their own
faults, incapable of controlling themselves, odiously sure of their
own cleverness, voluble in argument, each displays the hubristic
confidence that he can outwit fate and escape all risk of cuckoldry.

Panurge is reminded by Pantagruel that such eventualities are
beyond his control; all a man can do is make up his mind
carefully and thoughtfully whether or not he wishes to marry
and then, putting his trust in God, learn to accept whatever fate
has in store for him.[10] Chrysalde, too, reminds Arnolphe that

cuckoldry is a matter of chance, not an event that can be avoided by dint of individual effort and ingenuity, and therefore not worth all the anxious forethought he gives to the question (ll. 1236–49, 1309–11). Panurge accuses Her Trippa of his own defects, particularly of his major defect of being blinded by self-love; Arnolphe, as he advances ineluctably towards the cuckold's state, mocks all other cuckolds as if they belonged to a lower order of men and suggests that his friend and adviser Chrysalde is probably a cuckold too (ll. 9–12, 21–45, 1306–8).

Both Panurge and Arnolphe speak with an assumed authority which makes them deaf to the opinions of others. Panurge rejects the advice of all those whom he consults, even of his wise friend Pantagruel, answering them with a mixture of bad and good arguments used in contexts which pervert their meaning; Arnolphe passes himself off as an expert who has studied cuckoldry for twenty years or more and knows everything worth knowing about the subject (ll. 1182–1205). To draw attention to the way in which Arnolphe follows Panurge in using good authorities to back bad arguments, Molière portrays him usurping the authority of the wise Pantagruel and casting his friend Chrysalde in the role of the foolish Panurge. Arnolphe greets Chrysalde's sensible arguments on the subject of marriage with the words used by Pantagruel to stem the flow of Panurge's false arguments in praise of debts and debtors:

> To this fine argument, to this profound discourse, I answer as Pantagruel answers Panurge: Press me to marry a woman who is not stupid, preach and prate from now till Pentecost; you will be amazed, when you have finished, to find you have not convinced me in the least. (ll. 117–22)

Pantagruel, of course, says nothing about marrying stupid women; he is answering Panurge's views on debtors by quoting Romans 13: 8: 'Owe no man anything, but to love one another' (*Tiers Livre*, V, 5–9, p. 54). Arnolphe takes Pantagruel's words out of context, changes their meaning, and uses them to support his own private convictions. He is following the procedure of Panurge, who misuses the authority of Plato, Plutarch and Christ to prove that it is Her Trippa – and not he – who is blinded by self-love (XXV, 51–81, pp. 178–80).[11]

Molière signposts his debt to Rabelais quite unequivocally;

the explicit textual allusion, a rare occurrence in Molière's plays,
is both a tribute to Rabelais and an invitation to the spectator to
see his comic portraits as the continuation of a tradition which
connects him directly with France's greatest comic writer.

All Molière's comic heroes are blinded by self-love. Instead of
learning to know themselves, and growing wiser, they love
themselves uncritically and sink into vice, folly or melancholy
madness. Like Panurge and Arnolphe, they magnify their own
importance in the general scheme of things, devalue those around
them who do not agree with them, and remove reason from the
public domain, turning it into an instrument whose only function
is to justify private passions and designs. Having failed to understand themselves, Molière's fools also fail to understand the
shape of the world they live in; their careers are a series of comic
blunders and accidents which result from what Célimène calls
'this great blindness which afflicts all of us in respect of ourselves'
(l. 968).

Molière's account of the workings of self-love was part of a
much wider movement which ran through the literature of
moral reflection of sixteenth- and seventeenth-century France.
Rabelais, Montaigne, Charron, Pascal, La Fontaine, La Rochefoucauld and La Bruyère all, in different ways and to different
degrees, took pains to underline the dangers of allowing self-
love to run unchecked and make people morally blind.

# 5

# Reason and the Ridiculous

1. Honest laughter

For Molière and his contemporaries laughter in itself was neither
rational nor irrational; it was rational only when the object of
laughter was genuinely ridiculous. If the laugher was without
taste and judgement, his or her laughter, too, would be tasteless
and arbitrary. Another seventeenth-century satirist, La Bruyère,
underlined the difficulties and dangers of the use of ridicule in
*Les Caractères*:

> We should not see the ridiculous where there is none: it spoils our
> taste, corrupts our judgement and the judgement of others; but,
> where something ridiculous does exist, we must see it, draw it out
> with grace, and in such a way that it will both please and instruct.[1]

Molière sometimes portrays fools who are ridiculous precisely
because they do laugh at things which do not deserve to be
laughed at. Arnolphe, for example, laughs indiscriminately at all
cuckolds: 'there are objects of satire on all sides and may I not, as
spectator, laugh at them?' (*L'École des femmes*, ll. 43–4). The
answer is that he should not: to mock cuckolds in this indiscriminate way, as well as being uncharitable, shows bad judgement. If
a quiet, good-natured fellow is cuckolded, people in general will
laugh at him discreetly, and a few good folk may even say that
it is a pity it happened. If Arnolphe himself were to be cuckolded,
the victims of his loud mockery would be quick to rejoice in his
misfortune (ll. 45–72). Anyway, as Chrysalde later points out,
there is nothing intrinsically blameworthy or ridiculous about
being cuckolded (ll. 1228–75).[2]

Another of Molière's indiscriminate mockers is Sganarelle in
*L'École des maris*. He seeks to laugh his older brother into silence
by mocking his fashionable clothes, while he himself struts
around the stage, boisterously self-assured, in clothes fifty or
more years out of date. The contemporary audience, sharing the
older brother's tastes, would have turned their mockery against

the younger brother, finding him all the more ridiculous for being so sure of himself (ll. 13–74).

The *marquis*, in *La Critique de l'École des femmes*, is seen to be ridiculous because, in his debate with the honest Dorante, he has no other weapon but his braying laughter and a noisy conviction that he must be right because all his undiscriminating friends and peers share his opinions (Sc. 5). The two *marquis* in *Le Misanthrope* also display this lack of judgement and laugh all through the portrait scene in which Célimène ridicules their acquaintances; they make no distinction between degrees of worth and find everyone not actually present in the room equally ridiculous; all, in their estimation, are without redeeming qualities (II, 4). Mockery of this kind attracts mockery in Molière's comic world.

## 2. The ridiculous and sound learning

The value of the laughter the satirist turns upon the follies of humankind, then, depends upon the quality of his judgement. It was widely agreed among critics and commentators that a good comic poet must have a thorough knowledge of humanity. We saw earlier how, to create acceptable characters, theorists considered that the poet must know and understand the functioning of the virtues and vices which constitute the subject matter of moral philosophy. To write a coherent play, he must know how the various virtues and vices govern behaviour and choice in hundreds of different predicaments. In addition, the comic poet must have the learning necessary for him to make proper use of laughter; to laugh at the right things in the right way he must have good judgement. As Dennis wrote in his essay on taste:

> If philosophy and a knowledge of the world are necessary to a comick poet for his forming his characters; if an acquaintance with the best authors among the antients and moderns be requisite for the attaining the vivacity and grace of the dialogue; why, then for the forming a true judgement of these, the same learning and the same experience are necessary. (*Critical Works*, I, p. 291)

The anonymous author of the *Lettre sur la comédie de l'Imposteur*, arguing from the same commonplace, considered that Molière was admirably qualified to write comedies. This letter, a defence of *Le Tartuffe*, contains an analysis of the 1667 version of the play and some general reflections on the nature of comedy.[3] It may have been written by Molière himself or, more probably, by a close associate or friend who composed his polemic in close consultation with him. The writer defends Molière by arguing that his portrait of hypocrisy in *Le Tartuffe* is true to life, that he portrays 'the truth with all the dignity with which it should be accompanied everywhere'. He goes further and suggests that, in painting vice, Molière has avoided all possible corrupting effects by taking

> every precaution that a perfect knowledge of the best ancient authors, a solid veneration for religion, profound meditation on the nature of the soul, the experience of many years and an extraordinary amount of work could furnish. (*O.C.*, I, p. 1169)

The anonymous author is claiming that Molière, before portraying the human condition, had first taken the precaution of turning himself into a consummate moral philosopher.

In the *Préface* to *Le Tartuffe*, Molière made a similar claim, in more modest terms, under his own name. While conceding that there had been times in the past when the theatre had become an instrument of corruption, plays like his own, he argued, 'in which learning and honesty hold sway', provided entertainment which was both innocent and salutary. Molière considered that his was honest, well-informed laughter.

## 3. The nature of the ridiculous

Among the reflections on comedy in the *Lettre sur la comédie de l'Imposteur*, the most interesting is on the nature of the ridiculous, described as 'one of the most sublime matters in the domain of true ethics' (p. 1173). The author's aim was to show how comedy works in Molière's plays, and to provide a moral and philosophical context to justify the satirist's use of the ridiculous.

The author reminds the reader of the philosophical commonplace that man is born with an innate capacity to reason – a view which had taken on new meaning in the seventeenth century with Descartes's insistence that common sense is the most widely and evenly shared human faculty, the very form and essence of man. Unlike Descartes, however, the anonymous

author argues that man can perceive reason through the senses as
well as through the mind. Providence combats the laziness and
weakness which are natural to man, and which would often
prevent him from mastering the complex processes of sound
reasoning, by making reason perceptible to the senses, giving
reason 'an external form and a recognizable appearance'
(p. 1173). When a man sees something which looks reasonable,
he is intuitively recognizing the truth and virtue which lie
behind it; this recognition is accompanied by the passions normally aroused by a knowledge of truth and virtue, joy mingled
with esteem.

When, on the other hand, a man sees something which looks
unreasonable, or ridiculous, he intuitively recognizes the ignorance and error underlying it and responds with the appropriate
mixture of joy and contempt. Following the Cartesian classifica-
tion of the passions in *Les Passions de l'âme*, the author says that
every perception must of necessity arouse either esteem or
contempt. For Descartes, these are simply the two divisions of
wonder, *admiration*, which is the passion which accompanies all
perceptions and in which all other passions have their origin.
The special emphasis of the anonymous author is on the notion
that both reason and unreason inspire joy – reason because the
perception of reason and truth always causes acute pleasure;
unreason because we experience an agreeable feeling of superiority when we see others behaving less sensibly than ourselves
(p. 1179).

According to this argument, all manifestations of reason and
unreason can fall within the domain of comedy, as the purpose
of comedy is to give pleasure.

The anonymous author goes on to state more precisely the
nature of reason and the ridiculous:

> The ridiculous then is the external and perceptible form which the
> providence of nature has attached to everything unreasonable, to
> make it recognizable to us and force us to flee it. To know the
> ridiculous we must know the reason of which it indicates the
> absence, and see in what it consists. Its character is none other, in its
> essence, than appropriateness, and its visible mark is decorum [*la
> bienséance*], that is the famous *quod decet* of the ancients: so that
> decorum is to appropriateness what Platonists say beauty is to
> goodness, that is the flower, the exterior, the body and the outward

appearance; decorum is reason made apparent, while appropriateness
is the essence of reason. This is why everything which looks fitting is
always based upon some reason of appropriateness, and that which is
ill-fitting upon inappropriateness; in other words, the ridiculous is
based upon lack of reason. (p. 1174)

## 4. *Bienséance*, *decorum*, and the golden mean

In alluding to the '*quod decet* of the ancients', the anonymous
author most probably had in mind a passage from Cicero's *De
Officiis*, one of the handbooks of the middle forms in the schools
attended by Molière and the educated men among his audiences.[4]
The phrase is 'quod decet, honestum est et, quod honestum est,
decet' (I, 94). This is the central element in Cicero's definition of
*decorum* or propriety. For Cicero, *decorum* is the quality which
results from constant observance of the golden mean; it includes
'temperance, complete subjection of all the passions, and moderation in all·things' (I, 93). He wrote of *decorum*:

> Such is its essential nature, that it is inseparable from moral goodness;
> for what is proper is morally right, and what is morally right is
> proper. The nature of the difference between morality and propriety
> can be more easily felt than expressed. For whatever propriety may
> be, it is manifested only when there is pre-existing moral rectitude.
> . . . For to employ reason and speech rationally, to do with careful
> consideration whatever one does, and in everything to discern the
> truth, to uphold it – that is proper. To be mistaken, on the other
> hand, to miss the truth, to fall into error, to be led astray – that is as
> improper as to be deranged and lose one's mind. And all things just
> are proper; all things unjust, like all things immoral, are improper.
> (I, 93–4)

The anonymous author's argument that we can see reason
instantly and intuitively, without resorting to complex intellectual cogitation, also reflects Cicero's assertion that the relation of
propriety to the cardinal virtues 'is so close that it is perfectly
self-evident and does not require any abstruse process of reasoning to see it. For there is a certain element of propriety perceptible in every act of moral rectitude' (I, 95).

Cicero had also emphasized the point repeated by the anonymous author that the behaviour of reasonable people will have
an external as well as an internal harmony and beauty:

For, as physical beauty with harmonious symmetry of the limbs
engages the attention and delights the eye, for the very reason that
all the parts combine in harmony and grace, so this propriety, which
shines out in our conduct, engages the approbation of our fellow-
men by the order, consistency, and self-control it imposes upon
every word and deed. (I, 98)

If the anonymous author's theory of comedy is adapted largely
from Cicero's views on *decorum*, Cicero's views in turn were
inherited from the Aristotelian philosophy of the golden mean.
*Bienséance, decorum* and the mean all describe the same doctrine:
the individual's duty to try, as far as possible, to do and say
the right thing in the right way and at the right time. According to the anonymous author, Molière has assimilated the
principles of the mean and practised them in his plays. Just as
Aristotle, in the *Nicomachean Ethics*, looked at each of the
different vices measuring their distance from the mean,
Molière explored in his comedies the various degrees of
ridicule which indicate how far his fools have strayed from the
mean.

The mean is synonymous with what the anonymous author
calls reason. It is not a fixed measure of right and wrong, of
sense and error, but varies with every change in circumstances.
Aristotle wrote:

> Matters of conduct and expediency have nothing fixed or invariable
> about them, any more than have matters of health. And if this is
> true of the general theory of ethics, still less is exact precision
> possible in dealing with particular cases of conduct. (*Nicomachean
> Ethics*, II, ii, 3–4)

Molière's moral world, like Aristotle's, does not revolve around
a fixed axis of moral certainties; the reason against which folly
and vice are judged is in a constant state of flux. Even the most
alert and well-trained minds find it difficult to keep track of
reason.

Yet Molière did not expect his spectators to bring to his plays
the furrowed brows of moral philosophers intent on gauging
the midpoint of virtue between the various excesses of vice. His
aim was to entertain. To do so, while at the same time giving a
true and telling portrait of the human condition, he used laughter
as the measure of reason and unreason. Through laughter, whole

audiences could join together in recognizing and mocking depar-
tures from the mean.[5]

## 5. The ridiculous made visible

The relationship between inner reason or propriety and outward
appearance is the key to understanding the way comedy functions in Molière's plays; by the simple mechanism of using the
stage to make external reality reflect underlying reality, he keeps
reason before our eyes at all times. Cicero wrote:

> the propriety to which I refer shows itself also in every deed, in
> every word, even in every movement and attitude of the body. (*De
> Officiis*, I, 126)

> As for us, let us follow Nature and shun everything that is offensive
> to our eyes or our ears. So, in standing or walking, in sitting or
> reclining, in our expression, our eyes, or the movements of
> our hands, let us preserve what we have called 'propriety' (ibid, I,
> 128).

Precisely the same point is made by the anonymous author of the
*Lettre* when he described *decorum* − 'la bienséance' − as 'reason
made visible'. The implication of this is that whenever a man
fails to follow the mean, it shows in his outward appearance.
Cicero lists many examples of the extremes of outward behaviour which follow from such failure: speech which is either
effeminate or coarse (I, 129); the opposing extremes of anger or
indolence and indifference in conversation (I, 136); over-fastidi-
ous neatness or slovenliness in dress (I, 130); a tendency to slouch
or, alternatively, to be in too great a hurry − 'If we do this, it
puts us out of breath, our looks are changed, our features
distorted' (I, 131).

We have seen in *L'Impromptu de Versailles* how closely Molière
adhered in his stage practice to the view that the outer man was
a faithful image of the inner man. In *L'Impromptu*, he showed his
actors how to turn the follies and vices associated with their
characters into concrete, visible and audible reality. The contrasting roles of the *honnête homme* and the poet pedant show how he
placed reason and unreason side by side on stage. His instructions
to Brécourt, who is playing the *honnête homme*, recall Cicero's
requirement that propriety should show itself 'in every deed, in

every word, even in every movement and attitude of the body'. Molière, playing himself in *L'Impromptu*, says to Brécourt: 'As for you, you are playing the honest man at Court, as you did in *La Critique de l'École des femmes* [that is, Dorante]; in other words, you must look self-possessed, speak in a natural tone of voice, and gesticulate as little as possible' (Sc. 1). Dorante's opponent, Lysidas, on the other hand, is to be the incarnation of vanity, affectation and false erudition. In *L'Impromptu*, Molière gives this role to Du Croisy:

> (To Du Croisy) *You* are playing the poet, and you must steep yourself in this character, emphasizing that pedantic look which is maintained even when mingling with courtly society, that sententious tone of voice, and that exactness in pronunciation which stresses every syllable and does not allow a single letter of the strictest orthography to escape. (Sc. 1)

The outer and inner impropriety of the pedant are in perfect harmony.

Reason and laughter are inseparable in Molière's comedies, but the spectator or reader is invited to approach reason through laughter, not the other way round. A child with a good pair of eyes has enough reason to enjoy much of the comedy in Molière's plays, because he or she will laugh spontaneously at anything which appears ridiculous. A too sober and earnest spectator, conscientiously looking for the meaning behind everything he or she sees, risks missing much of the fun. However, the people best equipped to enjoy Molière's plays were the humanists among his contemporaries who combined informed judgement with attentiveness, a quick understanding, an uncluttered mind and a readiness to be amused.[6]

# 6
# Body and Soul: A Physiology of Laughter

## 1. The moral origins of visible folly

In making inner character visible in outward appearance, Molière was doing more than adapt classical views on propriety to refine the comic acting techniques of his troupe. The Ciceronian view that the health of the soul could be gauged from outward appearance had been elevated to the status of a science in seventeenth-century France. La Bruyère wrote in *Les Caractères*:

> There is nothing [in our movements] so casual, so simple and so imperceptible that it does not display characteristics which give us away. A fool neither comes in nor goes out, neither sits down nor gets up, neither keeps silent nor stands on his feet like an intelligent man. ('Du mérite personnel', 37, p. 110)

Such a view derived in part from contemporary accounts of the physiology of the passions. Descartes, in his *Passions de l'âme* (1649), sought to establish a close correlation between the appearance and movements of the eyes, changes in complexion, the various expressions of the mouth, the attitudes and gestures of the body and the nature of the particular passions affecting the soul. Le Brun applied such physiological theories literally in his painting; influenced by Descartes, he practised and taught the theory that the artist should make a study of the meanings of eye and lip movements, of bodily gesture and attitude, so as to portray these meanings in painting. There were parallels in the art of rhetoric which involved a study of the passions in order that the orator might be able to orchestrate gesture, facial expression and voice in such a way as to persuade his listeners through appeals to their eyes and ears as well as to their understanding.[1]

A further implication of the correlation between the inner and outer man was hinted at in Molière's instructions to the honest man and the pedant in *L'Impromptu*. The honest man was instructed to avoid all excesses of physical gesture, facial expression and tone of voice in order that the body might cease to be conspicuous and allow the qualities proper to the soul - reason, moderation and propriety – to dominate. In the case of the pedant, appearance and tone of voice were to be made obtrusively unnatural and inappropriate in order to show that the voice of the rational soul had been silenced. It is implied that the health of the soul can be gauged from the degree of prominence displayed by the body. Such a view was implicit in Cicero's analysis of propriety, and in the theory of comedy outlined in the *Lettre*. Descartes, in his theory of the passions, made this view explicit. According to Cartesian physiology, a soul which is easily swayed by the passions inhabits an ill-controlled body likely to exhibit, among other symptoms, 'changes in colour, fits of trembling, languor, fainting, laughter, tears, groans and sighs' (CXII). When a soul has achieved control of the passions, on the other hand, the body reflects the equilibrium of the soul; all excessive external symptoms disappear, so that a calm demeanour is the mirror of a soul at peace.

A theory of comedy which reflects the view that the health of the soul can be threatened by the appetites and humours of the body derives from both Christian and classical ethics. However, Descartes's recent restatement of this view, with its precise descriptions of the bodily symptoms accompanying disorders of the soul, gave new prominence to a dualistic view of humanity.

According to Descartes, the soul, by its nature, is entirely free and can and should operate independently of the body. The body, he argues, is merely a mechanism blindly and automatically pursuing its own interests. This bodily mechanism, which of itself is good and useful, becomes dangerous if it is allowed to run on unchecked, because it tends to enslave the soul, turning it into the passive servant of the body. The soul, however, with careful nurture and years of practice, can reverse this process and achieve full control over the body, gradually modifying its interlocking mechanisms and training it, as a hunter might train a gun dog, to abandon its normal patterns of behaviour and learn new ones. Total success is achieved when the body is retrained to follow the patterns set for it by the rational soul.

The comic implications of this dualism were most clearly exploited by La Bruyère, whose comic world is peopled by fools whose souls lie buried and helpless inside machines which have run out of control. His fool, for example, is presented as a simple animal mechanism. Like the lowing bull or the singing blackbird, the fool has a very small repertoire of sounds and actions which are repeated unceasingly:

> The fool is an automaton, he is a machine, he is a spring; mass shifts him, keeps him turning, for ever, and always in the same direction, and with the same even motion; he is uniform, never different from himself: if you have seen him once, you have seen him at every moment, in every period of his life; he is no more than a lowing bull, or a whistling blackbird: he is fixed and determined by his nature and, one might even say, by his species. What shows least in him is his soul; it is inactive, it does not exert itself, it is at rest. (*Les Caractères*: 'De l'homme', 142, p. 295)

La Bruyère suggests that it is only at the moment of death, as the soul begins to rise up through the wrecked and lifeless machinery of the body, that the fool begins to live:

> Then his soul thinks, reasons, infers, concludes, judges, foresees, does precisely all those things which it used not to do; it finds itself freed from a mass of flesh in which it was as if buried and without function, without movement, or at least without any which is worthy of the soul. (ibid, 143)[2]

La Bruyère's courtiers, Cimon and Clitandre, are typical portraits. The power driving their mechanism is the need to be seen; 'their profession is to be seen over and over again':

> Anyone who could portray them would express rush, restlessness, curiosity, activity, would know how to paint movement. They have never been seen sitting down, never still and in one place: have they ever been seen walking? You see them running, talking as they run, asking questions without waiting for a reply. They are coming from nowhere and going nowhere; they pass and pass again. Do not delay them in their headlong rush, you might cause their mechanism to run down. (*Les Caractères*: 'De la Cour', 19, pp. 205–6)[3]

## 2. Farce and moral perspective

La Bruyère's systematic use of mechanistic language when

contrasting body and soul suggests that he at least was directly influenced by the dualism and the physiology of Descartes. With Molière, the case is less clear. As a writer and performer of farces, he belonged to a tradition in which laughter had always been provoked by the sight of men and women whose bodies were running out of control. However, the formula of the moralist and satirist, according to which loss of rational understanding and control is measurable in a person's outward appearance, though perhaps implied in traditional farce, had not been exploited systematically. While the satirist combines laughter with censure, the writer or performer of farces is usually content to inspire laughter on its own.

In Molière's early farces, we laugh at characters who fail to control their speech and actions, but we do not feel inclined to judge them. The pedant in *La Jalousie du Barbouillé* could undoubtedly be described as a fool whose mechanistic behaviour reflects his lost grip on day-to-day reality and common sense, but he is so unreal, so harmless and amusing in his excesses, that we laugh at him with good-natured indifference, caring little for the moral implications of his behaviour.

However, from *Les Précieuses ridicules* (1659) onwards, Molière often combined laughter at the absurd appearance of men and women with censure of the poor judgement and flawed understanding which lay behind their comic exterior. Indeed, the very act of disapproving enriches the audience's laughter. The precious women who appear in *Les Précieuses ridicules* and then in *La Critique* and *L'Impromptu de Versailles* are farcical figures provoking laughter, but in their case our pleasure is the more acute because our laughter is also a response to their vanity and bad judgement. Élise, in *La Critique*, warns us that the precious Climène is 'the stupidest creature who ever attempted to reason', so that we look forward to finding her foolish before she even appears on stage:

> she is [precious] from head to toe, and the most affected creature in the world. It seems that her whole body comes apart, and that her hips, her shoulders and her head work on springs. She always puts on a languishing and vacuous tone of voice, pouts to make her mouth appear small, and rolls her eyes to make them look big. (Sc. 2)

When she appears, a few moments after this introduction, much of the audience's pleasure comes from sharing Élise's judgement: Climène minces on to the stage, radiant with self-love, heavily made up and absurdly coiffed, and the audience, united in pleasurable mockery of this travesty of womanhood, is quite ready to condemn whatever arguments she has to offer.

## 3. Passion, folly and appearance

In the case of Arnolphe, in *L'École des femmes*, Molière presents with method and consistency a comic exterior which performs as the image of a malfunctioning soul. Arnolphe's folly is not of such a kind as to be immediately evident in his clothes – he is traditionally soberly dressed in black – but it is expressed through-out the play in his voice, his facial expressions and his bodily movements. We see him not as a clown, but as a man who is losing control of his life and his reason.

In the opening scenes, exulting in the misfortunes of other cuckolds and rejoicing in the imminent success of his own long-term strategy, he crows, laughs and struts with odiously self-satisfied pride, self-love, confidence and contempt for others. On occasion, as in the scene where he displays most clearly his lust for power and domination over Agnès, he becomes an incarna-tion of evil: he rubs his hands, he contorts his face, and his eyes shine as he gloats over her simplicity and asserts: 'As I please I shall form this soul; it is like a piece of wax in my hands which I can mould to whatever shape I choose' (ll. 809–11). With a speed which enhances its comic effect, Arnolphe's euphoria readily changes to anger. On discovering that his rival, Horace, has gained access to Agnès, he is overcome with rage, exhibiting, according to one of the servants, the symptoms of one who has been bitten by a rabid dog (l. 392). We learn that he trembles, has difficulty breathing, sweats profusely and cannot stay still (ll. 393–4, 403–4, 1000–1, 1008).

In the fifth act, the ill-regulated Arnolphe falls prey to yet another passion which brings with it another set of symptoms for Molière to exploit comically. He is stricken with a slavish, abject love, the lovesickness to which melancholics are especially vulnerable; the new symptoms are a lover's sighs, an expiring gaze and extravagant gestures of self-sacrifice (ll. 1586–1604).

This lovesickness is combined in Arnolphe with another dangerous passion, which Descartes calls 'humilité vitieuse', or 'baseness', a state in which people 'abase themselves shamefully,
before those from whom they hope for some profit or fear some
harm' (*Passions de l'âme*,CLIX). It is this passion which prompts
Arnolphe to overturn the values which have shaped his life and
promise Agnès that if only she will marry him she will be free
to do as she likes – even, it is implied, to cuckold him if she
chooses (ll. 1596–7). Baseness gives way in turn to a vindictive
desire for revenge and then, at the close of the play, to such a
mixture of rage and despair that his rational faculties are unmanned and cease to function: he leaves the stage 'tout trans-
porté, et ne pouvant parler': 'beside himself with rage, and
unable to speak' (l. 1764).[4]

Even in the case of Alceste, a man of some weight and charm,
capable of inspiring respect and love in the sensible and tasteful
Éliante as well as in the coquettish and stylish Célimène and the
prude Arsinoé, Molière portrays a man whose body has been
allowed to usurp the functions of the soul. Ruled by his black bile,
his melancholic lovesickness, his jealousy, his unbridled philautia
and misanthropy, all passions which begin in the body and, if
allowed to grow unchecked, inhibit the action of the soul, Alceste
loses his judgement, fails to understand the world and himself, and
so condemns himself to failure, loneliness and despair. He is an
attractive man made unattractive by his seemingly wilful slide into
melancholy madness. All the bodily manifestations which make us
laugh – his bilious, gesticulating anger bursting out in all manner
of inappropriate situations, his strident jealousy, his ardent protesta-
tions of misanthropy, registered in his facial expressions and
sneering tones – are symptoms of his moral condition. They inspire
laughter and a succession of different judgements on the inadequacy
of his social performance as the action of the play advances.

In the case of Alceste, the laughter and the blame are tempered
by affection and sadness because he is at least as much sinned
against as sinning and also because, like a number of Molière's
contemporaries, we are not ashamed to admit that Alceste's
follies are not far removed from our own. Yet for all the
subtlety and profundity of this portrait, it is based on the
familiar comic mechanism of a body escaping from the control
which ought, in sensible people, to be exercised by the soul.

In the cases of Madame Pernelle, the stubborn, ill-tempered mother of Orgon who wishes to impose her own repressive religiosity on an entire household, and of Philaminte, the tyrant wife and mother of *Les Femmes savantes*, Molière emphasizes the discrepancy between what a womanly woman should be and what these women have become by giving their roles to men. The masculine body and voice then become visible and audible reminders of the extent to which femininity, intuition, gentleness and judgement have been destroyed in these women by the bodily passion of lust for power.

The clearest example of Molière's use of the animality of the human body to illustrate the destruction of the soul is in Tartuffe, the hypocrite who lays claim to a high degree of spirituality. From the start, Molière draws attention to the grossness which gives the lie to his spiritual pretensions. He is presented as a penniless tramp (l. 63), a glutton who eats enough for six and belches at table (ll. 191–4), who can eat on his own and at a single sitting a couple of partridges and half a leg of mutton (ll. 238–40) and who drinks heavily (ll. 254–5); he is big and fat, with a florid complexion, bright red lips and red ears (ll. 234, 647). All this we learn before he appears. When he does appear, his performance is dominated by very obvious carnal lust, his eyes drawn to Dorine's low neckline, his voice suave and insinuating with Elmire; soon, gesture follows appearance as his questing fingers fondle Elmire's dress.

Molière turns Tartuffe's eyes, ears, lips, movements, build and deportment into a hyperbolic statement of his moral worthlessness.

## 4. Kinds of laughter

The perspectives of the laugher are capable of endless variations. Each comic character – and, indeed, each comic situation – should elicit the kind of laughter appropriate to it. There is a wide gap, for example, between the often indulgent smile with which we follow the behaviour of Alceste and the almost incredulous distaste which colours our laughter at the behaviour of Tartuffe.

The degree and kind of amusement the spectator feels also varies from scene to scene within plays: in the case of Alceste, our wry smile as he asks Éliante to marry him in order to satisfy his desire for revenge upon her cousin Célimène is combined with strong disapproval, whereas we smile with unreserved pleasure when he tells the prude Arsinoé that he feels quite unattracted by her (ll. 1246–76, 1716–22).

The satirist invites us to vary our moral response to different kinds of fool in the same play. The three pretentious women in *Les Femmes savantes*, for example, are all comic, but the bullying mother and the spiteful, jealous daughter combine folly and vice which inspire laughter and censure, while the harmless Bélise, a fantasizing old maid who believes that all men are in love with her, is simply absurd and inspires laughter which is uncoloured by moral considerations. The two pedant scribblers in the same play both attract mockery for their easily inflamed authorial vanity and their insincere mutual flattery, but while we mock Vadius with good-tempered laughter, we feel a deeper distaste for the cold-blooded fortune-hunter Trissotin.

By such frequent variations, Molière can control very precisely the comic, moral and satirical perspectives in his plays. He can provoke for each folly and each vice the appropriate blend of laughter and censure. Through the manipulation of character, situation and action, he can guide the spectator's judgement, persuading him or her painlessly to share his values and insights into human nature. When it suits him, he removes the element of censure from our laughter altogether. Monsieur de Pourceaugnac, for example, in the play of that name, is guilty of nothing more serious than being rich and inconvenient. In his role of rich suitor and obstacle to the happy marriage of the young lovers, he becomes a comic butt, a ludicrous, ill-fitting outsider who is the legitimate target for a series of practical jokes. It would, however, be quite inappropriate for us to feel any moral disapproval of Pourceaugnac. Any moral assessment, on the contrary, would convict the young people of thoughtless cruelty and see Pourceaugnac as their innocent victim; but in an unreal world where fun and laughter are the matter of the play, a moral response would be absurd. The overture for three voices which reminds us that love conquers all, the very title of the play, *Monsieur de Pourceaugnac* – suggesting that the comic squire hails from some country village famed for its piggeries – and the reminder in the opening scene that the young lovers, with their two professional schemers, are going to lay on a series of comic routines for our entertainment, are invitations to the audience to abandon all thought of the real world and give themselves up to fantasy and pleasure.

Monsieur Jourdain, in *Le Bourgeois Gentilhomme* (1670), arouses laughter at yet another level. The behaviour of the *bourgeois* is seen to be morally wrong, but we are invited to enjoy his errors without dwelling too much on their possible consequences. These consequences are sketched out for us: Monsieur Jourdain is squandering his wealth in an attempt to gain entry into an aristocratic elite for which he is entirely unfit; he neglects his wife, trying to arrange a liaison with a *marquise*, and threatens his daughter's happiness by seeking to marry her to an aristocrat. Molière takes care to draw the sting from each of these follies: the *bourgeois* is so rich that his profligacy does no lasting harm; his wife, played by a man, is a tough *bourgeoise* who can look after herself, and Monsieur Jourdain, in any case, is such an inept suitor that Dorimène, his *marquise*, remains unaware of his intentions; the threat to his daughter Lucile is introduced late in the play (III, 3), never becomes acute, as her father has no particular aristocrat in mind for her, and is soon overcome. Molière provides a moral framework for the comedy, then plays the moral issues down. *Le Bourgeois Gentilhomme* is without the tension and menace which pervade *Le Tartuffe* and, to a lesser degree, *L'École des femmes* and *Les Femmes savantes*, or the hint of melancholy which colours our amusement in *Le Misanthrope*. His treatment of Dorante, the aristocratic adventurer who, like Tartuffe, is worming his way into the household by a false display of friendship and using his skills and influence to fleece the rich *bourgeois*, is a clear indication of the lack of importance of moral issues in *Le Bourgeois Gentilhomme*. While Tartuffe was led off to prison, to the relief of family and audience, Dorante is portrayed as a sympathetic figure who can be easily forgiven and drawn into the family's scheme for outwitting Monsieur Jourdain.

The same comic mechanisms are at work in this satirical portrait of social climbing as in the more pointed satirical plays. The audience witnesses the spectacle of a body in which the soul – will, judgement and common sense – lies dormant, while passion – an amalgam of vanity, envy and ambition – is given free rein; but now the moral overtones of such a demonstration are allowed to fade into the background, giving way to sheer pleasure in the absurdity of the comic hero's behaviour.

Aspiring to aristocratic grace, finesse and education, the *bourgeois* is an incarnation of vulgar self-satisfaction. Vulgarity is displayed in his figure, his face, his clothes, his tastes in music and dancing, his language, his treatment of all those around him and his absurd social aspirations. His ignorance of etiquette, a particularly rich source of comedy for an age which cared so much about etiquette and practised it with such skill, is illustrated by the complex ritual of bows which he memorizes and practises in preparation for meeting the *marquise*; designed to display the highest degree of respect, the ritual collapses as the *bourgeois* moves the *marquise* back a few feet, like a piece of furniture, in order to make room for his last bow (III, 16).

In his pursuit of education, Monsieur Jourdain chooses, with unerring instinct, that branch of learning which best suits his nature; having rejected logic, moral philosophy and physics, he elects to study orthography, beginning with pronunciation. His first steps in education lead him, not upward towards the refinement of the soul, but backward and downward, to the unlettered sounds of babies and animals. He struts and stumbles round the stage, arranging his face in unnatural fixed grimaces; he brays like a donkey: 'I,O, I,O', grunts like a pig: 'U, U', babbles like a baby: 'FA, FA' and 'DA, DA', and growls like a terrier: 'R,R,RA; R,R,R,R,R,RA' (II, 4). Animality is rampant in Monsieur Jourdain, but it is the harmless animality of donkeys and yapping terriers, without the menacing, brutish characteristics exhibited by such creatures as Tartuffe.

Molière exploits a vast range of different kinds of amusement and laughter in his plays. The few examples I have chosen could be expanded to include every situation, speech and comic routine in his collected comedies. Our laughter varies in kind and degree from moment to moment as we watch, often giving way to other emotions such as pathos, anger or affection. It would be as inappropriate to respond to the world's follies with the same fixed smile as it would to apply a fixed and preconceived moral system to the constantly changing situations we meet in everyday life. Laughter, like judgement, must take account of changing circumstances.

# 7
## *Honnêteté*

### 1. Comic structures and content

I have focused so far upon the origins and parts of Molière comedy, on its purposes and on the nature and functions of the ridiculous. I have looked at the framework and internal mechanisms of comedy, discussing the subject matter of the plays only when the analysis of dramatic forms made it necessary. In fact, questions of content have cropped up in every chapter. The structures of Molière's comedy carry with them the assumption that they can function effectively only when combined with content: we have seen, for example, that characters are not merely stage figures but faithful portraits of recognizable types, each representing his or her own point of view with consistency; groups of characters are involved in coherent actions which reflect patterns of behaviour observable in society in general; the laughter inspired by the plays should be well-judged so that the pleasure of spectators might be healthy and even beneficial; indeed, the laughter itself should perform the office of judgement, acting as a spontaneous and instant measure of the degree of folly being exposed on stage; the comedies contain the assumption that audiences possess an innate sense of propriety and a shrewd and quick perception of the golden mean.

In this chapter and those which follow, my focus changes. I shall look at Molière's comedies from the point of view of their content, examining certain perspectives, topics and themes important to his work as a whole. However, though viewed from a different angle, it is the same Molière and, as form and content in his plays are so well-matched, a look at the meanings in his comedies inevitably raises more questions of dramatic technique.

### 2. The ideals of *honnêteté*

Behind most of Molière's plays is an assumption that playwright and audience will hold similar views – for the duration of the play, at least – on the right and wrong ways to behave in the situations in which he places his characters.

Molière shared the Aristotelian view – a commonplace of seventeenth-century moral philosophy – that since true reason is single, the opinions of all clear-thinking, honest people must share much common ground. An individual whose reasoning leads him or her to adopt a private view of human affairs, a view which cannot be shared by other sensible people, must of necessity be reasoning badly. It is hardly surprising, then, that Molière held many assumptions in common with contemporary moralists. One of these was a belief in the importance to social behaviour of the observance of the code of *honnêteté*.

This protean ideal, so central to the work of La Rochefoucauld and Pascal, set the standards of behaviour, conversation and manners which every courtier aspired to follow. Such, however, is the variety of meanings and emphases attached to the term that our understanding of the moral underpinning of Molière's comedies is scarcely advanced by the statement that his plays reflect the values of *honnêteté*. The word was used to describe qualities ranging from the highest integrity to the merest veneer of good manners displayed by people of good birth.

In its highest sense, *honnêteté* described the condition of those rare men and women who had learned to know their true natures and how to live within them. This involved first knowing the nature of man in general. The *honnête homme* must never forget that man is *the* rational animal. Moral worth, then, comes from doing that which is most truly natural to man – from exercising reason. Seneca wrote, in answer to the question 'What then is reason?', 'It is copying nature'; and, in response to the question 'What is the greatest good a man can possess?', 'It is to conduct oneself according to what nature wills' (*Epistles*, LXVI, 39). Reason, a gift from nature, is the source of all virtues: 'Virtue is nothing else than right reason. All virtues are reasons' (LXVI, 32). This conviction that reason is the source of all that is good in man, reformulated and given a different emphasis, was to form the basis of Cartesian rationalism. Even Pascal, for all his sceptical arguments underlining the limits of reason, argued that man's worth and dignity came from thought; a central aim in his *Pensées* was to persuade his reader to think rationally.

A second, equally widespread assumption about human nature was that man, as Aristotle had affirmed, was *the* social animal *par excellence*. For the seventeenth-century moralists La Rochefoucauld, La Fontaine and La Bruyère, to follow nature was to act in accordance with reason in a social context. The focus of their portraits of the human condition was the defects of men and women in their relationships with one another.

The satirical and comic portraits of these moralists remind us of the third and last defining characteristic of the human being: man, alone among animals, is capable of laughter. In different ways, La Rochefoucauld, La Fontaine and La Bruyère all viewed man through a perspective of laughter, and their readers were invited to display a firm grasp of reason by laughing or smiling with them at their pictures of unreason at work among men and women.

In addition to knowing man in general, and studying the ways of reason, sociability and laughter, each individual man or woman had to undertake the no less difficult task of learning to know his or her own individual nature. La Rochefoucauld wrote:

> There is a manner which fits the appearance and talents of each person; we always lose when we leave it in order to adopt another. We must learn to know the manner which is natural to us, never abandon it, and seek to perfect it as far as we are able. (*Réflexions diverses*, III, p. 113)[1]

La Fontaine made a similar point in 'L'Ane et le petit Chien', when he wrote: 'Let us not exceed our talents / We would do nothing with grace' (IV, v). La Fontaine's *Fables* could serve as a handbook to the *honnête homme*; they portray a rich and varied array of characters for whom success or failure is a reflection of how well each learns to live within his or her own nature.

In his pursuit of the self-knowledge which will permit him to live in harmony with his own nature, the *honnête homme* must seek, above all, a knowledge of his own weaknesses. La Rochefoucauld wrote: 'False honest people are those who hide their faults from others and from themselves. True honest people are those who know them perfectly and confess them openly' (*Maximes*, 202, p. 62).

A true knowledge of human nature in general and of his own nature in particular will teach a man what he can and cannot do. As La Fontaine says in his fable 'Rien de trop', 'There is a just measure which the master of nature wants us to observe in all things' (IX, xi).

To observe this 'just measure', the *honnête homme* must acquire good judgement, which will enable him to know nature, to know the self, to appraise circumstances accurately, and to recognize reason. As La Rochefoucauld points out, 'You can sometimes be a fool with intelligence, but never with judgement' (*Maximes*, 456, p. 84). The whole enterprise of La Rochefoucauld in his *Maximes* and La Fontaine in his *Fables* might be described as the sharpening of both their own judgement and the judgement of their readers. La Rochefoucauld wrote:

> Honest people must approve without prejudice whatever deserves approval, follow whatever deserves to be followed and never be too pleased with themselves. But to achieve this requires a considerable sense of proportion and great precision of judgement; we must know the nature of good in general, and what is appropriate to us and follow in accordance with reason the natural bent which guides us towards the things which bring us pleasure. (*Réflexions diverses*, XIII, p. 126)

## 3. *Honnêteté* and the social graces

If reason, moderation and judgement are the soul of *honnêteté*, it is clear, especially from La Rochefoucauld's analyses, that these qualities should be reflected in a man's appearance and social behaviour. Not surprisingly in a society in which *honnêteté* was so highly prized and so difficult to achieve, emphasis easily moved from the effort to be an *honnête homme* to the determination to look and sound like one. The ideal of the *honnête homme* became inextricably tied up with the figure of the ideal courtier. Such a figure must be well-born, pleasing to his king, have style, grace, *sprezzatura* – an appearance of calm indifference – and an easy, flexible manner in his social intercourse. While *honnêteté* could, on occasion, refer simply to honest behaviour, it was more often used to mean courtliness.

In this second sense, the word became associated with a

particular class, as only men and women of good birth and those in their immediate circles could aspire to the role of courtier. Vaugelas, for whom the terms *galant* and *honnête* were synonymous, defined this sense of *honnêteté* in his *remarque* on the meaning of *galant*: the term

> embraced many qualities . . ., in a word, it was a compound whose elements are a certain *je ne sais quoi*, or good grace, the air of the Court, intelligence, judgement, urbanity, courtesy and gaiety, all without constraint, affectation or vice. With all these one might make up an *honnête homme* after the manner of the Court.[2]

The moral qualities of understanding, judgement and integrity are present in Vaugelas's definition, but there is a strong suggestion that they would be worth little without the indefinable grace, polish and ease of manner of the accomplished courtier. Vaugelas makes us feel that his *honnête homme* was not just any honest man, but an 'honnête homme à la mode de la Cour', with the numinous quality which could be acquired only from long hours spent at court.

In this sense, *honnêteté* describes a strategy to be deployed in one's social performance; it became hard to distinguish between *honnêteté* and *habileté*, 'skill' or 'cleverness'. La Rochefoucauld wrote: 'It is difficult to judge whether straightforward, sincere and honest behaviour is the result of probity or cleverness' (*Maximes*, 170, p. 59). In another maxim, he uses the term *habileté* where one might have expected *honnêteté*: 'Sovereign cleverness consists in knowing the exact value of things' (244, p. 67).

For La Rochefoucauld, cleverness was a useful quality. Twenty-five years later, however, when La Bruyère observed that the distinction between *habile* and *honnête* had almost disappeared, he gave strong pejorative connotations to both terms: he defined 'the clever man' as 'a man who conceals his passions, understands his own interests and sacrifices many things to them, who has learned how to acquire wealth or how to hang on to it' and the *honnête homme* as 'one who does not commit robbery on the highways, who murders no one, and whose vices are not infamous' (*Les Caractères*: 'Des jugements', 55, pp. 312–13). La Bruyère felt acutely the devaluation of both the meaning and practice of *honnêteté* in his own generation; it was only among the old, he claimed, among survivors from the generation of Molière and La Rochefoucauld, that true examples of '*honnêteté*, consideration and politeness' were to be found (ibid, 83, p. 320).

## 4. *Honnêteté* as a code for all

If *honnêteté* in its debased sense referred only to etiquette, it still retained – in some contexts, at least – the purer and older sense of the standard of behaviour to be followed by good men and women. In this sense the term is indistinguishable from Ciceronian *decorum*, and implied a rigorous moral code. *Decorum*, for Cicero, 'is essential to moral rectitude in general' ['ad omnem honestatem pertinet'] (*De Officiis*, I, 98). Ciceronian *decorum*, like seventeenth-century *honnêteté*, demanded that people should learn to follow nature; for Cicero, this led directly to the practice of the four cardinal virtues:

> If we follow nature as our guide, we shall never go astray, but we shall be pursuing that which is in its nature clear-sighted and penetrating (Wisdom), that which is adapted to promote and strengthen society (Justice), and that which is strong and courageous (Fortitude). But the very essence of propriety is found in the division of virtue which is now under discussion (Temperance). (*De Officiis*, I, 100)

It is clear that in this sense *honnêteté*, or propriety, could easily be extended to apply to men and women from any background, at every level of society. La Rochefoucauld observed, in a *Maxime* published posthumously: 'Honesty belongs to no one condition in particular, but to all conditions in general' (61, p. 107). La Fontaine's *Fables*, portraying creatures of every status from insects to lions, reflecting all social levels, show clearly how the concepts of honesty and following nature can be universally applied. Molière, too, portrayed all conditions, from the power-ful and nobly born Dom Juan to the serving-man of a peasant farmer, Colin (*George Dandin*). Dom Louis, in *Dom Juan*, recog-nizes that *honnêteté* can belong to all conditions when he says that he would esteem the son of a porter who conducted himself as an *honnête homme* more highly than he would the son of a king who had behaved as badly as his own son (IV, 4).

The key to this universal *honnêteté* was that each individual should follow nature in the light of his or her condition and milieu. In this more general sense, one of Molière's most delightful honest women is the kitchen maid Martine in *Les Femmes savantes*. When Philaminte accuses her of impropriety because she fails to follow Vaugelas's advice on good usage, the audience is clearly expected to find more impropriety in the mistress's behaviour than in Martine's (ll. 459–62). As Chrysale says, it is enough for her to be a good cook: 'Vaugelas doesn't teach you how to make good soup; and Malherbe and Balzac, so knowledgeable about fine words, would perhaps have been perfect fools at cooking' (ll. 532–4). Martine is following nature when she says to the learned women: 'Lor! I ain't done no studyin' like yous, an' I talks straight out like us does at 'ome' (ll. 485–6). A kitchen maid lacks the education to learn from books, and Martine is right to leave learning to priests in pulpits (l. 1662). She will learn her version of *honnêteté* through running a kitchen.

My argument is not that Cicero, La Rochefoucauld or even La Fontaine was writing with the lower orders in mind, merely that, in essence, their arguments about propriety and *honnêteté* were applicable to everybody. They were writing for an educated and polished public for whom the notion of *honnêteté* included the requirements of grace, urbanity, a well-stocked mind and easy, courtly manners. Molière – though he, too, wrote for this cultivated elite – addressed at the same time a wide spectrum of the public. As well as portraying people from many conditions, he also performed before them. While it would have been inappropriate for Cicero and La Rochefoucauld to attempt to pitch their arguments at a level which might appeal to the uneducated, who could not read, it was wholly appropriate for Molière to address himself to the pit as well as to polished courtiers. The audiences at Molière's plays would have expected him to ridicule folly at all levels; the low-born would have enjoyed his portraits of foppish *marquis* just as much as courtiers enjoyed laughing at George Dandin and Monsieur Jourdain.

The workings of *honnêteté* could be understood and practised by men and women of all conditions. Molière's audiences, high and low, if they came to his comedies with a ready wit and open minds, were well able to see when figures on stage failed to follow nature, when they abandoned justice and moderation, and when their judgement proved inadequate to deal with day-to-day problems. Molière appealed to the blunt common sense of ordinary people as well as to the discerning minds of those who were able to place his subtle explorations of moral problems against the writings of other earlier students of human nature. As Molière wrote in *La Critique*, in answer to the *marquis* who scorns the common folk in the pit of the theatre:

> I would happily trust to the approval of the pit, because, among them, there are many capable of judging a play according to the rules, and the rest judge it by the best possible method, which is to allow oneself to be guided by things and not by blind prejudice, forced enthusiasm or a ludicrous excess of delicacy. (Sc. 5)

## 5. Molière, comic poet and *honnête homme*

The *honnête homme* hoped to be taken for a man and nothing more. His highest achievement was to be fully human. As Pascal wrote:

> One must be unable to say he is a mathematician, or a preacher, or a rhetorician, but that he is an honest man; this quality of universality alone pleases me. When you see a man and remember his book, it is a bad sign. (*Pensées*, 35)[3]

The *honnête homme* must share all human qualities:

> Universal people are called neither poets, nor mathematicians, etc.; but they are all that, and judges of all of them. You cannot guess what they are. They will talk about whatever you were discussing when they came into the room. (34)

Pascal mocks society's habit of labelling people: 'you do not pass in society as skilled in verse, if you have not put the sign *poet* over your door' (34).

There are indications that Molière shared this view. His famous portrait of Damon in *La Critique* – probably a self-portrait – tells how Damon was invited to supper on the strength of his reputation as a witty writer; his hostess and her guests stared at him expectantly, waiting for the stream of witticisms which must inevitably accompany his every action. In fact they were disappointed, as Damon, a naturally taciturn figure, remained silent (Sc. 2). Molière is mocking those who expect to find in a comic poet anything other than an ordinary man.

He would have agreed with the Chevalier de Méré, the most articulate exponent of the code of *honnêteté* among Molière's contemporaries: 'an honest man has no profession. Even if he knows something thoroughly, and is obliged to spend his life at it, it seems to me that his way of behaving and his conversation should betray no signs of it'.[4] This attitude would explain why Molière rarely discussed stagecraft and dramatic theory; he would not have wished to play the part of the professional playwright, bristling with the jargon of his trade. When he did enter into polemical debate with his opponents – in *La Critique*, *L'Impromptu* and the *Préface* and *Placets* to *Le Tartuffe* – he wrote of the theatre with the attractive, natural style of an *honnête homme*, defending himself with urbanity, resting his case on broadly based common sense and taking care never to display the wounded vanity of the author. Molière saw himself as an *honnête homme* writing for 'les honnêtes gens'. One recalls his remark in *La Critique*, 'it is a strange undertaking to make honest people laugh', and his insistence in the *Préface* to *Le Tartuffe* that while some plays are indeed corrupt, his plays exhibit 'learning and honesty'.

Molière's *honnêteté* was also reflected in his attitude to classical authority and erudition. The *honnête homme* should be well informed, but his learning should never be on show. For the *honnête homme*, the only acceptable authority for an observation was whether or not it made sense; a sound and well-judged statement did not become any more sound just because Plato had once said the same thing. Pascal made this point succinctly when he affirmed: 'It is not in Montaigne, but in me, that I find everything I see there' (*Pensées*, 64). Pascal is neatly illustrating his point as he makes it, as he borrowed this observation from Montaigne, who had written: 'Truth and reason are common to everybody, and no more belong to those who first expressed them than to those who express them afterwards; it is no more according to Plato than according to me, since he and I under-stand it and see it in the same way' (*Essais*, I, 26, p. 152).[5] Molière was making a similar point in *La Critique*, when he said that the so-called rules of good composition were just a few straightforward, common-sense observations, 'and the same common sense which made these observations in the past can easily make them any day without the help of Horace and Aristotle' (Sc. 6). The same attitude underlies his mockery of Lysidas for preferring technical Greek terminology to current linguistic usage: 'Make your conversation more human,' says Dorante, 'and speak to be understood. Do you think a Greek name gives more weight to your reasons?'

As a comic poet, it was natural and appropriate for Molière to study human nature and, as an *honnête homme*, it was equally natural and appropriate for him to present his discoveries without reference to sources. To attempt to acquire a well-informed, rounded view of human nature without consulting the recognized source-books on the subject would have displayed the kind of blind and dogmatic preference for one's own private opinions over everyone else's which he so often ridiculed. If we are to take seriously the claim made for Molière in the *Lettre sur la comédie de l'Imposteur* that he composed his plays from a basis of sound learning, we should assume that he was widely read.

In fact, evidence of Molière's familiarity with the literature of moral reflection is everywhere in his plays. Boileau recognized this when, in his 'Stances à Monsieur Molière sur la comédie de *L'École des femmes* que plusieurs gens frondaient' (1662), he wrote: 'How learnedly you jest! . . . Your muse speaks the truth amusingly and with profit; everyone learns something in your school; everything there is beautiful, everything good; and your most comic words are often a learned sermon.'[6] In subsequent centuries Voltaire and Balzac, too, saw in Molière a consummate philosopher. Balzac, who learned so much from Molière's vast *comédie humaine*, compared D'Arthez, his idealized portrait of the complete author in *Illusions perdues*, with Molière, insisting that both were philosophers before they became great writers:

> D'Arthez did not believe there could be any exceptional talent without profound metaphysical learning. He was proceeding at this moment to plunder all the philosophical riches of ancient and modern times in order to assimilate them. He wanted, like Molière, to be a profound philosopher before writing comedies.[7]

# 8
# *Judgement*

## 1. Montaigne and judgement

The question of judgement has recurred in a variety of contexts in earlier chapters. The comic poet must have judgement for the understanding and forming of character, for conducting the central action of his play in such a way as to imitate the patterns of action observable in human behaviour in general and in the contemporary world in particular, for recognizing what is truly ridiculous in the actions of men and women, and for knowing how to combine all these elements in comedies which would charm, please and amuse audiences who prided themselves on their urbanity and taste. Judgement is a prominent theme in the plays themselves; in the comedies on marriage and on religious and social hypocrisy in particular, Molière offered his audiences a rich array of fools whose plans and ambitions are frustrated because they make incorrect judgements about themselves and the world they live in. Finally, in order to enjoy the plays, to appreciate the justness of Molière's judgement and to savour the amusement which comes from the spectacle of so many misjudgements on stage, the spectator must have sound judgement, too; whether his or her judgement arises from natural good taste or from a thorough and well-assimilated knowledge of the art of poetry, of the humanities in general and of moral philosophy, the spectator must share some of the qualities of judgement, taste and imagination of the comic poet himself.

We have seen that good judgement was the key to *honnêteté*. The moral writings of Pascal, La Rochefoucauld, La Fontaine, Le Chevalier de Méré and La Bruyère, though intended to please the reader and engage his or her attention, were also exercises in improving the writer's and the reader's judgement. Their works were conversations with their readers, a comparing of notes between like minds on the frailties and oddities of the human condition. 'Intelligence and discernment are formed through conversations', Pascal wrote in the *Pensées* (6). These writers, like Corneille, Racine, Boileau and Molière himself, were prominent figures in a society which spent much of its leisure time practising the arts of conversation, polishing epigrams, defining words, making fine distinctions between ideas, feelings, passions, virtues and vices.[1] The more educated and cultivated French courtiers, like their English counterparts at the court of Charles II, 'were at leisure to observe their frailties; to watch the turns and counterturns of their humours, and trace the windings of them to their very springs'.[2]

On questions of judgement, the discussions of seventeenth-century moralists were nourished by Montaigne. His *Essais* (1588), which address the reader as a friend, are like conversations – with past writers, with acquaintances, with the reader – and Montaigne's purpose was to sharpen both his own and his readers' judgement. A glimpse at Brunschvicg's notes on the text of Pascal's *Pensées* shows clearly how Pascal's lucid reflections on human nature were formed in response to his readings of the *Essais*. The presence of Montaigne in La Fontaine's *Fables*, La Rochefoucauld's *Maximes* and La Bruyère's *Caractères* is less obvious, but can be felt everywhere. Montaigne was a Socrates to seventeenth-century French moralists. The fact, too, that Montaigne wrote in the vernacular made him a particularly popular source for writers who were consciously refining and perfecting the French language. The *Essais* provided a rich fund of material which they used in the same way as Montaigne himself had used his sources. They absorbed his ideas, added to them, changed them in the light of other sources, made them their own and expressed them in a language which suited their own tastes and the tastes of their readers. They have followed Montaigne's recommendation to the good student: 'Let him conceal everything which has helped him, and reveal only what he has done with it' (I, 26, p. 152).

Molière, too, was affected by the *Essais*. I shall look at some specific examples of Montaigne's influence on Molière in later chapters on pedantry and medicine. My aim here is to look at a more pervasive influence which spreads through Molière's theatre as a whole. Montaigne helped Molière to know himself and to find his own distinctive voice. I am not suggesting that Molière was a follower of Montaigne: 'A man who follows another', Montaigne wrote, 'follows nothing. He finds nothing, indeed seeks nothing' (*Essais*, I, 26, p. 151). The nature of the two writers' projects is so different that obvious influence would be surprising. Molière had to reduce the infinite complexity of life to the discipline of well-structured one-, three- and five-act plays. To create coherent dramas, he stripped his characters of unnecessary idiosyncrasies in order to heighten their representative value and sharpen the conflicts which provide dramatic and comic tension. Montaigne, on the other hand, revelled in the complexity, variety and inconstancy of life, doubting whether an orderly view of the human condition was even possible:

> I leave it to masters of arts, and I am not sure if, with something so tangled, so slight and so random, they will succeed in arranging in columns this infinite diversity of faces, in stilling [life's] inconstancy and putting it in order. Not only do I find it difficult to relate our actions to one another, but I find it difficult to take each one on its own and attach the appropriate dominant quality to it, so equivocal are they, showing different colours under different lights. (*Essais*, III, 13, pp. 1076–7)

The major character in Montaigne's *Essais* is Montaigne himself, and much of the interest of his study comes from his freedom to dwell upon the oddities and inconsistencies of a particular temperament and character.

Nevertheless, if one examines the perspectives behind Molière's and Montaigne's different accounts of the human condition, the common ground is extensive.


## 2. Unclouded judgement

For Montaigne, judgement is the eye through which a man can know himself and the world, and it must be kept clear. It is a gift of nature which education and study can nourish or destroy, but cannot create. Judgement should be protected from strong external influences which might overwhelm it. When the opinions of good authors complement our own, we should absorb them and then, preferably, forget where they came from. Once they are properly digested, opinions from whatever source will bear our own individual imprint. If we allow others, however wise, even Plato or Aristotle, to usurp the function of judgement, we become slaves, and our souls die: 'Our strength and freedom are snuffed out' (*Essais*, I, 26, p. 151). Judgements may be irresolute and remain suspended in doubt – the state of doubt is, after all, appropriate to man whose natural condition is ignorance – but they should never be second-hand.

The need for a direct apprehension of things, unobstructed by a screen of ill-digested learning which blinds the individual to immediate reality, is central to Montaigne's definition of good judgement.

The freshness and immediacy of Molière's vision were the qualities which first struck his contemporaries and have continued ever since to surprise each new generation. His portraits were new, alive, accurate and distinctive. They appealed to everyone, even children. A suggestive and possibly apocryphal anecdote tells how Molière encouraged his actors to bring their children with them on days when he was giving readings of new plays so that he could observe and learn from their natural and untutored responses.[3] We recall that in *La Critique* he praised the judgement of common folk in the pit of the theatre because they judged plays 'by the best possible method, which is to allow oneself to be guided by things, and not by blind prejudice. . .' (Sc. 5).

His concern to keep judgement free, open and unobstructed lay behind Montaigne's distrust of expertise and erudition. He considered that the fields of medicine, the sciences and the different divisions of scholastic philosophy were dominated by eminent experts making all kinds of confident, absurd, unverifiable and contradictory claims. In the case of experts such as these, judgement has been smothered by erudition. As we shall see in later chapters, Molière's delightful farces on medicine and pedantry reflect these sceptical views of Montaigne.

Both Montaigne and Molière distrusted all those who believed they knew best: according to Montaigne, 'affirmation and obstinacy are sure signs of stupidity' (*Essais*, III, 13, p. 1075). Not only Molière's pedants and doctors, but all his leading fools suffer from the illusion that they are very much wiser and more knowledgeable than everyone else. Such confidence blocks their vision and destroys their judgement.

## 3. Learning through things

Once a child or an adult has cleared his or her judgement of all the lumber which prevents it from functioning properly, they can learn from everything. Good judgement, according to Montaigne, is acquired through direct experience of things, not from theories: 'a page's mischief, a *valet*'s silliness, a conversation at table'; as part of his education, a young person 'should sound out the range of each man: a herdsman, a mason, a passer-by . . . ; even the foolishness and weakness of others will be instruction for him' (*Essais*, I, 26, pp. 155–6). Every kind of contact with the world – through conversation, through events, through observation of the actions, humours and characteristics of himself and of others – can sharpen judgement and understanding. It is our knowledge of things which equips us to evaluate the arguments of philosophers: 'All the most profitable philosophical writings, against which human actions must be measured as against a yardstick, can be matched with examples' (I, 26, p. 158).

Montaigne's young apprentice, studying the world like a connoisseur, digging out examples of every kind of human behaviour, has much in common with Molière as he portrayed himself in *L'Impromptu de Versailles*, gathering and enumerating examples of folly and vice in court society as he assembles material for future plays.

Molière also shared with Montaigne a sense that bad behaviour was much more interesting than good. Among all the things we see in the world around us, it is the examples of foolish or vicious behaviour that teach us most. 'The wise', says Montaigne, quoting Cato, 'have more to learn from fools than fools from wise men' (*Essais*, III, 8, p. 922). Neither Montaigne nor Molière was so presumptuous as to imagine that he could teach a fool anything. Montaigne wrote: 'Silliness and abuse of good sense cannot be cured by a simple warning' (III, 8, p. 937), while Molière's Philinte points out that there is no greater folly than trying to set the world to rights (*Le Misanthrope*, ll. 157–8). The fool, on the other hand, by offering such a rich display of follies, feeds the judgement of the wise man. Montaigne finds it easier to learn from bad examples than from good; it is horror of cruelty, not love of clemency, which leads him to be clement;

incongruity catches the attention more effectively than harmony; when he sees a bore he attempts to be agreable, the spectacle of weak men makes him wish to be strong, and the sight of men who are harsh encourages him to cultivate gentleness (III, 8, p. 922). Montaigne's remarks constitute an eloquent defence of the didactic value of Molière's gallery of fools and villains. I doubt if anyone has ever modelled him- or herself on Molière's well-behaved characters – on the good-natured Horace (*L'École des femmes*), the upright and honest Cléante (*Le Tartuffe*), the excellent Philinte (*Le Misanthrope*) or the stylish and amusing Clitandre (*Les Femmes savantes*), but we might make considerable efforts to avoid being taken for a Tartuffe; we would not like our friends to see us making fools of ourselves, like an Arnolphe or an Alceste; and most women would be distraught to be taken for a Philaminte (*Les Femmes savantes*) or, worse still, a Béline (*Le Malade imaginaire*). Molière's plays exploit the timeless truth that most people, like Montaigne, are keener to avoid vice than to attain virtue. They are even keener, of course, to avoid ridicule – especially in France, where 'c'est le ridicule qui tue' ('ridicule kills').

## 4. Satire and self-knowledge

Montaigne's search for error is primarily within himself: 'By making public and censuring my own imperfections, someone else will learn to fear them' (*Essais*, III, 8, p. 922).[4] Molière's satirical gaze, as a playwright portraying fictional characters, was directed outwards upon the world around him. In fact, Montaigne and seventeenth-century moralists saw self-knowledge and knowledge of the world as interdependent. Montaigne wrote: 'This great world . . . is the mirror which we must look into in order to know ourselves from the proper angle' (I, 26, p. 157). The theme was taken up again by La Fontaine; in 'L'Homme et son Image', a fable addressed to La Rochefoucauld, he says that the faults we perceive in others are so many mirrors which reflect the faults which lie within ourselves (I, xi). Through a proper perception of the faults of others, we can learn to know our own. Montaigne wrote: 'So many humours, sects, judgements, opinions, laws and customs teach us to be sound judges of our own, and teach our judgement to recognize its imperfection and its natural weakness: which is no mean training.' He adds: 'There are those, who are not the worst of men, who seek no other pleasure than to see how and why each thing is done, to be spectators of the lives of other men in order to judge and regulate their own lives' (I, 26, p. 158). This is the position of Molière as satirist; it is also the position he invites his audiences to take up as they watch his comedies.

Most men, however, can see only the faults of others, as La Fontaine – after Aesop, Erasmus and Rabelais – shows in the fable of the two wallets, one of which contains our own faults and is carried on our backs, where we cannot see them, while the other, containing the faults of others, is carried in front, where it is in full view (I, vii).[5] Such men are unable to grasp the real significance of the faults of others because they are blinded by self-love. In his last fable, 'Le Juge Arbitre, l'Hospitalier, et le Solitaire', in which he leaves as his final and most important message to his readers the reminder that to learn self-knowledge is our first duty, La Fontaine captures the relationship between knowledge of self and knowledge of the world succinctly: 'If you cannot see yourself, you can see no one' (XII, xxix).

Molière's portraits of his monomaniacs who, blinded by self-love, fail to know either themselves or the world around them show how closely he shared the perspectives of Montaigne and La Fontaine. La Fontaine and Molière did not write about themselves, but they shared Montaigne's view that self-knowledge was the first qualification for knowing anything.

## 5. Judgement and laughter

For Montaigne, and for seventeenth-century moralists and satirists, lucidity and laughter were inseparable. Montaigne explained why he thought laughter the proper response to the human condition in his brief chapter 'De Democritus et Heraclitus' (*Essais*, I, 50, pp. 301–4). He reminds the reader that all human affairs are matter for testing judgement, but makes no pretence of ever wishing to cover every aspect of any subject in his *Essais*; he reserves the right to range widely over human affairs, to pick and choose, to look at things from unusual angles, to change his standpoint, to end his reflections in the doubt and uncertainty appropriate to a man whose natural condition, or 'maistresse forme', was ignorance. The result of this testing of his judgement was that he saw the human condition as irremediably comic.

Montaigne keeps his judgement constantly alert and active, but the human soul, which he is judging, is constantly changing. To judge it properly, he must see it at all times, at table as well as at war, and note how differently it functions in different people and in the same people at different times. If Alexander played chess, he no doubt showed as much impassioned commitment to winning the game as he did to leading his glorious advance on India. This ludicrous game, according to Montaigne, offered an accurate picture of the human condition, with all its laughable passions and vanities; the chess-player strains every nerve, displays anger, resentment, hatred, impatience and an overwhelming ambition to win a game any true gentleman would do better to lose anyway.[6]

We can respond to man's pitiable condition in one of two ways: we might respond, like Democritus, with laughter, or, like Heraclitus, with pity and tears. Montaigne believed that, of the two, Democritus showed the sounder judgement. Heraclitus esteemed man too highly in pitying him; human qualities, by their very nature, deserve contempt rather than commiseration. Timon, who will be reincarnated in Molière's Alceste, was a fool to hate mankind, accusing men of every kind of corruption; in doing so, he overestimated man's capacity for both good and evil. Diogenes, contemptuously ignoring mankind as offering nothing of interest, incapable equally of good and evil, exemplified a more appropriate response.

Montaigne concludes his chapter with a statement which modifies the commonplace Aristotelian view that laughter is one of the properties special to man, a quality which distinguishes him from all other creatures. This had been Rabelais's view expressed in the 'Poème liminaire' of *Gargantua*: 'It is better to write with laughter than with tears, for laughter is the property of man'.[7] Montaigne agreed, but adapted this axiom so that it became: 'The condition which is particular and proper to man is to be deserving of laughter as much as it is to laugh' ('Nostre propre et peculiere condition est autant ridicule que risible') (I, 50, p. 304).

The contrasting perspectives of Heraclitus and Democritus recall Aristotle's observation in the *Poetics* that tragedy places man in a magnifying perspective in order to make him a more worthy object of admiration and pity, while comedy diminishes man by exaggerating his weaknesses. Montaigne, however, is arguing that the Heraclitean, or tragic, perspective is inappropriate for man, and that the comic poet has no need to exaggerate man's limitations in order to inspire laughter. Man is already small and laughable by his very nature, and the comic writer has only to offer us a faithful portrait of him to invite mockery.

According to this view, the occupation of the satirist and comic poet, who both finds mankind laughable and invites man to join in the laughter, is the perfect career for a man of judgement.

Both Montaigne, explicitly, and Molière, by his practice, saw laughter as the truest possible response to the human condition. Faced with the folly which surrounds him – and, more importantly, with the folly he finds inside himself – a man who fails to laugh displays defective judgement. For the *honnête homme*, laughter is born of truth. The chosen audience of both Montaigne and Molière – though both, especially Molière, had a much wider appeal – was an elite of *honnêtes gens* of great discernment and taste, whose main pleasure and pursuit was teasing out old and new examples of folly and sense from their own and other people's behaviour. La Rochefoucauld, La Fontaine, La Bruyère and even Pascal addressed themselves to the same elite. All shared Montaigne's sense that the useful and pleasure-giving occupation of tracking down folly and sense was the one best suited to honest men and women whose highest ambition was the achievement of the freedom and lucidity which came from recognizing, with Socrates, that ignorance is the natural and proper condition of humankind.

For Montaigne, the most agreable context in which to exercise one's judgement was in conversation with honest men: 'The most fruitful and natural exercise of our minds is, in my opinion, conversation. I find it the most pleasant of all the activities in our lives' (*Essais*, III, 8, p. 922). Conversation with 'low and weakly minds' will do us considerable harm. It is with only very few men, Montaigne says, that discussion and argument give him pleasure – with those whom one might call 'honest and clever' [*honnestes et habiles*]. All that such men seek from one another is 'privacy, company and conversation: the exercise of their souls, without any other profit'. It is not necessary for such conversation to be weighty or profound; its characteristic qualities are grace and pertinence. All that is said bears the mark of 'a mature and constant judgement, blended with generosity, openness, gaiety and friendship' (III, 3, p. 824).

Much of the pleasure of such conversation comes from shared lucidity, the clarity of vision which was the ideal of the seventeenth-century *honnête homme*. Montaigne's *Essais* are, essentially, conversations of this kind, between the essayist and his readers. Molière's plays, too – especially the high comedies, *L'École des femmes*, *Le Tartuffe*, *Dom Juan*, *Le Misanthrope* and *Les Femmes savantes* – can be seen as conversations in which the comic poet and his audience share a lucid and amused view of human folly. To bring his honest and urbane spectators into the very heart of his actions, he provided them with lucid and modest spokesmen on stage, in such figures as Chrysalde, Cléante, Elmire, Dom Carlos, Philinte, Éliante, Ariste, Henriette and Clitandre, a community of *honnêtes hommes* and *honnêtes femmes*. Such figures are no more immune from human folly than the spectators in the audience or the other characters in the play, but they know both themselves and the world, and so take neither themselves nor other people too seriously.

# 9
## Sociability, Reason and Laughter

1. Sociability and the cardinal virtues

The first two special human properties, reason and sociability, were commonly seen as inseparable, as it was shared reason which united people in fellowship with one another. As Cicero wrote in *De Officiis*, when seeking to retrace 'to their ultimate sources the principles of fellowship and society that nature has established among men':

> The first principle is that which is found in the connection between all the members of the human race; and that bond of connection is reason and speech, which by the processes of teaching and learning, of communicating, discussing and reasoning associate men together and unite them in a sort of natural fraternity. (I, 50)

To follow nature, then, men must cultivate reason – not primarily as a speculative activity, but in the context of their relationships with others. Everywhere in Molière's plays, we see men and women either suffering from or enjoying their relationships with one another, and hear them discussing and analysing them in an attempt to get them into some kind of order.

As a comic writer, Molière was less interested in social harmony than in the different ways in which relationships fail when men and women abandon nature and reason. Some of his figures do succeed in following nature and reason, and their behaviour shows us the standards of sociability from which his fools fall short. The most articulate of Molière's sensible people, his *raisonneurs*, are in fact quite modest figures; they do not pride themselves on their wisdom, or consider themselves qualified to express authoritative views on the great and universal topics of marriage, religion, philosophy and medicine; they are simply level-headed people caught up in the ill-run affairs of their family or friends. When they do argue, it is because the crooked behaviour and reasoning of their interlocutors force them to do so. Their purpose is not to preach a philosophy of life but to head off disasters, avoid injustice, reconcile parents with children, save people in their immediate circle or family from making fools of themselves and, in general, to do what they can to promote the happiness of those around them.

In essence, Molière's *honnêtes hommes* and *honnêtes femmes* are doing nothing more remarkable than remind their fellows that neglect of the cardinal virtues, justice, prudence, temperance and fortitude, leads inevitably to social conflict and unhappiness. These are the virtues which Aristotle, Cicero and moral philosophers generally considered essential to the pursuit of happiness and the achievement of social harmony. Prudence, according to Aristotle in the *Nicomachean Ethics*, 'is a truth-attaining rational quality, concerned with action in relation to the things that are good and bad for human beings' (VI, v, 4). 'The first office of justice', Cicero wrote, 'is to keep one man from doing harm to another' (*De Officiis*, I, 20). Temperance, or moderation, enters into all that is said and done, for it is – again in Cicero's words – 'the science of doing the right thing at the right time' (ibid., I, 142). Fortitude, combining courage with persistence, is essential to the proper functioning of all virtues. As Cicero wrote, the cultivation of the cardinal virtues was essential to that perfect happiness which is felt when 'good men of congenial character are joined in intimate friendship' (I, 55).

## 2. Sociability in *L'École des maris*

In the opening scene of *L'École des maris* (1661) the two brothers discuss the individual's role in society. Sganarelle expresses a philosophy based on blind self-love. The first evidence of the wrongness of his views strikes the audience even before he speaks. He is so far out of tune with his times and his milieu that he is dressed in the clothes of a past generation. As his older brother points out, he has abandoned moderation; in questions of dress, good taste requires that one should neither be too fashionable nor lag behind the conventions of one's generation (ll. 41–54). When Sganarelle first appears on stage, the audience is struck by the jauntiness, bordering on boorishness, of his bearing. He lacks the poise of a mind and body in harmony with nature. When he breaks into speech, he is condemned still further. A good man's conversation, according to Cicero, 'should be easy and not in the least dogmatic', and his voice 'free from strain, yet neither faint nor shrill' (*De Officiis*, I, 133–4). In fact, Sganarelle is quick-tempered and abusive, repeatedly insulting his brother by insinuating that his age (Ariste is twenty years older) has weakened his brain and left him unfit for cogent argument.

Sganarelle's dialectic is undermined before we have time to hear it. Once we do hear it, we quickly see why. The burden of his argument is that he does not care what other people think and has only himself to please. With this argument, he undermines the social foundations of reason. For him, his brother and anyone else who happens to disagree with him are fools (ll. 9–10). Cicero argued that 'we should . . . in our dealings with people show what I may almost call reverence toward all men'; 'indifference to public opinion' – precisely the position of Sganarelle – 'implies not merely self-sufficiency, but even total lack of principle' (I, 99).

The subsequent action of *L'École des maris*, demonstrating Sganarelle's excessive self-satisfaction, his vindictiveness and cruelty, shows that his theoretical position is merely a disguise for behaviour dictated by the excesses of personal whim and passion unmoderated by common sense. Ariste, on the other hand, is seen to be sensible, fair-minded, modest and deeply respectful of the freedom of others, especially the freedom of the woman he hopes to marry; in fact, he practises all the cardinal virtues. Sganarelle's behaviour leads to frustration, failure and isolation, while Ariste's leads to the prospect of a happy marriage.

## 3. Sociability and misanthropy

Molière draws attention to the close thematic link between *L'École des maris* and *Le Misanthrope* (1666) through Philinte, who teasingly invites Alceste to see the parallel between Alceste and himself and the two brothers of *L'École des maris* (ll. 99–101). Alceste can be seen as a more articulate and attractive version of Sganarelle, while Philinte shares the tolerant urbanity of Ariste.

The main action in *Le Misanthrope* is an exploration of contrasting attitudes to sociability and integrity; the relative strengths and weaknesses of a number of different approaches to the question of how one should behave in society are illustrated in a series of social encounters which produce a rich harvest of comic improprieties. Most characters – Célimène, Arsinoé, Oronte and the two *marquis* – use social contacts to satisfy their own vanity and so lose touch with the demands of integrity. Alceste, a melancholic, blindly pursuing a false ideal of private integrity, forgets that man, by his very nature, is a social being; he wraps himself in a cocoon of melancholic self-absorption; in the midst of the social bustle of *salon* life, he retreats into a corner to nurse his black despair (ll. 1583–4). Typical of the melancholic, he is sure in his heart that, touched by genius, he stands above the common run of men; he alone, he feels, understands fully the corruption of mankind. In a world where reason was considered, by its very nature, to be the fruit of fellowship and conversation with one's fellow men, Alceste, in his wilful isolation, is well on the way to madness. Between these extremes of social flightiness and melancholic misanthropy, Philinte and Éliante tread the difficult course, in a turbulent and hypocritical society, of combining integrity with an appropriate degree of sociability.

The play's structure is already in place by the end of the opening act. The first three characters to appear take up the principal standpoints described by Aristotle in his discussion of the quality of agreeableness in the *Nicomachean Ethics* (IV, vi). Alceste is one of those 'surly or quarrelsome' people 'who object to everything and do not care in the least what pain they cause' (IV, vi, 2). Opposite him, Molière places another extreme – Aristotle's obsequious man who, because his ingratiating manner has an ulterior motive, is also a flatterer; this figure, Oronte, is one of those people 'who complaisantly approve of everything' (IV, vi, 1). The purpose of Oronte's flattery is to trap others into praising his poetry. The third position, between these two extremes, is represented by Philinte; his character has no special name, but Aristotle dwells upon the qualities which distinguish this middle disposition:

> It is clear that the dispositions described are blameworthy, and that the middle disposition between them is praiseworthy – that is, the tendency to acquiesce in the right things, and likewise to disapprove of the right things, in the right manner. But to this no special name has been assigned, though it very closely resembles friendship; for he who exemplifies this middle disposition is the sort of man we mean by the expression 'a good friend' .... A man of this character takes

everything in the right way not from personal liking or dislike, but from natural amiability. He will behave with the same propriety towards strangers and acquaintances alike, towards people with whom he is familiar and those with whom he is not. (IV, vi, 3–5)

Philinte is acquiescent when no harm will come of it; when he is caught in the gushing embrace of a man he barely recognizes, he responds in kind, displaying the proper degree of innocent social hypocrisy; he considers it worthwhile to feign enthusiasm for Oronte's insipid sonnet in an attempt to avoid a quarrel between Oronte and Alceste (I, 2). In contrast, Alceste is driven into an uncontrollable rage by both these trivial incidents. When it comes to more serious questions, such as the bilious hatred that the melancholic Alceste turns upon people in general, making him into a laughing stock and cutting him off from society, or the important matter of Alceste's love for the incorrigibly flirtatious Célimène, who would make him an utterly unsuitable wife, Philinte is not in the least acquiescent. He is open and frank in his criticisms and clear and firm in his advice to his friend. Philinte treats mere acquaintances with bland and easy good humour, reserving his inner self for his friends. Alceste, on the other hand, making no distinction between persons or situations, turns his anger equally against friends, mistress and rivals. Such conduct makes social relations impossible. Oronte, too, destroys the real value of social intercourse by his readiness to sell friendship to anyone who will repay him with flattery.

It is through the central couple of Alceste and Célimène that Molière explores the dangers of dogmatic integrity and excessive sociability most profoundly. Both have considerable merits: they are intelligent, lucid in their general analysis of human vice and folly, and each has great personal magnetism. In both, the social instincts common to all people are especially strong. Alceste, who is in love with Célimène, is experiencing one of the strongest of social pulls, the attraction which enslaves a lover to his mistress. Célimène, young, beautiful, free, intelligent, witty and coquettish, is surrounding herself with admirers who will applaud her brilliant social performance. Both Alceste and Célimène end the play isolated and unhappy because of their failure to achieve a reasonable balance between sociability and integrity.

Alceste devotes himself to integrity with such ferocious

single-mindedness that he is driven into hatred of all men, with the sole exception of himself – some of them because they are unjust and cruel, and the rest because they do not hate wicked people with sufficient venom (ll. 118–22). His devotion to virtue first destroys his relationships with his fellow men and secondly, by filling him with hatred, undermines his own virtue and integrity, for no one, least of all the hater himself, can profit from such hatred. All theorists of the passions agreed that an excess of hatred was detrimental to happiness and a danger to the health of the soul. Furthermore, he puts himself in the worst possible position from which to distinguish between the true and the false, between right and wrong, by closing his ears to the arguments of other men and women, all of whom he despises, and retaining love and respect for himself alone. His judgement is entirely at the mercy of melancholic self-love, unregulated by the correcting perspectives of others.

Alceste's bad judgement is revealed in most of his behaviour, but two incidents in particular show how far he has strayed from good taste and reason. One – a trivial example – occurs in the sonnet scene, where he fatuously asserts that the banal and dated jingle he quotes to Oronte captures the essence of true and unaffected passion (ll. 390–413). Philinte, appropriately, can only laugh at such a judgement. The second and more serious example is his proposal of marriage to Éliante (IV, 2). He confesses in his jealous rage that his proposal is motivated by the wish to punish Célimène. In his melancholic self-absorption he fails to see that he is treating Éliante with contempt, breaking every rule of *honnêteté* and propriety. He has lost sight of nature, reason and justice. As Philinte says, echoing Montaigne and St Paul, 'too much virtue can make us blameworthy; perfect reason flees all extremes and requires that we be virtuous with sobriety' (ll. 150–53). [1]

If the pursuit of virtue in melancholic isolation is the cause of Alceste's failure, it is the opposite fault of cultivating sociability without respect for integrity that leads to Célimène's downfall. Her social, coquettish games draw her into a web of lying and deceit; when her lovers compare letters and her duplicities are revealed, her social achievements, which have absorbed all her energies, collapse and leave her friendless. Her unreflecting pursuit of a brilliant social life leaves her isolated. Her strongest feelings are for Alceste, but no one, least of all Célimène, can tell whether or not she loves him. As Éliante says, 'How can one tell whether she loves him or not? Her heart is not really sure of what it feels; it loves sometimes without knowing it and, at other times, thinks it loves when in fact it does not' (ll. 1181–4). She is too busy playing social games to know the pleasure of love, and too addicted to the piquant amusements of malicious gossip to have the time and generosity needed to cultivate true friendship.

## 4. Alceste and laughter

If Alceste's melancholia undermines his reason and sociability, it also deprives him of humanity's third special defining quality – the ability to laugh. Alceste and Philinte illustrate Montaigne's and Molière's views on the relative values of the tragic and the comic perspectives discussed in Chapter 8. Alceste is unaware that his intemperate behaviour makes of him a natural butt for laughter; he refuses to listen when Philinte points this out to him (ll. 104–8).

Molière shows Alceste inspiring laughter in other characters inside the play as well as making the audience laugh. From the opening moments Philinte is amused by Alceste's disproportionate rage on seeing him greet a comparative stranger with every appearance of affection; Philinte makes light of this trivial incident, arguing that it is scarcely a hanging crime. His amusement, however, merely increases Alceste's anger, provoking the familiar lame response of people who take themselves too seriously: that this is no laughing matter (ll. 29–34). Again in the second scene, when Philinte laughs at Alceste's absurdly sincere delivery as he recites his favourite pastoral ditty, Alceste turns on him in rage, denouncing his friend as 'Monsieur le rieur' (ll. 388–416). In the portrait scene it is Célimène's turn to laugh at Alceste, with a rapid and accurate satirical sketch of a man whose whole social performance is dictated by a deep need to contradict everything and everybody (ll. 669–80). Again Alceste complains bitterly that the laughers are on Célimène's side (l. 681).

Blind to the ridiculous inside himself, Alceste is also blind to the ridiculous which can be seen all around him. Plunged in melancholy, he cannot profit from the therapeutic power of laughter. He has not learned that human folly is more deserving of laughter than of tears and rage. Alceste shares the defective judgement of Timon, the most famous of misanthropists, who, according to Montaigne, took life too seriously:

> For what we hate, we take to heart. This man wished us harm, passionately desired our ruin, fled our conversation as something dangerous, wicked and depraved. (*Essais*, I, 50, p. 304)

Philinte, on the other hand, does not take human wickedness too seriously. He is phlegmatic rather than bilious and melancholic. As he says to Alceste:

> Like you, I observe every day a hundred things which would have turned out better if a different course had been followed; but whatever I may encounter with each step I take, you don't see me flying into a rage like you; I take men quietly, as they come, and accustom my soul to putting up with what they do; and I believe that, in court or in town, my phlegm is as philosophical as your bile. (ll. 159–66)

Philinte is no less clear-sighted than Alceste or Timon in seeing human vices and injustices:

> I see the faults against which your soul murmurs as vices attached to human nature; and my mind is no more offended by the sight of a dishonest, unjust and greedy man than by vultures hungry for carnage, monkeys playing mean tricks and raging wolves. (ll. 173–8)

Philinte's philosophical phlegm is evident in his arguments with Alceste: while the latter stamps and rages, Philinte merely smiles at his friend's excesses. Philinte's cool mockery reflects the attitudes of Democritus and Diogenes; he also shares the perspectives of Montaigne and of Molière himself. Montaigne had written:

> It seems to me that we can never be despised beyond our deserts. Pity and commiseration imply some esteem for the thing one pities; the things we mock, we consider worthless. I think there is less misfortune than vanity in us, less wickedness than silliness; we are not so full of evil as of inanity; we are less wretched than vile. (*Essais*, I, 50, p. 303)

Diogenes is to be preferred to Timon, for while the latter raged,

Diogenes 'held us in such slight regard that we could neither trouble him nor upset him by our corruption, and he avoided our company, not from fear, but out of disdain for our conversation' (p. 304).

Philinte, in other ways, is quite unlike the traditional Diogenes, a figure who cared little for social conventions. Nor is Philinte a cynic. He does not laugh or mock without reason, and he does his best to save Alceste from his own folly. He is an urbane, polished Diogenes, fit to move in the highest court circles. Beneath his polish, urbanity and skilful social hypocrisy, however, Philinte is a lucid, generous but mocking judge of human weakness and folly. It is an argument implicit in the action of *Le Misanthrope* that this blend of tolerance, polish and goodwill with detached and gently mocking lucidity provides a sound basis for enjoying one of the most delightful of human pleasures, the pleasure men and women can take in the company of their fellows.

In contrast, the melancholic Alceste is without judgement, knows little pleasure in life, is shorn of the capacity to laugh either at himself or at others and, for an urbane seventeenth-century audience, is heading for insanity. He wishes to leave the civilized world and bury himself in the country (ll. 1803–6) where, according to Dorine's description of country life in *Le Tartuffe*, he will be able to visit the wives of the bailiff and the tax-collector, and watch puppet shows and performing monkeys (*Le Tartuffe*, ll. 660–66).

The issues of sociability and reason are at the heart of *L'École des maris* and *Le Misanthrope*. Other comedies by Molière focus upon different topics such as avarice, social climbing, preciosity, false learning, tyranny, pedantry, religious hypocrisy, medicine or hypochondria, but in all his portraits of human behaviour one finds the recurring, underlying pattern of fools failing to cope with the demands of sociability and reason.

# 10
## Families

### 1. A microcosm of society and state

It was a commonplace of moral philosophy that the skills needed to live happily in the wider human society were first learned in the family. Cicero wrote:

> For since the reproductive instinct is by nature's gift the common possession of all living creatures, the first bond of union is that between husband and wife; the next, that between parents and children; then we find one home, with everything in common. And this is the foundation of civil government, the nursery, as it were, of the state. (*De Officiis*, I, 54)

Most of Molière's plays are set in a domestic context. As the tragic poet portrayed kings and the fabulist animals, the comic poet, from the earliest origins of New Comedy, portrayed families. The countless conflicts and dramas involving husbands and wives, parents and children and masters and servants provided ideal subject matter for the comic playwright wishing to portray humankind in a belittling perspective. The home was the natural domain of comedy. If the courts of kings offered a magnificent and universally recognizable setting for the great dramas affecting the destinies of nations, the home provided a humble, equally universal and even more familiar setting for the countless little dramas which could bring happiness or unhappiness to ordinary men and women. The problems facing families may be on a smaller scale, but they are no less complex or intractable than those facing statesmen, and, what is more, it is in the individual's relationships with his or her family that human bonds are tightest and moral obligations clearest. For ordinary men and women, it is in the family that rational behaviour gives most pleasure and irrational behaviour causes most distress.

Molière's audiences would have shared a number of assumptions about how families should behave. The model is simple and, for most ordinary people, has changed little over the centuries: parents should be just, affectionate, prudent and generous towards their children; children should love and respect their parents; wives should be loyal to their husbands and run their homes efficiently, while husbands should love and respect their wives. Molière's audiences over the ages, whatever their private experiences of family life, have had no difficulty in recognizing and endorsing such a view. In his portraits of family life, Molière makes use of this universal familiarity to explore deviations from archetypal patterns which audiences instantly recognize.

## 2. A testing ground for folly and sense

Though Molière made frequent use of families, his plays are not primarily about families. Each play focuses on a different kind of folly or vice, often introduced into the home by an intruder, which then infects one or more members of the household; the nature and degree of the folly or vice can then be gauged from the damage it inflicts upon family life. In the intimate circle of the home, the effects of injustice are magnified, and follies which can often remain hidden in a wider society, where individuals are less closely involved with one another, become major obstacles to happiness and justice.

An extreme example of such disruption occurs in *Le Tartuffe*, where Molière uses the family to underline the special dangers which follow when a ruthless villain claims for his schemes the combined authority of God and the Church. Tartuffe wins the confidence of the father, Orgon, and, through him, rules the whole house, gains control of the family's money and comes close to committing Orgon to prison and turning the rest of the family out on to the street. The dual cause of the family's downfall is a hypocrite's scheming and the gullibility of a husband and father. The extent of Orgon's folly is revealed most clearly by his treatment of his wife and daughter. Elmire is his second wife, much younger than himself, attractive and attentive, and a kind stepmother to his grown-up children. Forgetting his duties as a husband, Orgon neglects her, loving Tartuffe in her place; in addition, in his new zeal, he seeks to force his wife to spend time alone with Tartuffe and so exposes her to the hypocrite's lecherous advances (l. 1174).

As a father, Orgon is still more unjust; Molière deliberately makes Mariane the most gentle, affectionate and obedient of daughters, so that when she pleads with Orgon not to force her to marry the lecherous hypocrite, we can feel to the full the cruelty of his intransigence (ll. 1276–1306). The audience is led to conclude that a father who can do all this in the name of religion has lost sight not merely of Christianity but of simple humanity and common sense.

### 3. Avarice and paternal love

In *L'Avare* Molière portrays another family at risk because of the folly of a father, but in this play, the sense of impending danger is less strong. Avarice, we are led to conclude, is less of a threat than religious hypocrisy.

The play shows how avarice robs a man of all properly human pleasures. It shows, too, the social effects of this vice, particularly its effects on the miser's immediate family. At the beginning, Harpagon is in a position to bring happiness to his family. His son and daughter, of marriageable age, are in love with two suitable but impoverished young people, and Harpagon is rich enough to provide for them all. By doing so, he would enjoy the deserved gratitude and love of his children and, more importantly, experience the pleasures of exercising to the full a father's love for his offspring. Instead, he seeks to marry his children to a widow and a widower, both rich as well as old. In addition, he starves them of money, forcing his son to raise money by gambling, and driving him into the hands of money-lenders. Then, to cap it all, he plans to remarry, reminding the audience that many a son and daughter were left without funds for their whole lives by vengeful or self-indulgent old men marrying young wives who might then outlive their stepchildren.[1]

These dangers, however, are merely hinted at. The main function of Harpagon's children is not to display the sufferings caused by avarice but to be the nucleus of a circle of normal people whose vitality, generosity of spirit and humanity provide the measure against which the inhumanity of Harpagon, 'the human of all humans the least human' (II, 4), can be measured. The charm, sincerity and verve of Cléante and Élise, of Valère and Mariane, who later turn out to be brother and sister, the inventiveness of La Flèche and Frosine and the generosity of Anselme provide a stream of humanity which contrasts with the aridity of Harpagon's anxious and lonely money-loving pleasures.

Within this broad opposition, Molière sets up more precise parallels. He casts the miser and his son as rivals for Mariane's hand to show the difference between human love and love which takes second place to love of money. Harpagon's courtship is seen to be ludicrous anyway as he is old, infirm and shabbily dressed, out of touch with the elegant etiquette of modern Paris; but, to make matters worse, he will not even recognize the convention that a rich old man courting a handsome young woman must at least spend money on her. As a result, his wooing is cold, drab and joyless. Cléante, on the other hand, young, good-looking and fashionably dressed, elegant in speech and manner, uses his father's money to lay on a succession of treats which reflect the more normal generosity of love and are a foretaste of a married life which will be stylish and rich in pleasures and excitements.

Another parallel opposes the two fathers. Anselme, like Harpagon, is the father of two children of marriageable age; he, too, is thinking of remarrying and, like Harpagon, has unknowingly chosen as wife the young woman his son wishes to marry. Unlike Harpagon, however, Anselme has no wish to press his suit against Élise's inclination. A minor character, Anselme is a rapid sketch of the good father. He has spent sixteen years searching for his wife and two children, whom he now believes to be dead. In the fifth act, when he discovers that Valère and Mariane are his missing children, and that his wife is still alive, the family affection which has been frustrated all those years is free to express itself and he happily puts his wealth at the disposal of his new-found family, offering to pay for both marriages, even agreeing to buy Harpagon a new suit for the weddings and to pay the *Commissaire* who had been called in to investigate the theft of Harpagon's *cassette*.

While Harpagon's avarice spreads misery and suffering on all sides, Anselme's generosity heals wounds and turns misery into joy. Most important of all, Anselme's money brings him happiness too. The respective fates of the two fathers are displayed in

the closing moments of the play. Anselme gathers the young
people around him and says: 'Let us go quickly and share our
joy with your mother'; while Harpagon, isolated in his manic
joy, adds: 'And I, to see my dear *cassette*'.[2]

## 4. Homes in chaos

In *Le Tartuffe* and *L'Avare*, an important minor theme is the
physical disruption of the household caused by false religious
zeal and avarice. In *Les Femmes savantes*, the spectacle of a house
turned upside down is central to the play.

The danger which threatens family life in *Les Femmes savantes*
stems from the vanity of women puffed up by false learning.
Molière designs a plot, as in *Le Tartuffe*, in which the family is
exposed to exploitation by an unscrupulous outsider; Trissotin is
not a criminal with a record, like Tartuffe, but he worms his
way into the family in order to marry one of the daughters and
get his hands on a good portion of the family's wealth. Again,
Molière places a flawed father at the head of the family: if
Chrysale had been stronger, his wife would not have been in a
position to turn the house upside down in the name of philosophy, and Trissotin would never have gained entry into the
family circle in the first place.

The satirical focus of the play is the three would-be learned
women of the title: the pivotal figure is Philaminte, a tyrant-
wife, tyrant-mother and tyrant-philosopher, played in Molière's
time by a man; she is supported by two coquettes: one, Bélise,
her sister-in-law, an old maid who fills her mind with imagined
Platonic lovers, the other, Armande, her daughter, a handsome
coquette and *précieuse* smarting from the loss of her lover. To
test and display the effects of learning on the three women,
Molière places them in a domestic context, a woman's first and
most natural sphere of influence and activity. The action of the
play quickly reveals that the women's bogus learning has made
them unfit to run a house and, worse still, has split the family
into irreconcilable factions.

Relationships were never likely to be harmonious in a household composed of a henpecked husband, a tyrant-wife, a disappointed old maid and two sisters who are rivals in love, but
Molière shows how false learning brings them close to breaking

down altogether. Supported by the authority of false learning, Philaminte usurps her husband's role and takes all the decisions without consulting him; she feels justified in giving free rein to her bullying instincts because, in her partnership with her husband, she sees herself as representing the soul; she alone can exercise reason, understanding and the will. In her estimation, her husband is a body, a mere shell, the empty husk of a human being. Running the house on philosophical principles, she has turned her servants into neophyte philosophers who care little for the things of this world and so neglect such mundane matters as cooking and cleaning; Martine, the only level-headed servant left, is dismissed because of her bad grammar.

The effects of false learning on Armande, the third *femme savante*, are equally serious. Having lost her lover to her younger sister by affecting scorn for the pleasures of the flesh, she is consumed with rage and jealousy. In her thirst for revenge, she joins forces with her mother in her campaign to make Henriette marry Trissotin. Henriette has dared to challenge her mother's authority by refusing to join her learned circle, and so – to punish her and, at the same time, to introduce her to the beauties of philosophy and letters – she is to be forced to marry the mincing, precious poet who cares only for her money.

The chaos of the household in which the family lives in *Les Femmes savantes* is a metaphor for a mind stuffed with erudition and bereft of judgement. For Molière as for Montaigne, memorized, untried learning places an impenetrable screen between the understanding and the real world, blotting out the light of reason and common sense. More interestingly, Molière also suggests through this portrait of family life that the affected world of preciosity and ostentatious erudition, with its vanities, factions and hypocrisies, provided a fertile breeding-ground for more dangerous vices than inflamed authorial vanity and bad taste.

Similar patterns can be seen in *Le Bourgeois gentilhomme* and *Le Malade imaginaire*, where the follies of a parent bring division and disorder into the family and the home. In the first of these, a *bourgeois* household is upset by an invasion of musicians, tailors, masters employed to teach Monsieur Jourdain the accomplishments of a perfect gentleman, and an impoverished aristocrat intent on spending some of the *bourgeois's* wealth. Here the comic register is lighter; the aristocratic intruder is seen to be harmless, the disorder is superficial, and the audience feels that the family will easily recover its equilibrium.

Family life in *Le Malade imaginaire*, revolving round the functioning of the hypochondriac's bowels, disturbed by the comings and goings of doctors and apothecaries, its funds threatened by medical bills and, more seriously, by the dishonest schemes of a stepmother pandering to the hypochondriac's desire to be indulged and sowing discord between him and his children, is more seriously disrupted. Behind all the laughter – and this is one of the most farcical of his plays – Molière suggests the bleakness, the lack of grace and seemliness, of a household dominated by hypochondria.

## 5. The servant as defender of the family

The laughter in Molière's family plays is inspired in the main by the fools and villains who come close to wrecking family life. However, the plays would not be comedies at all if Molière did not also portray an alliance of the sound people in each household who fight off these threats and achieve, at least for the sensible and innocent members of each family, the restoration of order and happiness.

This conflict between folly and sense, which varies only in detail from play to play, is clearest in *Le Tartuffe*, where the threat to the innocent is most acute. Though it is in fact the King who in the end rescues the family, Molière permits his audience to take comfort from the sheer size and talents of the alliance of figures opposed to Tartuffe: the resourceful and resilient Elmire, Cléante, urbane and balanced in his judgements, Dorine, irrepressible and full of sense, the young and energetic men, Damis and Valère, and the submissive but quietly determined Mariane inspire faith that, somehow, sense will triumph in the end. In balancing the forces of good and evil, sense and folly, Molière is careful always to place enough people and resources on the side of the good and the sensible to permit his audience to retain just the degree of optimism necessary for it to laugh rather than weep at the follies and vices paraded before it.

The figure of the loyal and clear-sighted servant has a special role in the various battles to restore order and sense to Molière's suffering households. Molière's good servants – all of them women – have a wisdom of their own, which is all the more sound because theirs is natural good sense. Their opinions have the special authority which comes from simplicity. As they do not derive their views from long-winded reasoning or unwieldy erudition, they are less likely to have their clarity of vision obscured by irrelevant considerations. Molière shares the view expressed by Montaigne in 'De la Praesumption':

> The condition of people least to be disdained, it seems to me, is the one which in its simplicity holds the lowest rank and shows us the best regulated social conduct. The morals and conversation of peasants, I find as often as not, are ordered more in accordance with the prescriptions of true philosophy than those of our philosophers. 'The common man is wiser because he knows just as much as he needs to know.'(*Essais*, II, 17, p. 660)

Montaigne was not idealizing peasants, as many writers of the eighteenth and nineteenth centuries were to do, but drawing attention to the fact that people with pretensions to learning or refinement often overreach themselves and, in their struggle for improvement, lose the good sense they were born with. Molière's delightful sketch of the peasants in *Dom Juan*, noisily completing their quarrel and laying their bets before getting round to rescuing the drowning men from the capsized boat, suggests that he, too, had no inclination to idealize the figure of the peasant (II, 1). A foolish peasant was as worthy of mockery as a foppish *marquis* or a garrulous pedant.

However, Molière did give considerable moral weight, in a number of his plays, to the figure of the untaught but clear-sighted servant. Dorine in *Le Tartuffe*, Martine in *Les Femmes savantes*, Nicole in *Le Bourgeois Gentilhomme*, and Toinette in *Le Malade imaginaire* all willingly take on the task of defending the true interests of their respective families. None of them rebels against the social order which places them so far below their masters. Indeed, they are driven into open argument only when the masters themselves fail to uphold the proper social order. Toinette speaks for all of them when she says to Argan: 'When a master isn't thinking what he's doing, a servant in her senses has a right to set him straight' (I, 5). Her task is to save Argan from marrying his daughter to a halfwit doctor. The whole

development of the quarrel in this scene is designed to show that
when a servant talking sense opposes a master talking nonsense,
the immediate social order on stage must be reversed to protect
the real, underlying and long-term social order which is under
threat. Toinette borrows her master's authority in order to
protect him and his family. It is Toinette who takes a paternal
tone, urging Argan to remain calm; it is she who presents an
orderly and convincing case, reminding Argan that a loving
father could not possibly marry his daughter to such a man as
Thomas Diafoirus. The so-called master, trembling and stamping
his foot like a child in a tantrum, can only scream, in an attempt
to dominate the situation: 'I am *not* good and I can be naughty
when I want to'. The reversal of roles reaches its logical climax
when Toinette threatens to disinherit Angélique if she dares to
obey her father's preposterous orders, while Argan, without a
shred of argument to defend himself with, attempts to beat her
with his stick.

Martine's instinctive sense of hierarchy and propriety, in *Les
Femmes savantes*, is outraged by Philaminte's bullying ascendancy
over her husband. The charm of her role comes from the way in
which Chrysale, impressed by her extraordinary courage in
standing up to his wife, adopts her as his ally and champion.
Martine shows up the follies of both her master and her mistress;
she exposes the pusillanimity of a master who needs the support
of a kitchen maid to give him the courage to disagree with his
wife and the wrongness of a wife usurping her husband's authority. Dorine, too, in *Le Tartuffe*, is thrust into the role of
attempting to redress Orgon's false reasoning: her aim is to save
Orgon from ruining his daughter's life and losing his own good
name by marrying his daughter to a low-born and ill-favoured
hypocrite and swindler. Nicole, in *Le Bourgeois Gentilhomme*,
shows up the absurdity of her master's pretensions by the
simplest, most natural and most lucid of responses: faced with
Monsieur Jourdain in his newly tailored would-be aristocratic
outfit, she displays all the wisdom the situation demands by
doubling up in uncontrollable laughter (III, 2).

All these servants speak in a language which, like Nicole's
laughter, flows naturally and spontaneously, as if springing up
from deep wells of unspoilt humanity. Their retorts are worth
more than laboured dialectic. The contrast between Dorine's

plain honesty and Tartuffe's twisted and lewd sophistry, for example, is caught in her response to Tartuffe when he covers her bosom with his handkerchief to protect his eyes from carnal temptation; she answers without hesitation that the sight of him naked from head to toe would leave her quite unmoved. Audiences no doubt smiled condescendingly when they heard Martine's rough speech, but they could not have doubted the rightness of her conclusion that Trissotin would make Henriette a poor husband: 'Why, if you please, land her with a scholar forever rabbiting on? It's a husband she needs, not a pedagogue' (ll. 1656–8). The very simplicity and roughness of their tongues is a guarantee of the truth and honesty of what they have to say.

Molière's *raisonneurs* defend common sense through complex, well-informed and well-balanced dialectic. His women servants, in contrast, have developed naturally, sharpening their judgements through contact with things not words, acquiring the habit of distinguishing between the true and the false without passing through the dangerous processes of study and learning. These portraits are a reflection of the great army of unsung women who ran the day-to-day lives of France's wealthy and aristocratic households and who, as nurses and housekeepers, were often the people most responsible for the practical upbringing of children.

## 6. Conservative values

Taken as a group, Molière's family plays are not intended to be a rounded picture of family life. Parents and children tend to share similar characteristics from one comedy to another. They face almost the same obstacles and complications, and their problems are ultimately sorted out in similar dénouements. Molière saw the family as a timeless institution and showed no desire to reform it. His interest was in the forces of unreason which threatened to destroy the old, reassuringly familiar patterns of family life. There is no evidence, for example, that he sought to encourage the young to break free from parental influence and marry according to their own private inclinations. In every case of a disagreement between children and parents, it turns out that the young lovers have chosen just the husband or wife a sensible parent would have wished his or her child to marry. Their choices fall comfortably within existing conventions. When the rich peasant farmer George Dandin does try to break new ground, marrying above his social status, the marriage is a failure and Dandin concludes at the end of the play that the only effective solution to his marital problems is to throw himself headfirst into the village pond.

The implied solution to the problems which beset Molière's families is not social reform, still less the abandonment of the family as an outmoded institution, but private reform. If parents and children could learn to obey the laws of nature, of prudence, justice, moderation, generosity and family affection, their clashes would melt away. There is an assumption behind the very genre of New Comedy, where the typical dénouement shows parents and children reconciled and lovers brought together in marriage, that happiness is to be found within family life. This is the view of Anselme in *L'Avare* who, believing his family dead, decides to marry again in the hope of enjoying in his old age 'the consolation of some new family' (V, 5). There is much wrong with the people who make up Molière's families, but the family as an institution is not under attack.

Molière's view of the family is of necessity profoundly conservative. Folly and vice bring unwanted change, upsetting existing plans and relationships. The family is the well-loved social institution with a lasting and well-tried code of values. By showing how contemporary follies and abuses threatened these values, Molière was showing how they also threatened the values of society as a whole.

# 11
## *Aristotelian Pedants*

1. The stereotype of the pedant

Among Molière's pedants, the earliest and most traditional are the farcical Aristotelian *docteurs* (not to be confused with medical doctors) who appear in *La Jalousie du Barbouillé, Dépit amoureux, Le Mariage forcé* and *Le Bourgeois Gentilhomme*.[1] There is evidence that *docteurs* had also played prominent roles in his earlier unpublished plays: the first farce Molière's troupe performed before the King and court, in 1658, was *Le Docteur amoureux*; other lost farces include *Les Trois Docteurs rivaux, Le Maître d'École,* and *Gros-René écolier*.[2] These figures belong to a long-established line of stage pedants common in farces of the fifteenth and sixteenth centuries. Among the comic stereotypes built up from the dominating characteristics of each of the trades and professions, the pedant, or *docteur*, based on the school and university teacher, was one of the the most frequent. Montaigne recalls, at the beginning of his chapter 'Du pédantisme' (*Essais*, I, 25, p.133), that the fool in the Italian comedies he saw in his childhood days was always a pedant. The stereotype of the pedant was simple: in academic robes, he was a talkative, pontificating figure, inordinately proud of his erudition, irascible, spouting bad Latin, quoting learned authorities, hopelessly out of touch with the real world, always ready to declaim some item from his rich store of rhetorical exercises – word-lists, encomiums (of himself), classical exempla and memorized summaries of the main branches of knowledge. Though in essence a satirical figure, the stage pedant, over the ages, had taken on a new and separate life as a clown, a useful focus for a wide variety of farcical stage routines.[3]

At first sight, Molière's four Aristotelian pedants fit quite comfortably into this picture. The *Docteur* (*La Jalousie du Barbouillé*), Métaphraste (*Dépit amoureux*), Pancrace (*Le Mariage forcé*) and the *Maître de philosophie* (*Le Bourgeois Gentilhomme*) are all stage clowns. Their function is to provide one or two lively farcical interludes or, in the case of *Le Mariage forcé* and *Le Bourgeois Gentilhomme*, episodes which help to characterize the comic protagonists, Sganarelle and Monsieur Jourdain. The *Docteur*, Métaphraste and Pancrace are so alike as to be interchangeable. Their memories are overloaded with learning, and the other more properly human faculties of judgement and feeling are destroyed in them; even their eyes and ears seem to have stopped functioning. All three of them are consulted in their capacity as learned men on particular family problems, but are so puffed up, so blinded by the spectacle of their own omniscience, so deafened by the sound of their own voices, that they never discover the nature of the problems upon which they are being asked to advise. As they have no eyes to see and no ears to hear, they can never respond appropriately to other people. Instead, odd words or half-heard phrases prompt them to launch into well-memorized but quite irrelevant rhetorical set pieces. The favourite theme for these orations is their own pre-eminence: the pedant in *La Jalousie du Barbouillé* can enumerate, with learned glosses on the symbolic value of each number, ten reasons to explain why he is such a learned doctor (Sc. 2). Pancrace is driven from the stage several times in *Le Mariage forcé*, still listing, as his voice fades into the wings, the countless disciplines of which he is master (Sc. 4). When called upon to listen, all three pedants drown the words of their interlocutors with *sententiae* extolling the merits of brevity until, driven mad by the frustrations of being expected to listen while others speak, they let go another flood of unstaunchable rhetoric which can be countered only by their being dragged or pushed off the stage. All three peddle the words, ideas and opinions of others. Métaphraste, especially, resorts to authority for all his statements, however trivial; in one conversation, he quotes from feudal law, Cicero, 'les Grecs', Virgil, Despautère's *La Syntaxe*, and Quintilian.[4] All four pedants – but particularly Pancrace and the *Maître de philosophie* – show through their displays of uncontrollable rage that their mastery of the theory of moral philosophy has brought them no practical benefit.

## 2. Pedantry and scholasticism

In fact it is not only to the tradition of farce that Molière's pedants belong; they are part of a strong current of Renaissance and seventeenth-century criticism of university and school education. The highly systematized Thomist Aristotelianism taught in all faculties and schools remained essentially the same throughout the Renaissance and the seventeenth century.[5] All the characteristics of Molière's pedant-clowns had already been exposed to censure and ridicule by Montaigne. In Montaigne's view, the scholastic method, which involved extensive memory training in order that pupils and students might learn by heart a vast body of predigested, systematically ordered material, taught the young to be vain and proud of their attainments, while failing to teach them judgement, self-knowledge and practical moral philosophy.[6] The masters themselves, according to Montaigne, were products of the system: inferior men, intent on parading their knowledge, fierce in their defence of scholastic dogma, excessively quarrelsome in disputes, incapable of conversing freely with others and utterly bereft of any of the talents needed to run a state, an army, or indeed anything which demanded a practical knowledge of the world. Their minds do not grow as they acquire more knowledge, but become overloaded so that they are bent double under the burden of their acquisitions and cannot function any more. Their learning is second-hand, so that they cannot think without the crutch of authority and quotation: 'We know how to say: Cicero says the following; these are the morals of Plato; these are the very words of Aristotle. But what of us, what do we ourselves say? What is our judgement? What do we do? A parrot could say as much' (I, 25, p. 137). The knowledge they do have is passed from hand to hand 'for the sole purpose of showing it off, of addressing others, of making a lot of noise over it' (ibid., p. 136). The content of their learning is never assimilated: 'more often than not, they listen neither to one another nor to anyone else, and . . . their memories are quite full while their judgment is perfectly empty' (ibid., p. 139). Their talk is copious but meaningless; Montaigne cites the case of a friend of his who, to amuse himself, kept up a day-long debate with a distinguished scholastic philosopher by inventing 'a string of gibberish, unconnected statements, a mosaic of disparate elements, except that it was often mixed up with terms relating to the matter of the dispute'; the philosopher is alleged to have answered each piece of nonsense as if it had been a sound debating point (p. 139). Their disputes are habitually conducted in a spirit of hostility and rage. As their first priority is to counter one another's arguments, they quickly lose sight of the truth: 'We learn to dispute only in order to contradict and, with each speaker contradicting and being contradicted, it follows that the dispute bears no fruit but the loss and destruction of the truth' (III, 8, p. 926).

In the seventeenth century, while Molière's scholastic education was still in progress at the Jesuit Collège de Clermont, Descartes, in his *Discours de la Méthode* (1637), reviewed his scholastic education, which he had received from the Jesuits at the Collège de la Flèche and which, in all essentials, was the same as the playwright's. Though Descartes's tone is less polemical than Montaigne's, and he professes to think highly of his teachers, his dismissal of their philosophy is no less damning: 'philosophy teaches us to speak plausibly of all things and to win the admiration of those less learned than ourselves'.[7] For Descartes, as for Montaigne, scholastic philosophy was concerned with appearances, not with truth:

> I have never observed . . . that the disputes practised in the schools have led to the discovery of any truth which had not already been known beforehand; for, while each speaker seeks to win, he is much more concerned with making his argument plausible than with giving due weight to the reasons on both sides. (p. 173)

Scholastic scientists look to Aristotle for answers to questions which he had never even asked. They are like ivy which can never rise higher than the tree on which it relies for support and which, once it has reached the top, tends to climb down again. Worst of all, however, they have perfected a method of argument which permits them to discourse with great confidence upon things of which they have no knowledge whatsoever:

> Their way of philosophizing is very convenient for those who have only very mediocre minds; for the obscurity of the distinctions and principles of which they make use permits them to speak boldly of all things as if they understood them, and to support everything they say against the most subtle and clever opponents, without there being any way of persuading them. (p. 174)

## 3. A unified cosmology?

Descartes was one of a host of figures, including Gassendi, Charron, Pascal and Boileau, who, for a variety of reasons and from differing vantage points, criticized the content, methodology and attitudes of Aristotelian philosophers intent on defending orthodoxy against the new ideas and discoveries which were revolutionizing both philosophy and science in the seventeenth century.[8] Molière was part of this modern movement; the fact that his stage pedants owed so much to tradition did not diminish their contemporary significance. His portraits of pedants show the knowledge of scholastic thought and pedagogy one might expect from a successful pupil of the Jesuits; they also show a lively awareness of the features of Aristotelianism under attack.[9] The unity of the old Christianized Aristotelian cosmology was disintegrating, to be replaced piecemeal by a fragmented, ever-changing group of separate sciences as Copernicus, Kepler, Galileo (astronomy and mathematics), Paracelsus, Vesalius, Harvey (medicine and anatomy), Bacon, Descartes, Gassendi and Pascal (philosophy, mathematics and physics) proposed new theories which grew out of observation, experiment or new philosophies. The defenders of scholastic philosophy and science were understandably unwilling to concede that any part of their reassuringly familiar, interlocking system might be in error, as they foresaw that the whole system might then fall apart. Molière emphasized this point in *La Jalousie du Barbouillé*, where the pedant seizes upon Villebrequin's remark that 'all are of one accord', saying: 'On the question of accord, would you like me to read you a chapter from Aristotle in which he proves that all the parts of the universe owe their continued existence only to the accord between them?' (Sc. 13).

The fear of losing this universal accord, even on the most trifling questions of terminological orthodoxy, lies behind Molière's satirical portrait of Pancrace in *Le Mariage forcé*. As Pancrace reverses on to the stage, following a dispute with a fellow Aristotelian, he trembles with rage, shaking his fist at his absent colleague, who has dared to speak of the 'form' of a hat, using the Aristotelian technical term reserved for living beings, when the proper term for an inanimate object should have been 'figure'. Even this slight departure from orthodoxy is enough to convince Pancrace that civilization is at an end:

Ah! Sganarelle, my good sir, all is overturned today and the world has fallen into general corruption; terrifying licence reigns everywhere; and the magistrates, who are appointed to maintain order in this state, should blush with shame for permitting a scandal as intolerable as the one of which I speak. (Sc. 4)

Pancrace's dissatisfaction with the magistracy is less absurd than it may seem; in 1624, the Paris *Parlement* did pass an Act forbidding people from holding or teaching views contrary to the doctrine of Aristotle.[10]

## 4. Plenum or vacuum?

A major element in the scientific revolution was the promotion of the empirical method and the invention of instruments which permitted scientists to pay more attention to the evidence of the senses. Significantly, Molière derives much humour from his pedants' blindness to empirical evidence. This is portrayed through the simple and effective farcical trick of making them metaphorically blind and deaf to the world. When Pancrace arrives on stage, he fails to see Sganarelle, who observes: 'His anger prevents him from seeing me' (Sc. 4). When he finally becomes aware of Sganarelle's existence, he is so bent upon airing his own knowledge that he has no ear for anything Sganarelle might have to say. Empirical evidence is gathered through the senses, and the pedants' habitual practice of dredging up and displaying remembered erudition leaves their senses with no time or opportunity to perceive immediate external phenomena.

   The clearest illustration of the pedant's contempt for empirical evidence can be found in Métaphraste's conversation with Albert in *Dépit amoureux*. Albert is worried by his son (in fact a daughter disguised as a son), who has sunk into a fit of melancholy, and confides his anxieties to Métaphraste. Instead of listening to Albert's evidence, the pedant listens for words or phrases which will permit him to display his erudition; he interrupts Albert's account with a false etymology and irrelevant allusions to a variety of classical authorities. Albert eventually manages to describe a scene which he alone witnessed the day before, a glimpse of his offspring retreating to a secluded woodland corner, and Métaphraste, who was not there and so could have nothing to add, translates his words into Latin and quotes Virgil evoking a similar scene. The pedant's words are all drawn from memory and have no connection with the living world to which Albert belongs. We sympathize with Albert, for all his ignorance, when he exclaims: 'How could this Virgil chap have said this, since I'm certain that, other than the two of us, there was not a soul in this quiet place?' (ll. 711–13).

In essence, Albert's complaint that Virgil could have had nothing relevant to add, as he was not there, is the complaint empirical scientists levelled against scholastic scientists who preferred the opinions of men who had been dead for centuries to the living evidence observable in the world around them. This problem of the conflict between ancient authority and the evidence of practical experiment lay at the heart of disputes on the question of whether or not a vacuum was possible in nature. The belief that nature was a plenum was fundamental to Aristotelian physics. Molière alludes to the question through Pancrace, for whom to admit the possibility of a vacuum in nature would be an absurdity: 'Rather than agree that we should say the *form* of a hat, I would agree that *datur vacuum in rerum natura*, and that I am only a fool' (Sc. 4).

Pascal has left an account of his dispute, in 1647, with an Aristotelian scientist, the Jesuit Père Noël, rector of the Collège de Clermont and formerly one of Descartes's teachers at La Flèche, on the question of the vacuum.[11] Their clash shows that, in his contacts with a living defender of scholastic principles, Pascal shared with Albert and Sganarelle the difficulties of communicating with a man who had no wish to hear what his interlocutor had to say. Pascal's empirical standpoint was that if experimental evidence showed that a space containing no known substance could be produced, then the hypothesis that nature abhors a vacuum should be abandoned. Theory and hypothesis, however venerable and however numerous and distinguished the figures who support them, are invalidated when there is a single piece of observable evidence which they cannot accommodate: 'on subjects of this nature, we do not base ourselves upon authorities: when we cite authors, we cite their demonstrations, not their names' (p. 523). To provide evidence of a vacuum, Pascal designed and performed a variety of experiments, based

on recent research carried out by Torricelli, tending to confirm
the probability of its existence. Noël, whose only concern was
to defend the scholastic axiom that a vacuum in nature was
impossible, countered Pascal's experimental evidence with a
variety of new and old hypotheses designed to show that the
space which appeared to be a vacuum could, in theory, be made
up of one or more of a variety of substances inaccessible to the
senses and as yet undiscovered.

The particular experiment discussed by Noël and Pascal involved filling a test tube with mercury, placing a thumb over
the open end, submerging the open end in a container half-
filled with mercury and removing one's thumb; the space
which then appeared at the sealed end of the test tube, Pascal
and others argued, was, so far as reason and the senses could
discern, a vacuum. Noël argued that experiment could not
prove that this space was a vacuum, that it might contain
invisible mercury vapours, that it might be made up of a
subtle matter, much finer than air, which could penetrate the
pores of glass, that it contained light and so must contain
luminous matter, and he backed up these hypotheses with a
variety of others which he invented or discarded whenever the
coherence of his argument appeared to require it.[12] Pascal tried
at first to answer Noël's arguments, but soon gave up. The
Aristotelian's whole procedure, according to Pascal, was to
move the argument away from a discussion of observable phenomena to a speculative discussion upon those properties of
nature which are inaccessible to human senses and understanding. In this dark domain, the light shed upon the mysteries of
nature by observation and experiment is extinguished; inventiveness and plausibility become the criteria for success, and the
search for scientific truth is forgotten in a battle of empty
words. As Pascal says of Noël, reporting his frequent changes
of opinion, he speaks as if his words had the power to shape
nature:

> I should like this Father to explain to me where his ascendancy over
> nature comes from, this control which he exercises so absolutely
> over the elements, which serve him with such meekness that they
> change properties as often as he changes his mind, while the universe
> modifies its behaviour to suit the inconstancy of his intentions.
> (p. 571)

In this satirical sketch of the Jesuit Noël, a foretaste of the polemical verve he will later turn against Jesuit casuistry in *Les Lettres provinciales*, Pascal invests him with magical powers over nature equivalent to those of Molière's Aristotelian doctors of medicine, when they claim that they have the power to create illnesses as well as to cure them. The same satirical point recurs in Boileau's *Arrest burlesque* (1671), a polemical tract ridiculing the University of Paris which, according to Boileau, was planning to ask the *Parlement* to issue a new decree forbidding the teaching of any doctrine other than Aristotelianism.[13] In this piece of legal burlesque, the officers of the University of Paris order a recent intruder, Reason by name, together with all followers of Descartes, Gassendi, Malebranche and others, to vacate its premises, leaving them to Aristotle and his followers, whose rights of sole succession and possession are to be enjoyed without disturbance. Nature, too, is ordered to mend its ways: the blood is commanded to refrain forthwith from its lately adopted illegal practice of circulating freely round the body, and the nerves, recently found to have attached themselves to the brain, are to return to the heart, where Aristotle put them.

## 5. The pedant and the *honnête homme*

Molière's satirical portraits of pedants, then, are echoes of much wider and more complex disputes in all domains of learning – theology, philosophy, the sciences, the humanities, medicine – where change and compromise were producing splits between the Aristotelians themselves as well as between them and the fissiparous new movements which grew out of new theories and practices. Molière's only direct involvement in the professional world of science and philosophy was as a schoolboy who learned his humanities, together with almost all educated men, from scholastic teachers, and as a patient who had to suffer the treatments prescribed by doctors. As satirist, he paints pedants with broad brushstrokes, showing no inclination to enter into the detail of their arguments. His picture of pedants as vain babblers, out of touch with the world and doing no real harm, lacks the satirical bite of his portraits of doctors, for example, who are shown blithely killing off their patients to preserve the sanctity of medical doctrine. His interest in pedants was twofold:

as a man of the theatre, he exploited their comic potential; also, as a man of taste and judgement, he found in the pedant – overconfident, garrulous, addicted to jargon, inattentive to other people, blind even to his own humanity – the antithesis of the *honnête homme* and a perfect butt for the laughter of courtiers. When Molière paraded his pedants before the King and the court, following his return to Paris in 1658, he must have judged that they would find a ready audience there.

It is striking that in *La Jalousie du Barbouillé* the pedant's first linguistic joke is the invention of a false etymology for the term *galant homme*. The joke would have reminded the polished courtiers in Molière's audience of the celebrated article in Vaugelas's revered and much consulted *Remarques sur la langue française* (1647), in which he discussed the meaning of *galant*. For Molière's pedant:

> the term *galant homme* comes from *élégant*! taking the *g* and the *a* from the last syllable, which makes *ga*, and then taking *l*, adding an *a* and the last two letters, which makes *galant*, and then adding *homme*, that makes *galant homme*. (Sc. 2)

For Vaugelas, the term captures the essence of *honnêteté*, and is the perfect antonym of pedant. He concludes, having discussed the meanings of *galant* with courtiers of both sexes, that the term is

> a compound whose elements are a certain *je ne sais quoi*, or good grace, the air of the Court, intelligence, judgement, urbanity, courtesy and gaiety, all without constraint, affectation or vice. With all these one might make up an *honnête homme* after the manner of the Court. (pp. 476–8)

The gallant courtiers, as they listened to the *docteur*'s absurd etymology, must have enjoyed measuring the distance between such learned fools and 'honest' men and women like themselves, urbane, witty, gracious and gay. Perhaps it was the spectacle of so much self-satisfaction that led Molière to abandon the type of the pedant in favour of other types, such as the *précieux* and *marquis*, who had hitherto escaped ridicule, and whom he found all around him in the polished circles of Paris and the court?

# 12
# *Medicine*

## 1. Medical pedants

Molière's doctors share most of the characteristics of his Aristotelian pedants. The younger Diafoirus, in *Le Malade imaginaire* (1673), a recent graduate from medical school, has precisely the qualities which, in Molière's view, would equip him for a career in either scholastic philosophy or medicine. His father, Monsieur Diafoirus, also a doctor, is proud of his son's education:

> He never showed signs of a lively imagination, nor of the quick intelligence you find in some; but it was these qualities which led me to foresee that his judgement would be strong, a quality essential to the exercise of our art. When he was little, he was never what you might call high-spirited or alert. You would find him always mild, peaceful and taciturn, never saying a word or playing any of those little games peculiar to children. It was a long, hard struggle teaching him to read and, at nine, he still didn't know his alphabet. 'Good,' I said to myself, 'it's the late-blossoming trees that bear the best fruit; it's harder to engrave on marble than on sandstone, but the inscriptions last longer, and this slowness of understanding, this sluggishness of the imagination, are marks of a sound judgement to come.' When I sent him to school, he found it hard; but he stiffened himself against difficulties and his masters always spoke highly of his assiduity and perseverance. Eventually, after much hard slog, he succeeded in graduating with glory; and I can say without vanity that, in his two years on the benches, no candidate has made more noise than he in the disputes of our School. He has made himself formidable, and no thesis can be advanced without his arguing the opposite case to its ultimate extreme. He is unbudgeable in dispute, strong as a Turk on principles, never modifies his opinions and pursues his reasonings into every last retreat of logic. (II, 5)

However, if doctors and pedants shared the same inflexibility, the same vanity and vindictiveness in dispute, they differed in other respects. Pedants were harmless figures of fun; grown men could look back with serenity upon their school and university

days; the posturing of their verbose teachers and professors
could be recalled with amusement – even, for some at least,
with nostalgia. Women of all stations and men from the lower
orders could live out their whole lives without ever having to
suffer at the hands of pedants. Doctors were more substantial
objects of satire. More people felt need of them (though the
majority were too poor to afford them); they commanded
much better incomes, and were more widely feared and revered.
The discrepancy between theory and practice in medicine, between the confidently prescribed cures and the sudden deaths
which often followed treatment, offered the satirist a rich source
of humour. Above all, medicine deals with the functioning of
the body and provided an inexhaustible fund of jokes, comic
gestures and farcical routines.

## 2. Farce without satire

Molière's earliest medical play, *Le Médecin volant* – a traditional
one-act farce, probably part of the repertoire of Molière's troupe
when he returned to Paris in 1658 – presents many of the
features which will recur in his later medical satires: a patient
who is suffering from nothing more serious than lovesickness, a
doctor who is a *valet* in disguise, some scatologicical humour, an
allusion to the alleged venality of doctors, and mockery both of
doctors' reliance on ancient authority and of their professional
jargon (Scs 2–5). In this play, however, the laughter is benign.
The scatological jokes revolve around Lucile's urine: Sganarelle
drinks it, likes the taste, asks for more, then, hearing that she
cannot produce more, prescribes a 'pissing potion'. The allusion
to doctors who can say nothing without reference to ancient
authority occurs in Sganarelle's citing of Galen and Hippocrates
to prove that a person is not well when he is ill. Molière will use
a similar joke in *Le Médecin malgré lui* (1666), where another
Sganarelle invokes the authority of Hippocrates for the wearing
of hats indoors at the beginning of a consultation (II, 2). The
mockery of medical jargon is equally good-humoured. The
ignorant Sganarelle quotes all the magic-sounding formulae he
can dredge up: an Arab greeting, half a line from Corneille's *Le
Cid*, a couple of fragments of Italian and Spanish and a Latin
liturgical phrase picked up in church: 'Salamalec, salamalec.

"Rodrigue, as-tu du cœur?" Signor, si; segnor, non. Per omnia saecula saeculorum.'

Molière goes out of his way to emphasize that the satire is friendly. He introduces an honest lawyer whose only function is to deliver an elegant encomium of doctors. 'One must confess', he says, 'that all who excel in any science are worthy of great praise, and particularly those in the medical profession' (Sc. 8). He underlines the special difficulties of medicine with an apposite quotation from the *Aphorisms* of Hippocrates, and quotes a line from Ovid to support the view that a doctor, however skilled, can never guarantee success. He recalls that doctors were once held in such esteem that people numbered them among the gods.

A modest polemical note is introduced with no hint of mockery when the lawyer expresses his hope that Sganarelle does not practise 'rational or dogmatic' medicine. Quoting Erasmus's adage 'experientia magistra rerum', the lawyer indicates his preference for empirical medicine. Molière appears to be supporting the campaign of doctors such as Joseph Duchesne, Jean Fabre, Estienne de Clave and David de Planis, who opposed the dogmatically based humoral medicine of such conservative bodies as the Paris Faculty and called for the use of empirically based chemical remedies.[1]

This urbane, well-informed and articulate lawyer is not a stock comic character. He shows a seriousness of tone and a familiarity with wider cultural and scientific questions quite foreign to Sganarelle, Gorgibus and the world of low farce.

This brief moment of warmth and approval for doctors was never to be repeated in the later medical plays.

## 3. Biting satire

Molière did not return to medical themes until 1665, in *Dom Juan*, just eight years before his death. The tone of his satire had changed: 'their whole art is pure hypocrisy', says Dom Juan, and 'it is one of the great errors among men' (III, 1). From 1665 until his last play, *Le Malade imaginaire* (1673), Molière's satire of all doctors, whether advocates of modern chemical medicine or of the conservative Aristotelian dogmatic approach taught in the Paris Faculty, was consistently biting.

We cannot be sure why Molière began to ridicule the medical profession in 1665. It has been suggested that it might have been a consequence of contacts with doctors resulting from his own ill health. Perhaps the deaths of his ten-month-old son in November 1664, and – just a few weeks earlier – of his friend the abbé Le Vayer, son of La Mothe Le Vayer, at the age of thirty-five, left him with bitter memories of doctors. These deaths occurred around the time Molière was writing *Dom Juan*, a few months before the first performance in February 1665. Gui Patin, doctor and prolific letter-writer, asserts that Le Vayer's doctors poisoned him with antimony.[2] Antimony, commonly prepared and administered as *vin émétique*, is the remedy which Molière singles out in *Dom Juan* as the most lethal of all the cures popular in his day. Sganarelle cites its use on a patient who, at death's door for six days, failed to respond to all remedies until the doctors administered 'de l'émétique'; its effect was immediate, Sganarelle boasts: he died instantly.

Molière's mockery of doctors, however, may have had nothing to do with his own personal experience. He used the *raisonneur* Béralde, in *Le Malade imaginaire*, to point out that 'it is not doctors he is mocking, but the folly of medicine' (III, 3). He belonged to the sceptical humanist tradition of Montaigne, who had written that many doctors were 'honest men, worthy of affection. It is not against them that I harbour ill feeling but against their art' (*Essais*, II, 37, p. 780). It is an anachronism to view Molière's distrust of medicine as excessive. The views he expresses through Béralde are no more extreme than Montaigne's. Like Montaigne, he believed that the mechanisms of the body were mysteries hidden from man's understanding, that man's best hope of recovering from illness was to trust patiently to the healing powers of nature, that sick men especially should avoid doctors as they needed all their strength to withstand their illnesses and had none to spare for fighting off the ill effects of medication. Both observe that doctors speak with great confidence about the theoretical functioning and malfunctioning of the body, but are powerless when faced with the problem of curing real illnesses.[3] Another sceptic, Pascal, who was also a scientist, shared the view that medicine was not a science. In a passage on the imagination in the *Pensées*, he points out in a matter-of-fact way, without polemical venom, that doctors and pedants were obliged to wear academic dress in order to capture the imagination of their public, because the sciences on which their expertise was based were wholly illusory (82).

It was doubly appropriate for Molière to parade doctors on stage: they were part of the heritage of farce and, in their stock roles as pedant-clowns, a rich source of visual and linguistic comedy; equally, their claims appeared genuinely absurd to a sceptical humanist; like Aristotelian pedants, they offered comic examples of would-be experts, looking back to a worn-out corpus of theory while remaining blind to the real complexities of the world about them.

## 4. Court doctors

*L'Amour médecin*, a *comédie-ballet* written at the King's request, composed and rehearsed – according to Molière – in five days was Molière's first full-blooded medical satire. It was performed at Versailles in 1665, seven months after *Dom Juan*. The play is a three-act entertainment, with a conventional plot, a slight central action and a musical tableau, with singing and ballet, at the beginning and end of each act. Molière used this light structure, with music composed by Lulli, to present a delightfully comic and bitingly satirical portrait of the doctors at court.

As the play was written at the King's request, it is not unlikely that he suggested the subject, too. At the very least, Molière must have sought prior approval for his play; the court doctors were important figures, close to the persons of the King and his immediate family, and neither Molière nor the courtiers would have laughed at them in the King's presence if he had not led the laughter. Allusions to particular doctors were quite clear to contemporaries. Bahys's stammer allegedly imitated a speech impediment of Jean Esprit, doctor to Monsieur, the King's brother; Des Fonandrès's horse, in place of the traditional doctor's mule, is an allusion to Guénaut, doctor to the Queen, and to his unconventional habit of visiting his patients on horseback; Macroton's slow speech was said also to be modelled on Guénaut's intonation; other court doctors and Des Fougerais, a successful Paris doctor, were also cited as possible models. Contemporary sources indicate that Molière made the allusions even clearer by having masks made for his actors which resembled leading doctors of the day.[4]

It is nevertheless fruitless to attempt to tie each of the doctors to a particular model. As we have seen, Molière gave Guénaut's horse to Des Fonandrès and his intonation to Macroton; he no doubt collected and rearranged characteristics from many models to construct five distinctive caricatural doctors. All five bear the stamp of the traditional stage doctor: they are wealthy; they agree that their patients, however healthy, always need expensive treatment; they diagnose illness with reference to the conventions of medicine, paying scant attention to the patient and none at all to her or his case history; they care more for the reputation of medicine than for the health of the patient – as Tomès says, 'A dead man is merely a dead man and of no consequence, but a neglected formality inflicts damage upon the whole body of doctors' (II, 3); finally, all have left behind them, in their rise to the top of their profession, countless dead and dying patients; as Filerin says, 'I've made my little pile, thank God. Let the winds blow, let it rain and hail, the dead are dead and I have enough put by to do without the living' (III, 1).

Superimposed on this general medical character, each of the five doctors represents something a little more precise. Tomès, as his Greek name indicates, was an advocate of bleeding; in this he represents the typical graduate of the Paris Faculty, practising humoral medicine (*G.E.*, V, p. 269). If Lucinde, the lovesick patient, is not bled instantly, Tomès asserts, 'she is a dead woman' (II, 4). He displays another distinguishing feature of the Paris doctor: he will have nothing to do with doctors from other faculties, as only Paris graduates can practise in the region of Paris; he boasts that on one occasion he allowed a patient to die rather than share a consultation with a doctor from outside (II, 3).

In opposition to Tomès, the arch-conservative from Paris, Molière portrays the ultra-modern horse-riding doctor, Des Fonandrès, who swears by chemical medicine, symbolized by his keenness to prescribe antimony. The contrast is crude, as befits the medium of farce, but it is clear that Des Fonandrès represents the empirical chemists from Montpellier who flourished at court, which was exempt from the jurisdiction of the Paris Faculty. Molière does not enter into the details of the rival claims of Paris and Montpellier. He now shows no more faith in the modern supposedly empirical medicine of the chemists than in traditional humoral medicine.[5] Both Tomès and Des Fonandrès are presented as dangerous fanatics, each believing absolutely in the efficacy of his chosen treatment. Each is quite sure that while his own method is infallible, that of his rival will prove fatal. Molière reflected and shared Montaigne's view that the irreconcilable differences of opinion between doctors interpreting the same symptoms were evidence enough that the claims of medicine had no basis in science (II, 37, pp. 770–76).

The next pair of doctors to take over the consultation, Bahys and Macroton, are quite different. Their priority is to sustain the reputation of medicine with a display of solidarity. Bahys with his stutter and Macroton with his slow speech are a delightfully absurd double act, but they do not fall out; they harmonize their diagnosis of Lucinde's condition with a consummate display of mutual deference and flattery. They begin cautiously, recalling the Hippocratic aphorism which emphasizes the difficulties and dangers of diagnosis and treatment. They give the patient value for money by dwelling lovingly and at length on the complexities of her very interesting condition: her humours are 'overcooked and have acquired that malign condition in which their smoke spreads through the region of the brain' (II, 5). Most important of all, Bahys and Macroton are wily old doctors who will prescribe radical treatments only as a last resort. Before turning to 'vigorous purgation' and bleeding, they recommend that Lucinde try 'little, harmless remedies, that is, little softening and cleansing enemas, juleps and refreshing syrups to be mixed in her *tisane*'. She is to be given a chance to recover on her own before being exposed to the more lethal remedies. Finally, the two doctors prudently offer no guarantee of success, consoling Sganarelle with the assurance that if his daughter must die, they will see to it at least that she dies 'according to the rules' (II, 6).

The fifth doctor, Filerin, is introduced to restore peace between Tomès and Des Fonandrès. Molière uses the artifice of putting him on stage with his fellow doctors and no non-medical witnesses, so that he can speak his mind, confess openly the failures of medicine, and outline the policies and procedures doctors should follow to hide them (III, 1). His speech is redolent of Montaigne's influence. He shares Montaigne's view that the scientific claims of medicine are fraudulent and that the success of the medical profession is built upon the gullibility of people unmanned by the fear of death. To conceal the lack of scientific certainties in medicine, Filerin calls upon doctors to keep their quarrels secret. Montaigne had said of doctors:

> They should have contented themselves with the perpetual discrepancies in the opinions of the principal masters and ancient authors of this science which are known only to those who are well-read, without showing the common people as well the controversies and inconsistent judgements which they nurture and keep going between them. (II, 37, p. 771)

Filerin says:

> Do you not see the harm these sorts of quarrels do us in the opinion of people? And isn't it enough that learned men see the contradictions and disagreements between our authors and our ancient masters, without revealing to the common people as well, by our debates and quarrels, the charlatanism of our art. (III, 1)

Molière shows Filerin enthusiastically developing Montaigne's argument that doctors are no worse than most people who try to profit from the silliness of others; flatterers, alchemists and astrologers all work on the same principle.[6] In short, Filerin argues, as medicine is built upon the gullibility of the patient, the doctors' highest priority should be to conceal their differences and present a public façade of perfect harmony and unity.

## 5. The Faculty of Paris

Molière's remaining doctors – two in *Monsieur de Pourceaugnac*, and Monsieur Purgon, Monsieur Diafoirus and his son Thomas in *Le Malade imaginaire* – are all fiercely loyal graduates of the Paris Faculty and staunch defenders of the principles and practices of humoral medicine. Molière portrays the Faculty and its graduates through the reductive perspective of comic hyperbole. Any redeeming features in the behaviour of individual doctors or of the Faculty as a body, however interesting to historians of medicine, were of no concern to Molière as satirist and comic artist. The picture he paints is delightfully clear, rigorously stripped of complications which might weaken the impact of the comedy, perceptive in its analysis of the general defects in the Paris Faculty's practices, and quite unfair on questions of detail.

Antimony, or *vin émétique*, the remedy associated with innovating doctors from Montpellier, is mentioned no more after *L'Amour médecin*. Paris doctors confined themselves to the three techniques for purifying the humours: enemas, bleeding and purging. In the mock graduation ceremony at the end of *Le Malade imaginaire*, the candidate answers all questions on the treatments appropriate to different illnesses with the same refrain:

> Clysterium donare
> Postea seignare,
> Ensuitta purgare.

On each occasion, the examining Faculty doctors congratulate him on his excellent reply. Bleeding is the favourite remedy of the two doctors in *Monsieur de Pourceaugnac*. They diagnose their healthy patient as a severe melancholic, and the first doctor opines with evident relish that it may prove necessary 'to open a vein in his brow'; 'let the opening be wide,' he adds, 'to let out the thicker blood' (I, 8). Monsieur Purgon, on the other hand, as his name suggests, is an out-and-out purger.

For Molière, Paris doctors, though conservative and backward-looking in their treatment, kill just as many patients as the antimony poisoners. The apothecary in *Monsieur de Pourceaugnac*, who has complete faith in his doctor, praises him for his decisiveness: 'he's not one of those doctors who make concessions to illnesses: he's a quick worker who loves to deal with his patients at speed; and when you have to die, it's over as quickly as possible' (I, 5). This doctor has already despatched three of the apothecary's children into the next world in less than four days. The remaining two are under his care, and the apothecary adds with satisfaction: 'he treats and governs them as he pleases, with no interference from me; and, as often as not, when I get home from town, I'm amazed to find that he's had them bled or purged' (I, 5). It is these out-and-out doctors who believe in the efficacy of their art who are the most dangerous. Monsieur Purgon (*Le Malade imaginaire*) is another of the same kind. According to Béralde, Monsieur Purgon

> is nothing but doctor from head to toe; a man who has more faith in his rules than in any mathematical demonstration, and who would think it criminal to wish to examine them; a man who sees nothing obscure in medicine, nothing doubtful, nothing difficult,

and who, with the impetuosity of conviction, an inflexibility born of confidence, with the brutality of common sense and reason, indiscriminately hands out purgations and bleedings, never hesitating over anything. You mustn't bear him ill will for any harm he does you: it's with unquestionable good faith that he'll polish you off and, in killing you, he's doing no more than he has already done for his wife and children and, if the need arises, will do for himself, too. (III, 3)

Molière did not embrace all doctors in this condemnation. Béralde encourages Argan, if he cannot do without doctors, to find another with whom he would be less at risk. A healthy man like Argan would have no difficulty surviving the anodyne treatments of a Bahys or a Macroton.


## 6. Medicine and authority

Molière presents a picture of the Paris Faculty obsessed with its exclusive rights and privileges. In the Paris region, they alone could practise; we saw how Tomès, in *L'Amour médecin*, let a patient die rather than share him with an intruder from another faculty. Their patients were their property and their income; in *Monsieur de Pourceaugnac*, the doctor, trying to recapture his escaped patient, describes him as 'a piece of property which belongs to me, and which I count among my effects' (II, 2).

Even more jealously guarded than the right to the exclusive exploitation of their patients was the right to determine the rules and laws of medicine. The Faculty of Paris, as seen by Molière, was a world-in-itself, isolated from medical scholarship and practice elsewhere in France and Europe; the candidate in the graduation ceremony in *Le Malade imaginaire* must swear to use no remedies except those approved by the Faculty of Paris. For Monsieur Diafoirus, the particular strength of his son is his refusal even to listen to new theories and discoveries:

> What pleases me most about him – and in this he is following my example – is that he holds on blindly to the opinions of our ancients, and has never wished to understand or listen to the so-called discoveries of our century on the circulation of the blood and other opinions of the same kind. (II, 5)

Diafoirus has no hesitation treating the fact of circulation as an opinion.

Molière's Paris doctors were isolated not only from other doctors but from the whole realm of empirical observation. As guardians of the hallowed principles passed down through generations of doctors, they could not risk opening their eyes, ears and minds to the evidence of the day-to-day illnesses under their care, for fear that what they observed might not tally with the theories of their masters. To highlight this blindness to evidence, Molière used the technique of presenting his doctors only with patients enjoying excellent health; first of all, they fail to notice that their patients have nothing wrong with them; then, with barely a glance at them, they launch into a mass of pre-learned theory which has no connection with the patients whose condition they are supposed to be discussing.

The strategy of Molière's Paris doctors is to keep their body of theories and codes of practice intact. To do this, they reduce the whole field of medicine to a verbally self-contained system; they banish the world of phenomena and experience from their discipline and replace it with a self-referential linguistic code. When asked to explain why opium induces sleep, the graduand answers:

> Quia est in eo
> Virtus dormitiva
> Cujus est natura
> Sensus assoupire.

The answer tells us nothing of the chemical composition of opium or of the body's responses to it. Instead, it is a perfect circle of words: opium brings sleep 'because it contains sleep-making properties whose nature is to induce drowsiness in the senses'.

The method harnesses the same scholastic techniques as those used by the Jesuit father Noël 'proving' that a vacuum in nature is impossible; it is a method designed to produce accounts of phenomena which will ensure that they fit into a preconceived cosmology and physiology.

In the cut-off world of Paris medicine, the candidate for examination need have no worries about the truth or falsehood of what he has learned. His knowledge will not be tested empirically. He is answerable only to the doctors of Paris who, so long as he parrots the orthodox views, will greet his every reply with the acclamation:

Bene, bene, bene, bene respondere:
Dignus, dignus est entrare
In nostro docto corpore.

[He replies well and is worthy to be admitted into our learning body.]

Where all the experts agree, who can question their authority? The need for unanimity in such a system is paramount. If agreement between the experts is to be the cornerstone of medical authority, then the experts must be seen to agree. It was easy enough for doctors to speak with one voice on the general principles of humoral medicine, but according to Molière, when it came to individual cases their diagnoses were so arbitrary that doctors regularly ran into the problem of incompatible opinions. When two Paris doctors are on stage together, the problem is easily solved; in *Monsieur de Pourceaugnac*, the second doctor listens while the first doctor speaks and then has only to deliver an encomium of his colleague's wisdom. Such is the beauty of the first doctor's diagnosis of melancholic hypochondria, according to the second doctor, that a mere layman would be proud to develop the symptoms described as a sort of homage to the doctor's wisdom and eloquence (I, 8).

However, when a doctor is invited to offer a second opinion in a case where he has not heard the opinion of the first doctor, problems arise. In *Le Malade imaginaire*, Molière presents the opinions of three doctors at once: the young Thomas Diafoirus, on no more evidence than one measurement of the patient's pulse, offers his diagnosis of Argan's condition; the earlier opinion of the absent Purgon is reported by Argan himself; the third doctor, Thomas's father, who is taking the pulse of Argan's other wrist, has the difficult role of agreeing with everything his son says and then of harmonizing his son's opinion with the quite different analysis of Purgon. For Thomas the illness originates in the spleen, while for Purgon it begins in the liver. Monsieur Diafoirus quickly intervenes with some obfuscating medical jargon designed to prove that their differences are only on the surface and that, medically speaking, spleen and liver are virtually the same thing. However, he then falls into the trap of offering an opinion himself, surmising that Purgon has prescribed a diet of roast meat for his patient; in fact, he had prescribed only stewed meat. Monsieur Diafoirus quickly brings the consultation to a close and leaves, having re-established his authority by declaring firmly that the grains of salt Argan takes with his eggs should always be counted in even numbers (II, 6).

Molière pushes his satire of Paris doctors to its logical extreme by suggesting that, in their own eyes, they have achieved the power and stature of kings and even gods. Pascal had accused Noël of arrogating a godlike position in relation to nature, inventing and ignoring phenomena to prove whatever he wished. Molière's Paris doctors behave in a similar manner. In the insular world of the Paris region, where every patient is in their power and only the medical opinions of the teachers and graduates of the Faculty of Paris are accepted, Paris doctors are omnipotent; they are free to create and remove illnesses entirely as they please. When the patient of a doctor in *Monsieur de Pourceaugnac* escapes before his treatment is completed, the doctor tells Oronte that if he finds him and fails to restore him to the doctor's custody, he will be 'struck down by whatever diseases the Faculty chooses' (II, 2). When Argan fails to observe the precise instructions of his doctor – he wishes to delay an enema – Purgon, in a blind rage, condemns his patient to a whole sequence of illnesses of increasing gravity which, he promises, will leave him incurable within four days and, soon after that, will lead to certain death (III, 5).

The quasi-divine powers which Paris doctors claim for themselves are compared mockingly to the divinely instituted powers of kingship. Argan's postponement of his enema is anathematized by Monsieur Purgon as an act of *lèse-Faculté*. The new graduate in the mock ceremony praises his elders in terms more suited to an encomium of *le Roi soleil*:

> Ce serait sans douta à moi chosa folla,
> Inepta et ridicula,
> Si j'alloibam m'engageare
> Vobis louangeas donare,
> Et entreprenoibam adjoutare
> Des lumieras au soleillo,
> Et des étoilas au cielo,
> Des ondas à l'Oceano,
> Et des rosas au printanno.

[It would no doubt be a mad, inept and ridiculous thing if I were to engage in praising you, and undertake to add light to the sun, stars to the sky, waves to the ocean, and roses to the spring.]

The student's gratitude to his Faculty teachers is expressed in even more excessive terms. He speaks as if he were offering thanks to his Creator:

> Vobis, vobis debeo
> Bien plus qu'à naturae et qu' à patri meo:
> Natura et pater meus
> Hominem me habent factum;
> Mais vos me, ce qui est bien plus,
> Avetis factum medicum.

[To you, to you I owe much more than to nature and to my father: nature and my father made me a man, but you, much more importantly, have made me a doctor.][7]

Molière was never to turn his doctors into the subject of high comedy; they were never to achieve the status of such figures as Arnolphe, Alceste, Dom Juan, or even Philaminte. They belonged to the world of farce, and on stage they performed as clowns, in clownish medical costumes, with funny voices and mechanical gestures. This is not to say that his medical plays were innocent farces with no satirical edge to them. On the contrary, Molière's choice of a farcical medium was a reflection of his low opinion of the medical profession. Doctors, like Aristotelian pedants, did not deserve more serious attention: their absurd scientific pretensions, their vanity and their cupidity made them natural figures of fun.

But Molière's blame did not fall too heavily on the doctors themselves; it was not entirely their fault that the whole discipline of medicine was built on uncertain foundations. To underline his view that it was the discipline itself that was absurd, Molière had his stage doctors use real diagnoses, with the correct technical terms; the first doctor's analysis of hypochondriacal melancholy in *Monsieur de Pourceaugnac* has been hailed as a masterly summary of seventeenth-century medical opinion on this condition (*O.C.*, II, 1402, n. 3). Molière felt that medical eloquence was funny enough to stand on its own, without any need of comic exaggeration. He blamed the public, too, for the state of medicine: the fear of death made people gullible and much too keen to spend money on their health; as Montaigne and Molière pointed out, doctors flourished and multiplied in response to public demand.

However, Molière's satire of doctors, for all the laughter they inspire, is much harsher than his satire of pedants; the audience is not allowed to forget that the models for these strutting clowns, in the real world, never tired of sending men, women and children to an early grave. Both the delightful humour and lightness of his portrait of doctors and the chilling realities of medical practice are captured in Molière's last words on the subject, and the last words he wrote for the stage:

> Vivat, vivat, vivat, vivat, cent fois vivat
> Novus doctor, qui tam bene parlat!
> Mille, mille annis et manget et bibat,
> Et seignet et tuat!

[Long live, long live, long live, long live, a hundred times long live the new Doctor, who speaks so well! For a thousand and a thousand years may he eat, drink, bleed and kill!]

# 13
# *Preciosity*

## 1. *Les Précieuses ridicules*

In putting Aristotelian pedants and doctors on stage, Molière was merely bringing up to date two of the stock figures of farce, and the scenes in which they appeared were played in a careless atmosphere of carnival. His portraits of modern pedants whose special learning reflected seventeenth-century culture were more individual and varied. His first satire on the precious movement, *Les Précieuses ridicules* (1659), was a one-act farce; the two 'precious' women of the title were coquettes and their admirers were two *valet*-clown figures, Mascarille and Jodelet. A few years later, in *La Critique de l'École des femmes* (1663), he painted a much more sober picture of a modern playwright and pedant in Lysidas, the central figure in a precious cabal which included a *précieuse* and a *marquis*. His most biting portrait appeared less than a year before his death, in *Les Femmes savantes* (1672), in the person of Trissotin, who combined the qualities of poet, pedant and fortune-hunter; Trissotin is supported by three precious bluestockings and a fellow versifier, Vadius.

In an age of increasing refinement and culture in the circles around Richelieu, Fouquet, and then Colbert and Louis XIV – circles in which, from the early 1660s, Molière was to become a leading figure – the satirist had opportunities to observe many examples of new and fashionable ways of putting knowledge and language to perverse uses. He saw groups of poets and their precious admirers forming coteries from which they attempted to control taste and fashion, banding together to decry the work of outsiders and to provide loud applause for their own productions. He heard poems of the slightest literary merit extravagantly praised by men and women competing to display superior sensitivity and advanced taste.

In itself preciosity is not comic. Elements of the precious, a search for elegance and refinement, for the spiritual, in thought, feeling and language, can be found in some of the great literature of all periods. Ronsard, Racine and Mallarmé were all, in some degree, precious poets. Molière portrayed a debased strain of preciosity. When Élise mocks Climène in *La Critique de l'École des femmes*, she says: 'Is there a woman whom one can more truly call *précieuse* than she, if you take that word in its worst sense?' (Sc. 2). It was only with this worst sense of the word that Molière was concerned. His purpose in *Les Précieuses ridicules* was to show up the folly of preciosity when it became the private code of vain and silly people who, while claiming to live only for the pleasures of the mind and soul, were in fact ruled by petty vices and passions.

To present his comic caricature of preciosity in *Les Précieuses ridicules*, Molière establishes a norm of gentlemanly honesty in the opening scene; La Grange and Du Croisy, two respectable and urbane suitors, have come to propose marriage to the two precious cousins. We immediately learn that the *précieuses*, who reject them as unworthy lovers, come from a humbler, much less polished, provincial background; their modest origins are revealed both by the rough speech of their father and uncle, Gorgibus, and by their own coarse and flirtatious demeanour which, in spite of their pretensions, betrays itself in all their words and gestures. They claim to be too good for their suitors, but we see that in fact they are not good enough. This discrepancy between the ideal image the *précieux*, both men and women, have of themselves and the banal reality of their true selves is doubly emphasized by Molière's choice of the pretentious *valets* of La Grange and Du Croisy to play the roles of the precious *marquis* and *vicomte*: we laugh to see the mannerisms of precious courtiers mimicked by noisy and vulgar servants. At the same time, we find it amusing and appropriate that the two girls should deem the servants more acceptable company than their masters.

Molière shows how an excess of preciosity leads men and women to abandon the roles for which nature has fitted them. The two girls are quite unself-knowing and seek to live according to rules drawn from the imagination, borrowed from the world of fiction and, in particular, from the precious novels of Mlle de Scudéry.[1] For them, marriage should follow a long courtship, strewn with obstacles and adventures, enriched with countless discussions on the different emotions and moods of love, and taking place against an elegant background of palaces and ornate gardens with hidden arbours and quiet walks (Sc. 4). Against this background, respectable and well-off suitors like La Grange and Du Croisy, who prosaically raise the question of marriage at a first meeting, are beneath contempt.

The precious women abandon nature, too, when they attempt to divorce mind from body and live only in the higher regions of the mind. They profess to be appalled at the thought of what marriage will lead to. Abandoning all modesty of language, Cathos asks: 'How could one bear the thought of lying down against an entirely naked man?' (Sc. 4). The comic mechanism at the heart of the play is revealed in this question: Molière's *précieuses*, while proclaiming their contempt for the pleasures of the body, in fact think of little else. Molière shared Montaigne's view that 'supercelestial opinions and subterranean behaviour' (saints apart) are always found together (*Essais*, III, 13, p. 1115).

The piquant contrast between the would-be spirituality of the *précieux* and their constant preoccupation with the body is evident in their appearance. Both the precious girls and the *valets* dress with the intention of displaying the very highest degree of refinement; in consequence they are slaves to fashion, obsessed with ribbons, feathers and gloves and absurdly overdressed; Mascarille even stoops to mentioning the cost of his feathers (Sc. 9). The two girls, to stress their superiority over ordinary women, make excessive use of make-up; this, too, rivets attention to their bodies. To drive the point home, Molière tells us, through Gorgibus, that their make-up is concocted from the lard of a dozen recently slaughtered pigs (Sc. 3). To prepare themselves for scaling the social and literary heights of Paris and the court, the two girls first smear their faces with pork fat.

Mascarille's farcical entry in a sedan chair is a metaphorical expression of the same truth. A gentleman who merely wishes to avoid the mud of the streets of Paris would leave his chair at the front door; a *précieux*, determined to demonstrate his superiority, insists on being deposited inside the room he is visiting and, as a result, is tossed around inside the chair all the way up the stairs and arrives dishevelled and bruised.

Molière exploits the delightful absurdity of the precious women's view that they can love with their minds only: as the

action develops, the precious exchanges between the four protagonists degenerate steadily into a display of full-blooded flirtation. They pay one another extravagant compliments, the men
declare themselves bowled over with love, show their wounds
and invite the women to touch them; Mascarille offers to pull
down his trousers to show off a terrific wound ('une plaie
furieuse'), adding that these are the things which 'show what a
man is made of' (Sc. 11). The special irony is that their flirtation
is made easier by the pretence that the life of the mind alone
matters; when all agree to ignore the existence of the flesh, there
is no need to feel constrained by the social conventions which
discourage obvious flirtation.

Molière shows the *précieux* reinventing the language of ordinary men in order to make it more fit to express the concerns of
the mind. Here, too, their efforts to rise above earthly matters
plunge them into involuntary earthiness. In an attempt to forget
their origins and shed their former selves, the country women
replace their baptismal names with pastoral names suited to
heroines in precious novels – Polyxène and Aminte; the two
*valets* present themselves as *marquis* and *vicomte*. To maintain the
ethereal grace of the imaginary world they wish to inhabit, they
seek to make language abstract, disguising the materiality of the
concrete objects which surround them. As with their attempt to
disguise the body with fussy clothes and excessive make-up,
their efforts to find abstract terms for familiar household objects
merely force these objects upon our attention. The awkward
and, at first, puzzling order to Almanzor, the newly renamed
servant, 'Vite, voiturez-nous ici les commodités de la conversation!' ('Quickly, convey to us the conversational commodities!'),
forces the listener to unravel the circumlocution and turn his
mind to chairs; also, in order to avoid the word chair, with its
suggestion of backsides, Magdelon inadvertently repeats *con*, the
'syllabe sale' of 'commodités' – pronounced *con-modités* in the
seventeenth century – and 'conversation'. The relationship between body and chair is further emphasized when Cathos invests
this increasingly sinister chair with a life and will of its own; for
a quarter of an hour, according to Cathos, this chair has been
stretching out its impatient arms towards Mascarille's backside:
'Don't be hard-hearted,' she pleads, 'do satisfy its desire to
embrace you' (Sc. 9).

On questions of literature and taste, Molière suggests that the *précieux* were ruled by vanity, clannishness and the need to be in the know. The neophyte *précieux* establishes his reputation by being seen in the company of the right people; he must always have the very latest information on who is writing what; and, as with most up-to-the-minute movements, his keenest interest will always be reserved for the very latest work, known only to him and the inner circle. As Magdelon says, 'These are the things that get you noticed in company; and if you don't know these things, I wouldn't give a fig for all the intelligence in the world' (Sc. 9).

After the dialogue on literary manners, Molière shows through a poetry-reading how a poet's reputation was made. Mascarille intones a little *impromptu*, already a little old for a spontaneous piece as he boasts that he had recited it to a duchess the day before. The poem, predictably, is without merit:

> Oh! oh! je n'y prenais pas garde:
> Tandis que, sans songer à mal, je vous regarde,
> Votre œil en tapinois me dérobe mon cœur.
> Au voleur, au voleur, au voleur, au voleur!

> [Ah! ah! I was not paying attention:
> While, without noticing, I look at you,
> Your eye furtively steals my heart,
> Stop thief, stop thief, stop thief, stop thief!]

As soon as Mascarille completes his reading, he and his two precious admirers launch into gushing literary appreciation, competing with one another to bring out the subtle effects hidden behind every word of his miniature masterpiece. In precious circles, the comedy implies, reputations are created and sustained by the simple technique of members of an in-group agreeing mutually to praise one another's work to the skies.

## 2. La Critique de l'École des femmes (1663)

In *La Critique de l'École des femmes*, a precious cabal of the kind the provincial girls of *Les Précieuses ridicules* yearned to belong to is portrayed in action. In this play the *précieuse*, Climène, is a Parisian whose precious credentials are well-established. Mascarille, the would-be *marquis*, is replaced by a real *marquis*, a fop and man-about-town who moves in literary circles and would claim to be an arbiter of good taste, but not a writer. These two belong to the same faction as Lysidas, a figure who combines the characteristics of pedant, critic and poet.

Whereas in *Les Précieuses* Mascarille and the precious women unite in admiration of a poem emanating from their own embryo *salon*, in *La Critique* the precious cabal has come together to savage the work of an enemy and outsider, Molière's first five-act masterpiece, *L'École des femmes*. Lysidas arrives at Uranie's house fresh from a *salon* in which he has played the gratifying role of a Mascarille being acclaimed for his genius; he apologizes for being an hour late because he has just been detained by *Mme la marquise*, who insisted on praising at some length a play he has just written. In spite of such praise, however, the public is bored by the work of Lysidas, and Molière portrays the cabal's jealousy and vexation that a play from outside their circle is filling the theatre, while their own plays, backed by the approval of all their allies and scholarly friends, are being performed to empty houses.

Through Lysidas, the *marquis* and Climène, Molière shows how a precious clique sets about ruining the reputation of a rival poet. The pedant, Lysidas, displays a formidable armoury of erudition, hoping that all opposition will be cowed into submission by his use of Greek terms in place of the more easily understood French ones. He is portrayed as a casuist who twists classical sources in order to prove that *L'École des femmes* is an ill-constructed play, breaking the rules of drama passed down from Aristotle and Horace. For example, his point that the lack of action on stage in Molière's play sins against the very name of drama – meaning action – is the argument of a sophist: action in the Aristotelian sense means what happens between the beginning and end of a play, and does not refer to particular actions on stage. The *marquis* has no arguments to level against *L'École des femmes* other than the fatuous self-satisfaction which convinces him he must be right; for him, the play is detestable because it is detestable, because the theatre was so crowded that people trod on his toes and disarranged his ribbons, and because his friend Dorilas, who was sitting next to him, also thought it detestable. Climène, the *précieuse* and the nastiest of the three, found the play so full of filth that it almost caused her to vomit. Her argument is that its author has so little sense of moral propriety that no decent person could enjoy his work: 'I would assert that an honest woman could not watch it without confusion, so much dirt and filth did I discover in the play' (Sc. 3).

The main techniques of the three allies are to support one another unquestioningly, to repeat the same arguments over and over again, and to close their ears to any points which might weaken or destroy their case.

## 3. Preciosity and family life

Molière's most developed satire upon the contemporary literary scene is *Les Femmes savantes* (1672). As usual, Molière aimed to give not a broad panoramic view of the literary world but a profound analysis of the kinds of actions, follies and abuses which could result from judgement distorted by the over-eager, self-loving pursuit of culture and refinement. The two themes underpinning the actions of the two one-act plays depicting precious circles are taken up again and explored more richly in *Les Femmes savantes*. The satire is further enriched by the portrayal of a tyrant woman, one of the types mocked by Juvenal in his satire on women:

> But most intolerable of all is the woman who as soon as she has sat down to dinner commends Virgil, pardons the dying Dido, and pits the poets against each other, putting Virgil in the one scale and Homer in the other. . . . She lays down definitions and discourses on morals, like a philosopher . . . . Let her not know all history; let there be some things in her reading which she does not understand. I hate a woman who is forever consulting and poring over the 'Grammar' of Palaemon, who observes all the rules and laws of language, who like an antiquary quotes verses that I never heard of, and corrects her unlettered female friends for slips of speech that no man need trouble about: let husbands at least be permitted to make slips in grammar! (*Satire* VI, ll. 434–56)

The central theme of *Les Femmes savantes*, however, touched on only obliquely in the earlier plays, is the relationship between body and soul. This theme – which Molière, like Pascal, had found in Montaigne, amongst others – is expressed in Pascal's famous *pensée*: 'Man is neither angel nor beast, and the misfortune is that he who would equal the angels sinks to the level of the beasts' (358).

To highlight the absurdities of attempting to perfect the soul independently of the body, Molière places his 'precious' cabal within a family circle: the cast includes two brothers and a sister from an older generation, two sisters of marriageable age, a husband and wife, servants and two suitors. The very structure of family life is dependent upon the body: courtship, marriage, children, sharing a house and eating together, the common elements in family life, are all reminders that, in Montaigne's words, 'the condition [of man] is astonishingly corporeal' (*Essais*, III, 8, p. 930). For Montaigne, neither the body nor the mind should be cultivated in isolation:

> It is true, as they say, that the body should not pursue its appetites in such a way as to harm the mind; but why should it not also be true that the mind should not pursue its appetites to the point where they harm the body? (*Essais*, III, 5, p. 893)

To illustrate the dangers of caring only for the body, Molière portrays a henpecked husband, a natural coward, concerned only with food and home comforts, indifferent to books, 'except for a fat volume of Plutarch to press my collars' (l. 562), and unable to protect his daughters from his wife's follies. 'My body is myself,' Chrysale says to his sneering wife, 'and I want to look after it. Old rag, if you will, my old rag is dear to me' (ll. 542–3).[2] Weak, self-absorbed and living in a small world bounded by food and fear, Chrysale has given up any thought of cultivating his soul, of running his family, curbing the excesses of his wife and promoting his daughters' welfare and happiness. Philaminte is right to feel contempt for this empty shell of a man.

Chrysale's error, however, is no graver than the opposing error of Philaminte and her allies, Bélise and Armande, who cling to the ennobling Platonic notion that the soul needs nourishment, while forgetting that the body needs feeding too. As a result, the life of the body suffers: the kitchen is ill-run, the servants neglect their duties in order to cultivate their minds, and the whole household lives in discomfort. More importantly, Armande, at marriageable age, is so contemptuous of the body that she has resolved to reject marriage because it is too carnal (ll. 9–14). Her attitude recalls Cathos's revulsion at the thought of sleeping against a naked man. Both Cathos and Armande exemplify in an extreme form what Montaigne presents as the strange but widespread habit of regarding the act of making love as shameful: 'Is it not bestial of us to call bestial the operation which makes us?' (*Essais*, III, 5, p. 878). By adopting such a pose, Armande is jeopardizing her chances of future happiness; her affected coldness has already led to the loss of her lover (ll. 129–50).

The most serious consequence of an exclusive concern with the soul, however, is that it allows the neglected body to run out of control. All three would-be-learned women are ruled by their passions, and for all three their supposed love of learning serves as a mask and a catalyst for their passions. Philaminte can pretend that her relentless bullying of all those over whom she has power is born of superior wisdom and is for the good of her victims. Her philosophical researches extend the range of her tyranny, providing her with new domains over which to exercise her whimsical and iron authority. Equally, her belief in her own intellectual superiority relieves her of the need ever to question whether or not her behaviour is just.

Her sister-in-law, Bélise, an ageing coquette, is ruled by feminine vanity; inspired by fashionable Platonizing discussions of love, she has imagined for herself a philosophy which permits her to believe that all men love her, but do not dare to show it openly; seen through this happy perspective, the behaviour of every man she meets takes on a most satisfying coherence. As her brothers point out, she has suffered the consequence which, for Montaigne, inevitably follows the separation of mind from body: she has gone mad (l. 397).[3]

Armande, in the bloom of womanhood, is a bully in the making. She has used her learned pretensions to torment her admirer, Clitandre, and reduce him to delicious despair by telling him with hauteur that he must learn to purge his love of all traces of the sensual and aspire to a perfect marriage of souls (ll. 1189–1212). Having, in consequence, lost her lover to her sister, she then places her learning at the service of her bitter jealousy, accusing her sister of being an inferior, earthbound, ill-educated creature, content to live the lowly life of a wife and mother trapped in domesticity (ll. 26–52).

Molière emphasizes the extent to which the three women are dominated by their bodies by making them speak – especially when they are discussing literature – in the language of the physical appetites. In particular, their appreciation of Trissotin's poems, in the third act, is expressed with a mixture of metaphors drawn from the world of food and sex. Armande 'burns' to hear his poems (l. 713); for Bélise, 'they are delicious meals poured into my ears' (l. 716); Philaminte says: 'On hearing these verses, one feels flowing deep inside one's soul a certain something which makes one swoon' (ll. 778–9). Trissotin, responsive to their mood, promises to satisfy their hunger by following up the modest dish of an eight-line poem with the more substantial 'stew of a sonnet' ('le ragoût d'un sonnet') (ll. 747–54).

All three of the learned women are incapable of self-knowledge because they pretend that the bodily part of them, in their case the dominant part, does not exist. Their lack of self-knowledge leaves them easy victims of blinding self-love and destroys their judgement. At the same time, and for the same reason, they show themselves incapable of knowing others; they undervalue Clitandre because he does not share their obsessions and tastes, and absurdly overvalue Trissotin, a mincing, untalented versifier and heartless fortune-hunter, because he panders to their literary whims.

## 4. Body and soul in equilibrium

Between Chrysale, who lives on good soup rather than fine language (l. 531), and the women, who wish to believe they live upon ideas, Molière places a group of figures who are content to live as ordinary people who hope to find happiness for both their bodies and their souls. Clitandre is their leading spokesman:

> For me, Madam, I notice, unfortunately, if you please, that I have a body as well as a soul: I feel it is too closely tied to the soul to be left to one side; I don't know the art of such separations; heaven has denied me this philosophy, and my soul and my body work in concert. (ll. 1213–18)

Love without the participation of the senses is too pure for Clitandre; 'I love with my whole self', he affirms, and equally, when he loves, his love is for the whole woman (ll. 1219–26). He shares Montaigne's opinion that 'philosophy has no quarrel with the natural pleasures of the body, so long as these are

enjoyed with restraint, and preaches moderation, not abstinence'
(*Essais*, III, 5, p. 892). Henriette has the important function of
reminding us that marriage is wholesome, normal and, if the
couple is well-matched, attractive (ll. 20–25). It is she who
points out to Armande that had their mother not had a lower
side to her nature, she would never have seen the light of day.
Who knows what little philosopher waiting to come into the
world might be suppressed if Henriette were to share her sister's
high ideals? (ll. 77–84).

Both Clitandre and Henriette are seen to have clear heads and
sound opinions, regulating their lives with prudence and modesty. Clitandre, after Juvenal, considers that learning in women
is acceptable so long as they have the good taste to conceal some
of their achievements. In fact, he is doing no more than extend
the definition of the perfect *honnête homme* to include women;
we recall that Pascal never wanted to meet 'an author' or 'a
poet', but a man; it is our humanity which must show, not our
qualifications. Clitandre is simply pointing out that a pedant in
woman's clothing looks even more incongruous than a pedant
in the shape of a man (ll. 215–30). It is Clitandre, too, who
reminds us of the commonplace that a learned fool is more
foolish than an ignorant one (ll. 1275–1312).

Henriette also is clear-sighted. Molière is careful to show that
she deserves none of the contempt which her mother and sister
heap upon her. When, for example, Trissotin is told that Henriette's family has lost all its money and he instantly renounces his
claim to her hand, leaving her free to marry Clitandre, the
audience might expect Henriette to share Clitandre's joy. Henriette, however, immediately sees the implications of what she
believes to be the new situation; without a dowry, and knowing
that Clitandre has very little money, she foresees a life of
married penury, likely to end in unhappiness and mutual recrimi-
nation, and insists that the match is no longer suitable (ll. 1749–
54). She does not agree to marry Clitandre until she hears that
the news of their lost fortune is only a trick designed to unmask
Trissotin's cupidity.

The other figures occupying the ground of common sense
between the two extremes are Martine and Ariste. Martine is
only a kitchen maid, but she displays the earthy common sense
appropriate to her condition. On the central issue of the compara-

tive roles of husband and wife, her wisdom boils down to the unshakeable and, in the context, sound conviction that the hen should not crow before the cock (l. 1644). Ariste's functions are to underline the culpable weakness of his brother Chrysale and the madness of his sister Bélise, and to invent a stratagem which will show up Trissotin's true character and permit a happy ending to the play (ll. 658–710, 351–96, 1687–1764).

## 5. Philosophy, literature and language

The affectations and pretensions of the three learned women, unlike those of the Aristotelian pedants and doctors of previous chapters, are up to date. In philosophy, they mingle Platonism, Epicureanism – which had been given new impetus by the work of Gassendi – and Cartesianism with elements from Christianity and Stoicism. They show no grasp of any of these systems, merely repeating the tags and catch-phrases associated with each of them: they admire the abstractions of Plato, Epicurus's atoms, Descartes's vortices and the sage of the Stoics (ll. 866–98). They have profited from the new instrumentation of empirical scientists, having used their telescope to see men on the moon and even, Bélise asserts excitedly, church towers (ll. 890–92). They are intent on outdoing Plato: his ideal Republic never got beyond the planning stage, but Philaminte will convert her women's academy into a reality (ll. 844–50). It will outdo Richelieu's recently founded *Académie française* by reconciling all scientific and philosophical systems, couching them in beautiful language, and unveiling the secrets of nature in a thousand experiments (ll. 872–6).

In fact, the learned women are guilty of many of the faults of the traditional pedants and doctors of farce: they conceal a lack of interest in and understanding of real phenomena behind a welter of almost meaningless words, they are puffed up by their learning, and they build up a common defence to support one another against outsiders. To these faults they add new ones: they are much more aggressive in using their jargon and their half-assimilated knowledge as a stick with which to beat the uninitiated; they brand all those who do not share their affectations ignorant and unpolished; and they are determined to avenge the wrongs women have suffered at the hands of men by demonstrating the superiority of their sex (ll. 851–76).

Molière underlines the modernity of his subject and the reality of the follies he is mocking by portraying a literary lion, the favourite poet of Philaminte's *salon*, who has unmistakable connections with the well-known living poet Cotin. Trissotin (Tricotin in an earlier spelling) is a wordplay on *sot* or *sotin*, meaning 'foolish', and Cotin's name; the name invented by Molière means 'thrice-foolish'. Molière did not consider it necessary to compose silly verse to caricature Cotin's precious compositions; he chose, for the farcical scenes of poetry-reading and appreciation in the third act, poems actually written and published by Cotin. Molière's satire of Cotin and his fellow poets is biting; he is presented as vain, money-loving, presumptuous, ludicrously self-assured and incurably pleased with himself – qualities which shine with equal brightness from the pages of his books, from his face and from his whole demeanour (ll. 245–68).[4] Molière felt sufficiently strongly about Cotin to depart from the Horatian principle he set out in *L'Impromptu de Versailles*, and observed in other plays – that the satirist should paint folly in general and never particular individuals. While Trissotin is a general portrait, another in the line of the comic poet's delightful and disturbing caricatures, it is clear that he was also intended to be seen as a portrait of Cotin. Real life and caricature, the satirist would have us believe, have made a perfect marriage in the person of this precious poet.

The vanity and fragility of the alliances between poets and writers like Cotin are exposed through Trissotin's quarrel with the proud Greek scholar Vadius, seen by most as a caricature of another well-known literary figure, Ménage.[5] When Trissotin first introduces Vadius to the three learned women, the two poets go through the familiar ritual of praising each other's work to the skies (ll. 936–86). Then Vadius is invited by Trissotin to comment on a sonnet which he had heard in another *salon* without hearing the name of its author. Unaware that the sonnet is by Trissotin, Vadius treats it as if it were written by an outsider and dismisses it as a worthless piece of doggerel. He has committed the unforgivable sin in precious circles of not knowing who wrote what. The unseemly, foot-stamping row which follows this error, with the promise on both sides to engage in a duel of pamphlets, is intended to reveal how thin were the polish and sophistication of such leaders of literary fashion in the *beau monde* (ll. 988–1044). In pursuing culture in the company of such figures as Trissotin and Vadius, the three women will find little food for the soul.

In the domain of language, the three women have fervently embraced notions very much in the air at the time. They believe that the French language is in need of purification and, like Juvenal's bluestocking, they are obsessive grammarians. They echo the *Académie française*'s determination, outlined in the *Statutes*, 'to work with all possible care and diligence to give definite rules to our language and make it pure, eloquent and capable of treating of both arts and sciences' (Article 24). They reflect and magnify the heavily prescriptive tone of the *Académie* in Article 43: 'The general rules which the Academy will make concerning language will be followed by all those of its company who write, whether in prose or verse.' They see themselves as disciples of Vaugelas and set themselves the task of rooting out all bad usage in their home.

The three women are in the lunatic vanguard of linguistic reformers: to ensure purification, all dirty syllables – such as *con* and *cul* – are to be removed from words (ll. 909–18, 1699–1700). They turn Vaugelas's urbane comments on usage in *Remarques sur la langue française* (1647) into inviolable laws. His observation that usage alone has authority in questions of language, that even kings must yield to this tyrant, appeals especially to Philaminte; if kings must bow to usage, it must indeed be an abominable crime for a kitchen maid to refuse to do so; in consequence, Martine is sacked (ll. 459–510). To expect a servant to acquire good usage – an achievement which, according to Vaugelas, required many years spent at court, mingling with the small elite of court figures with a sure command of good usage – is an indication of how little Philaminte understands about language. As with philosophy and literature, the three women's claims to expertise are shown to be baseless, and their use of the patchy knowledge they do have is narrowly repressive. If Armande has her way, the whole French language will be impoverished and put in a straitjacket: each meeting of their academy will begin with a list of words to be eliminated from all prose and verse (ll. 899–908). In a comic and exaggerated form, the learned women's interventionist linguistic policies resemble those of the *Académie française*.

The attitude which informs all Molière's satire of precious, learned and literary figures in contemporary *salon* circles is a strong distaste for all the affectations which turn literature and philosophy into private domains, guarded by those who claim to hold the only keys which can admit new initiates. Since he wrote as one of the most successful and lionized writers of his age, it is hardly surprising that his satire shows no signs of professional jealousy, but it does reveal contempt for much of the writing of his contemporaries, for the kinds of affectation which created the climate in which such writing could succeed, and, as his portraits of Lysidas, Trissotin and Vadius show, for many of the individuals themselves. It is clear, for example, that he wished to destroy Cotin's reputation completely in *Les Femmes savantes*; contemporary evidence suggests that he succeeded.[6]

# 14
# Le Tartuffe

## 1. Comedy and topicality

Two of Molière's greatest plays, *Le Tartuffe* (1664) and *Dom Juan* (1665), from the moment of their composition to the present day, have continued to be a focus for controversy. Both tackle religious subjects normally beyond the range of the comic stage, and both reflect a lively interest in some of the most topical political, moral and theological issues of the time. There has been much disagreement among literary historians as to the precise focus of Molière's satire in these plays. Modern critics, partly in response to this confusion, tend to play down the religious elements and concentrate instead on dramatic techniques and on the timeless questions of human nature raised.

Those with an interest in Molière as a seventeenth-century playwright, however – and, indeed, the many who are puzzled by the structural oddities of these comedies – will feel the need to follow up allusions to contemporary issues as fully as possible. The plays raise many questions. Why, for example, did Molière depart from all the conventions of comedy to end *Le Tartuffe* with the direct intervention of the reigning monarch, an ending which modern directors and theatre-goers find ponderous and contrived? Why does the action of *Le Tartuffe* take place under such a brooding weight of menace that, up to the moment when the King intervenes, the audience fears that the forces of evil may prevail? Such a mood is foreign to the traditions of New Comedy. The case of *Dom Juan* is stranger still. Is it even a proper comedy? No one can be said to be happy in the dénouement; the eponymous hero is not, in any normal meaning of the term, a comic character; its episodic structure can easily seem bitty; characters appear and disappear without obvious reason; they are sometimes inconsistent – when Elvire comes on stage for the second time, she has undergone a transformation from vengeful, scorned wife to angel of love and mercy; for some, the supernatural elements in the play, especially the burning of Dom Juan in hell-fire, are simply too strange to carry conviction on the comic stage. Such an ending is certainly untypical in Molière's *œuvre*.

The study of theatrical conventions and dramatic techniques does not explain such oddities. We need to find out which aspects of contemporary life Molière was imitating. We cannot expect to follow the internal order of a well-constructed play if we do not know what the play is about.

## 2. Jansenists, Jesuits and the *Compagnie du Saint-Sacrement*

Of the possible targets for Molière's satire in *Le Tartuffe*, the most frequently named are the Jesuits, the Jansenists and the *Compagnie du Saint-Sacrement*. The case for the Jansenists is weakest; it is argued that Molière is satirizing Jansenist rigorism – perhaps as a riposte to their attacks on the theatre as a danger to morals – through his portrait of a household plunged into gloom by the strict control over the family's social life and pleasures exercised by Tartuffe and Orgon. In fact, there is little to suggest that Molière is mocking rigorism – Tartuffe is leading a most self-indulgent life; what he does hold up to ridicule is the use of false rigorism as a means of controlling the lives of others. It was not a common accusation that the Jansenists used rigorism to cloak self-indulgence and cupidity; Tartuffe simply does not have the characteristics which would make him recognizable as the caricature of a Jansenist.

A stronger case has been made for the *Compagnie du Saint-Sacrement*. Raoul Allier, in *La Cabale des dévots* (Paris, 1902), has shown how this group of powerful men worked together to defend what they saw as the interests of the Church, placing their members and allies in important posts, and seeking to promote their own policies through existing institutions. He argues that Tartuffe's underhand methods and the clear indication that he belongs to a cabal of like-minded schemers could be allusions to the practices of this *Compagnie* (pp. 389–92). However, Allier himself draws attention to the weaknesses in his case: the members of the *Compagnie*, though misguided, were genuine high-born zealots working to promote what they considered to be the true interests of the Church, while Tartuffe, a low-born villain, womanizer and trickster, uses the cover of religion to pursue his own narrowly self-interested ends (pp. 407–8). Another weakness in Allier's case is that the *Compagnie du Saint-Sacrement* appears to have been successful in keeping out of the public eye; Molière's audiences, who had flocked to see his satirical portraits of such familiar figures as the pedant, the *précieuse*, the *marquis*, jealous husbands and tyrant fathers, would not have known whom they were laughing at. It was unlikely that Molière, so famous for his telling portraits of well-known groups, should suddenly choose to portray such shadowy, little-known figures.

The strongest case can be made for the Jesuits. Tartuffe is presented as a master of the very latest casuistic techniques, and – particularly following the phenomenal success of Pascal's satire of new casuistry in the *Lettres provinciales* (1656–7) – the use of lax casuistry was associated more with the Jesuits than with any other Order. Among many other signposts which would have been clear to contemporaries, perhaps the clearest was Molière's choice of a name for Tartuffe's close ally, the silver-tongued bailiff who, with ten of his men, takes possession of Orgon's house and announces, with every assurance of Christian zeal, that the family must vacate the premises by the following day: the bailiff is called Monsieur Loyal, after Loyola, the founder of the Society of Jesus.[1]

Tartuffe himself, however, is not presented as a Jesuit: he is planning to marry Orgon's daughter, and Jesuits could not marry. Equally, Jesuits, like Jansenists and members of the *Compagnie du Saint-Sacrement*, did not behave like Tartuffe. There were Jesuits of many kinds: some were outstanding scholars and preachers; many were famous as teachers, missionaries or confessors; they saw themselves as apostles of the Counter-Reformation, determined to promote the authority of Church and Pope; among the Jesuits of Paris, there were many polished men of letters and courtiers. Perhaps there were some out-and-out scoundrels among their number, too; in such a large, successful and rapidly expanding organization it would be surprising if this had not been the case. But the typical Jesuit, even with the help of comic perspective, was not a likely model for the villainous Tartuffe. I suspect it is the contrast between the better-known

Jesuits – such distinguished men as Petau, Rapin or Bourdaloue – and the gross, unstylish figure of Tartuffe which has discouraged historians of literature from recognizing *Le Tartuffe* as a specifically anti-Jesuit satire.[2]

However, a Jesuit model for Tartuffe did exist: the figure of the caricatural Jesuit, a creation of polemical literature. In the numerous anti-Jesuit tracts published and circulated in France and all over Europe, the enemies of the Jesuits, jealous of their power, appalled by what they saw as Jesuit ruthlessness in pursuing their own policies and interests, built up a composite picture of the scheming, embezzling, hypocritical, spying Jesuit, ready to go to any lengths to please those whom he found useful, but vindictive and pitiless in ruining those who opposed him or attempted to halt the spreading influence of the Society of Jesus.[3]

To see how Molière, among so many others, came to condemn the activities of the Jesuits in such strong terms, it is necessary to look briefly at some aspects of the history of the Jesuits in France.

## 3. The Jesuit of polemical caricature

There were a number of characteristics particular to the Society of Jesus which provoked controversy in France and elsewhere. The simple fact of the Society's extraordinarily rapid expansion from its foundation in the early 1530s to the point where, by the end of the sixteenth century, there were Jesuits in most great centres, everywhere in the world, was a major source of friction: they had taken over as the major providers of Roman Catholic schools; become confessors to the powerful; opened new churches; achieved fame for their stirring preaching, their mastery of the theory and practice of rhetoric, the plays performed by their pupils, their theological scholarship and their missionary successes. Though many welcomed this new and exciting movement, others resented the Jesuits' presence and disliked their methods of self-advertisement which, to them, appeared thrusting and ostentatious.

The problem was exacerbated by the equivocal legal relationship between Jesuits and bishops: the Jesuits had a peculiar status, halfway between monk and priest; as members of an Order,

they owed obedience to their own general but also, and especially, to the Pope, to whom all senior Jesuits had sworn a special
fourth vow of loyalty; as priests working in the wider community they were – in theory, at least – subject to the jurisdiction
of the local bishop; quarrels with local priests and, on occasion,
refusal to obey a bishop's orders when these clashed with Jesuit
policy often caused serious disruption in the dioceses in which
they worked.

In France, the Jesuits met opposition in the *Parlements*, in the
University of Paris, from the Huguenots, from many of the
clergy and bishops – especially those who wished for some
measure of independence from Rome in the Gallican Church
– and from the Jansenists, who accused them of teaching heretical doctrines on grace and criticized their scholarship and their
lax use of casuistry. In 1594 their enemies in France, who
accused the Jesuits of inspiring Chastel's attempt upon the life
of Henry IV, persuaded the King to expel them for promulgat-
ing casuistic opinions which allegedly encouraged regicide.
After the Edict of Rouen (1603), permitting their return on
strict conditions, anti-Jesuit polemics in France grew in number
and vindictiveness again. Their enemies blamed them for the
assassination of Henry IV in 1610.[4] They saw the Jesuits as
agents and spies of Spain, France's major political enemy, infil-
trating French institutions, usurping the rights and privileges of
honest Frenchmen, corrupting their morals through lax casuistry, misappropriating their funds, using their schools as recruit-
ing grounds for the Society and taking children away from
their parents. They resented, too, the fact that from 1604 the
confessors to Henry IV, and then to Louis XIII and Louis
XIV, were all Jesuits with constant close access to the reigning
monarch.

Towards the middle of the seventeenth century, both before
and after the appearance of Pascal's *Lettres provinciales* (1656–7),
polemical attacks on the Jesuits focused more and more upon
their alleged misuse of casuistry.[5] As the leading confessing
Order, the Jesuits were of necessity specialists in casuistry – the
domain of moral theology concerned with cases of conscience.
Earlier attacks on Jesuit casuistry had centred on their views on
tyrannicide and regicide. Under the influence of Pascal, in
particular, the emphasis changed to a broader attack upon the

whole range of casuistic opinions. Pascal argued that their lax
casuistry was undermining the traditional teachings of the
Church. He accused them of using casuistry to serve political
ends, arguing that lax casuistry had become an instrument for
pleasing and conciliating the rich and powerful in order to
extend the influence and power of the Society (5th Letter, pp.
43–6). In polemical literature generally, a picture emerges of
Jesuits who presented a uniformly pious exterior, who were
ruled by ambition and pride in their Order, and who worked
together secretly as an international force to promote policies
agreed in Rome and Spain; to spread their influence, they
became adept at attracting funds; they were compliant in serving
their powerful allies, and ruthless in crushing their enemies. As
their numbers grew, their enemies in France accused them of
invading every corner of French life.

From the evidence of *Le Tartuffe*, Molière shared this hostile
view of the Jesuits. This did not place him in an odd and
fanatical minority. The clergy of Paris in general, many French
bishops, most *parlementaires*, Pascal, Racine, La Fontaine, the
doctor Gui Patin, *le grand* Arnauld and the Jansenists, and many
other groups and individuals who viewed the Jesuits from a
great diversity of standpoints, showed the same hostility. Molière's satire, like Pascal's *Lettres provinciales*, found a huge and
eager public.

## 4. A political satire

The action of *Le Tartuffe*, in a simplified caricatural form, traces
what Molière saw as the Jesuit invasion of France. He has
translated into a domestic context, suited to the genres of New
Comedy and farce, a major national and political drama. The
political importance of the play is reflected in the fact that even
with the support of the King – to which Molière alludes with
gratitude in the *Placets* of 1664 and 1667 and the *Préface* of 1669
– it took five years and at least two revisions of the text for him
to win the right to have it performed freely and openly. In the
same *Placets* and *Préface*, Molière made it clear that 'the famous
originals' of his portrait were numerous, powerful and determined; and that in his opinion his career in the theatre would be
over if the King allowed these 'tartuffes' to succeed in having

the play banned (*O.C.*, I, pp. 892–3). In *Le Tartuffe*, Molière has briefly restored to comedy the function of Old Comedy, central to the plays of Aristophanes, of presenting on stage matters of importance to the public and the state. By portraying a scheming casuist and hypocrite worming his way into a good, dependable French family, attracting alms with loud demonstrations of piety, flattering the head of the house, usurping his power and wealth, and turning treacherously against him once he has him in his power, Molière added his voice to the many others who condemned Jesuit activities in France.

The extraordinary and monstrous character of Tartuffe is constructed from two apparently incompatible sets of qualities. He is a consummate schemer who easily outwits his victim, implements a clever strategy for taking over his house and his wealth and, at the same time, arms himself with enough of his victim's secrets to have him jailed should he ever need to. The other set of characteristics, his self-indulgence, gluttony and carnality, show Tartuffe as a careless, ill-disciplined rogue whose hypocrisy is transparent to any reasonably clear-sighted person. Each of these sets of qualities is built up from different elements of anti-Jesuit polemics.

Tartuffe the schemer is shown putting into practice the policies of the infamous fictitious Jesuit of one of the most widely disseminated anti-Jesuit tracts, the *Monita secreta* (1612), usually attributed to Jerome Zaorowski, an expelled Polish Jesuit. Molière could have read one of the many Latin editions of this tract or the French translation, *Advis secrets de la Société de Jésus* (1661), probably published in Paris but giving Paderborne as its town of publication to help protect the printer. In this cleverly conceived and skilfully written little tract, the polemicist presents his text as a set of secret instructions from a very senior Jesuit to be communicated only to other Jesuits of the fourth vow. Only professed Jesuits take the fourth vow and the reader is encouraged to believe, as he reads the instructions, that he is entering into the very heart of the Society and sharing in its most secret counsels. He is to learn the techniques and tactics which – the polemicist alleges – have made it possible for the Jesuits to spread so rapidly in so short a time. The Jesuit is instructed in a strategy for attracting alms and support when spreading to new territories:

He must go to far-off places where he will receive alms, even the smallest contributions, after having displayed the poverty of our members. These must then be handed to the poor, in order to edify those who do not yet know our Society and to encourage them to be more generous towards us. (I, iii)

This is how Tartuffe first ensnares Orgon; with the new convert's enthusiasm, Orgon describes his first encounters with his spiritual mentor to Cléante:

Having been informed by his boy, who imitated him in everything, of his poverty and of what kind of man he was, I offered him gifts but, modestly, he always wanted me to take some of them back. 'It's too much,' he would say to me, 'half as much would do; I don't deserve to inspire such compassion'; and when I refused to take the money back, before my very eyes, he would distribute it among the poor. (ll. 291–8)

In the sixth and seventh chapters of the *Monita*, the fictitious Jesuit instructor explains to his advanced pupils how they should set about gaining control of wealth in private hands. They should, when possible, choose wealthy widows as the objects of their campaign but, the instructor says, his advice on how to approach rich widows holds good for merchants and rich, married *bourgeois*, too. The heart of the Jesuit's strategy must be to teach the widow to turn to him and him alone for advice on all matters, to persuade her that her Jesuit confessor is 'the sole source of her spiritual advancement' (VI, v). Dorine tells us that Orgon stands in just such a relationship to Tartuffe: 'He admires him on every occasion, cites him at every turn; his least actions appear to him to be miracles, and all his words are so many oracles to him' (ll. 196–8). The Jesuit, according to the *Monita*, should also make use of confession to discover the state of the widow's finances and learn all her secrets (VI, vi; IX, iii–iv). Again, Dorine tells us that Tartuffe is 'the unique confidant of all his [Orgon's] secrets, and the prudent director of all his actions' (ll. 187–8). Tartuffe's success in laying his hands on secret incriminating papers belonging to Orgon is a crucial element in his plan to put him in his power.

The Jesuit should, at the same time, isolate his widow or rich *bourgeois* from all contacts with society (VI, ii). We learn in the opening scene that Orgon's family is suffering from the pall which has descended over the household since Orgon has been persuaded to put an end to visits from friends (ll. 79–82). The Jesuit's chosen victim should also be isolated from his own family, the main obstacle to an outsider hoping to gain control of his or her affairs (VI, x). Orgon's estrangement from his wife, children, brother-in-law and even servant is a central theme of *Le Tartuffe*; it is one of his proudest boasts that Tartuffe has taught him to love no one: 'He detaches my soul from all loving-relationships, and I would see brother, children, mother and wife die without caring that [snapping his fingers] for it' (ll. 276–9). A childless widow or *bourgeois* is always to be preferred, but if the Jesuit has chosen one with children, he must, if he is to gain control of her or his money, sow hostility between parent and child: 'Mothers must be taught to vex their children with scolding and censure from their earliest youth' (VIII, i). Stirring his family into a rage, as Orgon himself proclaims, is his greatest joy (l. 1173).

Behind this quite savage satire, both in the *Monita secreta* and in *Le Tartuffe*, lies the accusation that the Jesuits have sacrificed Christian principles to political expediency. In the *Monita secreta*, where the polemical message is explicit, the Jesuits are portrayed working to increase the resources and power of their Order. Molière, who does not name the Jesuits, paints a similar state of mind and similar behaviour, detaching the crime from the Society of Jesus and attaching it to his caricature of a hypocrite. His method was to portray a set of follies and vices and leave his audiences to decide who might be guilty of them. If the cap fits, wear it.


## 5. Jesuit policy and Christian doctrine

Tartuffe uses the language, external appearance and authority of Christianity and the Church, while undermining, by the code of conduct he follows and preaches to others, everything that Christianity stands for. In the most detailed and cogently presented seventeenth-century attack upon the Jesuits, the *Lettres provinciales*, this is the picture Pascal painted of the Society of Jesus. Throughout his letters, Pascal's argument was that the Jesuits had traded the substance of Christian doctrine for the appearance of ecclesiastical success; in order to embrace as many people as possible within the Church, they had reshaped doctrine to soften its demands and accommodate it, wherever necessary, to the foibles and even the vices of men and women. He argued, too, that the Jesuits had confused the glory of God with the glory of the Society of Jesus; they had redefined heresy so that it no longer consisted in holding beliefs contrary to the traditional doctrines of the Church, but in professing views critical of the Jesuits (15th Letter, p. 183). To express his anger against the Jesuits, Pascal borrowed the words of a Capuchin friar, Valeriano Magni, a contemporary who, like Pascal, found himself the object of Jesuit attacks on his good name; Valeriano's denunciation captures the essence of Pascal's view:

> These kinds of men, who make themselves unbearable to the whole of Christendom, aspire, under the pretext of good works, to the highest honours and to domination, distorting to serve their own ends almost every law – divine, human, positive and natural. They attract, through their doctrine, through fear, or through hope, all the princes of the earth, whose authority they abuse in order to bring success to their detestable intrigues. But their wrongs, although so criminal, are neither punished nor stopped; on the contrary, they are rewarded and they commit them as boldly as if they were rendering service to God. Everyone recognizes them, everyone speaks of them with execration, but how few are capable of standing up against such a powerful tyranny; that is what I have done. (quoted in 15th Letter, p. 188)

In the person of Tartuffe, Molière has scaled down this awesome power to a comic level, but the same characteristics recur. Tartuffe equates the will of God with his own desires; all his crimes are carried out in the name of God and under the cloak of religion. He aspires to dominate and control the small world of which he has chosen to make a conquest; to achieve this, he wins the head of the house and, as soon as he is sure of him, abuses his authority. He moves the boundaries between good and evil to suit his changing interests and desires at different points in the play: the clearest example is his change of attitude to Orgon; while Orgon believes him to be a saint, no praise is too high for him, but as soon as Orgon sees through his hypocrisy, Tartuffe declares him to be a traitor who must at once be jailed. He is in league with others, all behaving in the same way and working to the same ends: we hear of his servant,

Laurent, who imitates all his master's ways (ll. 203–10) and meet the bailiff, Monsieur Loyal, who has come to take possession of Orgon's house (V, 4).

Perhaps the most striking parallel between Tartuffe's behaviour and the behaviour of the Jesuits as described by Valeriano Magni and Pascal is that its dishonesty is known to all, yet apparently unstoppable; though Tartuffe's scheming is crude and most members of the family see through him instantly, the audience is made to realize that only the last-minute intervention of the King can save the family from him.

## 6. Tartuffe as casuist

Tartuffe the schemer would be a grim figure, too sinister for the world of comedy, if Molière had not combined with the cold, calculating side of his character an unregulated, sensual nature which makes him succumb readily to any temptation of the flesh. Fat, florid, red-lipped, thirsty, greedy, belching, deep-sleeping and, above all, easily roused by the sight of a woman's flesh, Tartuffe is altogether a man, an epitome of all the base appetites which afflict the genus. His status as a man, and nothing more, is proclaimed with delightful irony by Orgon when, lost for words to describe such a paragon, he can only say: 'He is a man ... who, ... ah! a man ... a man in short' (l. 272). When Tartuffe appears on stage in Act II, roaring like a braggart-soldier about his hair shirt, his whip and his charitable good works, his real nature is immediately revealed as his eyes fix upon Dorine's low-cut dress and he advances towards her unfolding his handkerchief in order to cover her bosom and protect himself from temptation. This oafish, self-deceiving, over confident and lecherous fat-man is a perfect hero of farce.

This side of his character has obvious comic functions, but it is also part of Molière's anti-Jesuit satire. Through Tartuffe's weaknesses of the flesh, Molière extends the range of his satire to include the whole field of lax moral teaching allegedly spread by the Jesuits' innovations in casuistry. Tartuffe's grossness and sensuality are intended not as an accurate characterization of Jesuit behaviour but as a comic portrayal of all the sins a self-indulgent rogue can commit while remaining innocent in the eyes of an accommodating casuist. Pascal claimed that the only sins which could not be rendered innocent by new casuistry were those committed 'with the formal intention of sinning and with no other purpose than sinning' (7th Letter, p. 69). In the midst of his earthbound enjoyment of the seven deadly sins, Tartuffe never does anything which cannot be shown by an expert new-casuist to be technically innocent. When he says to Elmire, 'Ah! for being a man of God, I am no less a man', he is not confessing to weakness but making the technical point that he can remain devout without sacrificing any of his animal appetites (l. 966). Tartuffe was not one of those gloomy ascetic Christians who were blind to a woman's beauty. Pascal quotes a passage from the Jesuit Le Moyne's *Peintures morales* ridiculing such a figure: 'For him a beautiful woman is a ghost; and these imperious and sovereign faces, these agreeable tyrants who, without help of chains, make willing slaves of men have no more power over his eyes than the sun over the eyes of owls'; Tartuffe would claim rather to have, in the words of Le Moyne, the 'honest and natural affections' appropriate to a warm-blooded man (9th Letter, p. 98).

Opponents of the Jesuits accused them of moving back the frontiers of sin, of making the Christian life accessible to all in order to swell the numbers of their converts and allies. Pascal's claim was that this new casuistry, none of it more than eighty years old, was taking the place of the Scriptures, the Church Fathers and the Councils, undercutting the Church's ancient authority and putting in its place new and debased doctrines (5th and 6th Letters, pp. 52–67). The new figures who have replaced all earlier authorities, according to Pascal's fictitious Jesuit father, are:

> Villalobos, Conink, Llamas, Achokier, Dealkozer, Dellacruz, Veracruz, Ugolin, Tambourin, Fernandez, Martinez, Suarez, Henriquez, Vasquez, Lopez, Gomez, Sanchez, De Vechis, De Grassis, De Grassalis, De Pitigianis, De Graphaeis, Squilanti, Bizozeri, Barcola, De Bobadilla, Simancha, Perez de Lara, Aldretta, Lorca, De Scarcia, Quaranta, Scophra, Pedrezza, Cabrezza, Bisbe, Dias, Declavasio, Villagut, Adam à Mandem, Iribarne, Binsfeld, Volfangi à Vorberg, Vosthery, Strevesdorf.

Pascal records his letter-writer's astonished response:

> 'Oh, my Father,' I said in panic, 'were all those people Christians?' 'What do you mean, Christians?' he replied. 'Wasn't I telling you

that these are the only people by whom Christendom is governed these days?' (5th Letter, pp. 52–3)[6]

Pascal concedes quite happily that severe Jesuits expected people who came to them for confession to follow God's law as closely as possible, but unfortunately, he adds ironically, the majority of people required confessors who were more accommodating. As a result, with the laudable aim of keeping everyone within the fold, casuists have sprung up on all sides, compromising, introducing ingenious sophisms and adapting their rulings and recommendations to suit each case (5th Letter, pp. 43–4). If a sin cannot be overcome, it must be redefined and reclassified. The Jesuits, according to Pascal, practised a dual policy: high standards were set for the truly devout by austere confessors, while ill-disciplined rogues needed less exacting confessors; the latter, however, in order to rise to the challenge of 'purifying' behaviour which was often gross and godless, had to be much more skilled in their handling of the sophisticated techniques of casuistry. Pascal recalls ironically that François Hallier had once said of Bauny, one of the more notorious casuists: 'Here is the man who takes away the sins of the world' (4th Letter, p. 32).

Tartuffe knows his new casuistry and has no fear of sin. He is pleased, too, to place his skills in this science at the service of his friends. When Elmire fears that adultery might displease God, Tartuffe replies:

I, Madam, can dissipate these ridiculous fears; and I know the art of alleviating scruples. God does truly forbid certain satisfactions:[7] but arrangements can be made with Him. There is (according to our various needs) a science of stretching the limits of our conscience, and of rectifying the evil of an action by the purity of our intention. Those are secrets, Madam, in which we can instruct you: you have merely to let yourself be guided. Satisfy my desire and do not be terrified. I will answer to you for everything and take the evil upon myself. (ll. 1485–96)

Tartuffe could have cited in support of these reassuring words a passage from Bauny quoted by Pascal, saying that a confessor 'can and must absolve a woman who has a man in her house with whom she frequently commits sin, if she has no honest way of getting him out of the house, or has some reason for keeping him there' (10th Letter, p. 113).

Tartuffe could easily provide opinions from specialist casuists to cover all his sins. He eats enough for six (l. 192), starts the day with four good draughts of wine (l. 255), eats a couple of partridges and half a leg of mutton at a single sitting (ll. 239–40), but according to Escobar, quoted by Pascal, he is not guilty of gluttony so long as he does not eat until he vomits (9th Letter, p. 101).

When Damis tells his father that he has just heard Tartuffe declare that he loves Elmire, Tartuffe deftly employs another casuistic trick to deceive Orgon without telling a lie. If a man, as often happened, wished to conceal a particular sin from his confessor – either to conserve his confessor's esteem, or to avoid having to admit that he has slipped back into the same sins as last time – he had only, according to Escobar and Suarez, 'to make a general confession and to lose this sin among all the others he is accusing himself of in general' (quoted by Pascal, 10th Letter, p. 108). Tartuffe abases himself before Orgon, confessing quite truthfully that he is a wicked man, an abject sinner, guilty of many a low crime, but not mentioning the particular sin of having tried to seduce his wife, and Orgon, impressed by such a striking display of humility, takes Tartuffe's side, throws his son out of the house and, for good measure, disinherits him in favour of the hypocrite (III, 6).

In condoning Orgon's decision to make him sole heir to his fortune, to which he has no right, Tartuffe justifies himself with more casuistic evasion. He accepts Damis's money – not for himself or from any desire to harm Damis, but because he, as a holy man, can put the money to a more godly use; his intentions are pure (ll. 1237–48). Another piece of sophistry is used to explain why it is right for the legitimate son of the house to be expelled while Tartuffe remains in residence: if Tartuffe were to withdraw, people would say that he was acting from political expediency and that his withdrawal was equivalent to an admission of guilt; his reputation could be compromised (ll. 1203–16). The best-known piece of casuistry is the double sophistry performed by Tartuffe and his disciple Orgon together. Orgon is persuaded to hand over incriminating papers to Tartuffe in order that he may be able to deny innocently, by an indirect lie, that he has any such papers in his possession. In fact, the whole suggestion is a trick practised by Tartuffe on Orgon: while pretending to offer him friendly support and subtle moral advice, he is really planning to put Orgon in his power so that, should the need arise, he will be in a position to ruin him (ll. 1576–92).

## 7. Tartuffe as lover

Tartuffe, overweight, repulsive, low-born and ill-bred, makes an unlikely stage lover. Elmire is an attractive and still quite young second wife to Orgon, of good background, elegant, generous with her stepchildren and patient and loyal with her husband. Much of the comedy of Tartuffe's lecherous pursuit of this paragon of womanhood comes from the fact that he is so obviously unsuited to such a task. The strong satirical suggestion, again, is that only Tartuffe's use of the cloak of religion could enable him to cross the social barriers which would normally prevent him from gaining access to a woman of Elmire's standing. Dorine points out that he was a penniless nobody until Orgon took him in (ll. 63–4, 482–6).

Paradoxically – and comically – it is also Tartuffe's use of a religious mask, and his mastery of Christian rhetoric, which permit him to make his gallant declarations to Elmire with so little groundwork. Dom Juan, a more effective and urbane seducer, proceeds quickly enough in his seduction of Charlotte, but he does so by practising the flattering arts and wiles of the seducer (II, 2). Tartuffe, with the confidence which comes from knowing that lust and adultery can be made innocent by new casuistry, dispenses with the normal preliminaries of the seducer; he can easily square God and his conscience, but forgets that it is not so easy to persuade an honest woman to accept his attentions. As soon as Elmire appears on stage in the third act, he begins to mingle the language of devotion to God with an expression of his devotion to her: the words 'body', 'desire', 'love', 'grace', 'cherish', 'thrilled', 'sweet', 'attractions', 'zealous transports', 'fervour' and many more combine to evoke an atmosphere which might pass for religious enthusiasm, but is really one of erotic excitement (III, 3).

There is nothing specially Jesuitical in the use of erotic language to describe religious experience; it is a trait common to most mystical writing. However, it is not to mystical literature

in general that Molière is alluding. Tartuffe is using arguments
and rhetoric which can be found in the *Peintures morales* (1640–
43) of Le Moyne, the well-known contemporary precious poet
and Jesuit. Le Moyne had attracted some of Pascal's severest
censure for his *Dévotion aisée*. His *Peintures morales* were also
cited by Pascal as a text which made a mockery of sacred things:
'Does not his whole book of the *Peintures morales*, in its prose
and its verse, display a spirit full of vanity and the follies of the
world?' (11th Letter, p. 130).

Le Moyne's text is written for the court, especially for the
women of the court: its style is precious, arch and florid; its
contents are leavened with images and conceits which would
ensure that the book could be consulted, discussed and read
aloud in *salon*, *boudoir* or *ruelle* without risk of striking a too-
solemn note. Read in the context of either theology or moral
philosophy, the *Peintures* are easily ridiculed. The second volume
is devoted entirely to the subject of love, and the chapter from
which Tartuffe could have borrowed his reasoning on love is
entitled 'The second rule for the sanctification of love: how to
contemplate the beauties of the body with the eyes of the spirit'
(pp. 838–65).[8] Le Moyne's stated aim is to encourage the flighty
courtier to find God in the features of the many fine women he
is likely to admire in the course of his daily life. He argues that
as men and women are made in God's image, it is legitimate to
love God in these earthly reflections of His beauty; and, secondly,
that just as in admiring the qualities of a work of art we are
really praising the hand that made it, we can admire God's
handiwork in the human bodies which He created and which so
effectively reveal His art. Provided sexual desire does not degenerate into 'amour brutal' ('animal sensuality'), it can enrich the
spirit:

> If we have eyes sufficiently purified to recognize the royalty of Jesus
> Christ in the pleasant and natural sovereignty which is imprinted
> upon beautiful women, we shall learn by this means to cherish His
> commandments and to accept with pleasure the yoke of His law
> upon our hearts and our heads. (pp. 861–62)

Le Moyne dwells upon the beauties of the body: 'the Creator
has made the human body as beautiful as we perceive it to be,
and has given it so many charms and ornaments, in order that it

might provide the beautiful robe or the fine dwelling-place of a still more beautiful soul' (p. 849). He is pleased with his reasoning, concluding: 'I believe I have done love a considerable good turn by the lesson I have just taught her' (p. 865).

Tartuffe extends the argument that the beauty of the outer robe is a kind of guarantee of the quality of its contents one stage further. His first compliments are paid to Elmire's dress, which he handles freely, exclaiming: 'Heavens! How wondrous is the detail of this stitching! The work of people these days has something miraculous about it; never, anywhere, have I seen anything finer' (ll. 919–21). His attention soon moves to the woman wearing the dress. Now, he sees Elmire as the curiously worked artefact who reflects the skill of her Maker: 'The love which binds us to eternal beauties does not smother in us the love of temporal beauties; our senses are easily caught in the spell of the perfect creations which God has shaped' (ll. 933–6). Faithful to Le Moyne's formulation, Tartuffe finds in Elmire both irresistible evidence of God's creative powers and a reflection of His beauty:

> His reflected charms shine in women like you; but, in you, He displays His rarest wonders: on your countenance, He has poured beauties in profusion which surprise our eyes and ravish our hearts, and I could not look upon you, perfect creature, without admiring in you the Author of nature and feeling my heart smitten with a burning love for the most beautiful of God's self-portraits. (ll. 937–44)

Tartuffe follows Le Moyne, too, in noting that God's image is likely to be reflected more faithfully in the very beautiful, such as Elmire, than in those who are less so. Le Moyne argues:

> God has imprinted upon us the light of His countenance and has made it a sign which shows in our faces; beautiful women, however, have received more of this light than others; and its meaning is clearer and more distinct in them. They are, therefore, among visible things, the most perfect images of God, and the most particular representations of His beauty. (p. 857)

Tartuffe could claim that his disconcerting blend of veneration of God and lust for woman is permitted by Le Moyne, who has taught him the means of purifying himself through that which defiles, how to turn an object of pleasure into a subject of virtue, how to light a divine fire from the matter of a sensual fire, and how to make oneself agreable to God through the inclination one feels for His creatures. (p. 866)

Le Moyne teaches, too, that beautiful people deserve 'respect and honour, they command almost religion and worship' (p. 851).

Certainly, Tartuffe has no hesitation in addressing Elmire in the language of prayer, making an offering of his heart, expecting nothing from his own infirmity, but waiting upon her bounty to see if she will bring him peace and bliss (ll. 953–8). He even commits the ultimate blasphemy of perverting the language of the Mass with his reference to 'l'autel où leur cœur sacrifie' ('the altar where [young lovers] make a sacrifice of their hearts') (l. 994).

## 8. The importance of secrecy

It is at once clear to Elmire and to the audience that Tartuffe has little to offer as a lover. He is without wealth, position, style and even superficial charm. However, he sets much store by one advantage he has over the loquacious young bloods he sees as his rivals. They are boastful about their conquests, while he, with his reputation to protect, will guarantee absolute discretion:

> People like us burn with a discreet fire; with us, you can be quite sure of secrecy: the care we take of our reputation provides a full guarantee to the loved woman, and with us you will find, if you accept our hearts, love without scandal and pleasure without fear (ll. 995–1000)

He returns to the question again, when he believes that Elmire is to be his, to reassure her that there is no harm in adultery: 'you can rest assured of total secrecy; there is any wrong in it only if it reaches the ears of the public; the stumbling block is the worldly scandal: to sin in silence is not to sin' (ll. 1503–6).

This characteristic of Tartuffe reflects another persistent theme in anti-Jesuit propaganda. The Jesuits were accused by their opponents of caring more about their reputation than about honesty, justice or virtue. Hence, it was argued, they would go to any lengths to protect their reputation and, if one of their number slipped into wrongdoing, would care little for the sin itself so long as it could be kept secret. A contemporary pamphlet, *L'Innocence persécutée*, a long anonymous poem circulated in manuscript form, accusing the Jesuits of collaborating with Colbert to ensure the conviction of Fouquet, made precisely this accusation: 'They place their virtue in the art of concealment; what no one hears about is not called sin.'[9]

According to another polemicist, Jarrige, a Jesuit who left the Order and then attacked it bitterly in *Les Jesuistes mis sur l'eschafaut* (1648), this use of secrecy to protect the Society's good name was widespread among Jesuits. He argued that Ignatius, in his rules on chastity, set such a high standard for Jesuits, requiring that they maintain 'angelic purity', that 'he has thrown them into despair of ever achieving success, and, being unable to show that they are angels, for they are too carnal, they have shown, especially recently, that they are men, and among those most attached to the senses and the flesh' (p. 44). Allegations of this kind add significance to Tartuffe's delightfully understated remark to Elmire: 'But, Madam, after all, I am not an angel' (l. 970). Jarrige claimed that Jesuits had bowed to expediency, shifting guilt from the act of fornication itself to the fact of being found out: 'all lascivious acts between man and woman which discretion has kept hidden were not sins before God, but simply those which came to the knowledge of men' (pp. 98–9). Jarrige claimed to have heard a woman saying she preferred Jesuits to other priests, as she found them 'more discreet' (p. 61).

## 9. Orgon's credulity

In terms of traditional comedy, Orgon plays the fool to Tartuffe's knave; he is the rich, naïve *bourgeois* who falls readily into the traps laid by the villain. His role of gullible fool has satirical functions, too. Within the microcosm of the family, he represents the figure in authority, who is manipulated by the ruthless hypocritical intruder. He also symbolizes, together with his mother, Madame Pernelle, those French men and women whose desire to defend the Church against heretics and libertines was so strong that they easily fell victim to the tricks of hypocrites who appealed to them in the name of God.

The theme of credulity runs through the play; both Madame Pernelle and Orgon confuse credulity with faith. They imitate Tartuffe, naming God and Heaven at every opportunity, making an ostentatious display of devoutness and claiming always to know the mind and will of God. As a result, they feel they have earned the right to condemn as sinners all those who do not share their noisy and aggressive religiosity. In the famous opening scene of *Le Tartuffe*, in which Madame Pernelle scolds the whole household, except for the absent Orgon, the comedy arises in part from the fact that it is not for their shortcomings that this shrill old woman is condemning them, but for their refusal to share her credulous adulation of Tartuffe. True morality is overturned: from inside her cocoon of credulity, this sour, elderly bigot feels entirely justified in proclaiming that God is on her side and that other members of the family, who have done nothing worse than receive visits from friends, are instruments of Satan.

Orgon uses similar perverted logic to discredit Cléante, Valère, and his own wife and children. His behaviour and reasoning are based on an assumption that his own wishes and the wishes of Tartuffe have divine authority and need no other backing, while the wishes and arguments of those who oppose them are contrary to the will of God and carry no weight. When Cléante tries to persuade Orgon that his trust in Tartuffe has been accorded too easily, Orgon responds by condemning his brother-in-law as a libertine, so damning Cléante and everything he says and relieving himself of the chore of having to find answers to his arguments (ll. 314–17). Cléante protests in vain that, for the credulous, 'a man's a libertine for having a good pair of eyes, and anyone who fails to adore empty grimaces has neither faith nor respect for sacred things' (ll. 320–2).

Valère receives similar treatment; when Orgon decides, without good reason, to break the promise he has made to Valère and to marry his daughter to Tartuffe instead, he shifts the blame for his change of mind from himself to Valère; it is Orgon who is breaking his promise, but by instantly convicting Valère, without evidence, of libertinism and gambling to justify his decision, the sin is transferred from the offender to the innocent victim.

Later, when Orgon is forced to choose between believing his

son Damis and trusting his friend Tartuffe, he is not content merely to convict his son of deliberate lying but, to punish him, sentences him to instant exile from the family home and deprives him of his rightful succession to the family fortune. Orgon, blinded by credulity, turns justice on its head: his punishment would be cruel even if his son had been lying; in fact, Damis is innocent and his father, with all his religious prating, has become a monster of injustice. When his wife, supported by the rest of the family, tries to persuade Orgon that Damis has been telling the truth, all are dismissed as liars; the credit they have earned in Orgon's eyes over years of family life proves worthless when balanced against Orgon's newly adopted faith (IV, 3).

His credulity is almost unshakeable; when Elmire is driven to playing the seductress to expose Tartuffe's hypocrisy and force her husband to abandon his faith in him, still, while Tartuffe prepares to take possession of her just a few feet away from his hiding place, Orgon hesitates. Only when Tartuffe himself states unequivocally that Orgon is a fool, asking to be led by the nose, does he finally emerge from under the table with his sight restored (IV, 5 and 6).

Molière's play shows how hypocrisy is fostered by credulity. In both the *Placet* of 1667 and the *Préface* of 1669, he complained bitterly that many genuinely good and devout people had been turned against him and his play by the specious arguments of hypocrites. Such good men, he writes in the *Préface*, 'from the warmth of their devotion to the interests of heaven, readily receive the impressions these people wish to give them' (*O.C.*, I, p. 884). Molière makes it clear that Orgon had been a good man before being blinded and corrupted by the combination of Tartuffe's hypocrisy and his own credulity; he had been a loyal Frenchman who had fought for his King in the troubles of the Fronde (ll. 181–2); it is partly in gratitude for past services that the King pardons him for having given shelter to a fugitive from justice (ll. 1935–44). Molière surrounds Orgon with a loyal and generous family, too, to suggest that before Tartuffe's arrival he had been an affectionate father and husband.

The satirical implication of the portrait of Orgon, when transferred from the context of the family to the wider context of the state, is that according to Molière many a good Frenchman, seduced by the appeal of the external trappings of religion, had lost his judgement, hardened his heart, turned against his friends and become an instrument of injustice. Orgon is not merely fooled and robbed; he has himself become a danger and a scourge to all those who should be closest to him.

## 10. Orgon's family

The family of Orgon, including the servant Dorine, represents the considerable number of discerning, level-headed Frenchmen who, Molière suggests, have no difficulty seeing through the machinations of hypocritical cabals, but who, especially if they speak out against them, are likely to suffer from their vindictive calumnies. Cléante and Valère, when they are accused of being libertines, are suffering the same fate as other opponents of the Jesuits, including Pascal and Molière. Pascal lists among the names given to him by Jesuit polemicists: 'ungodly, buffoon, ignoramus, joker, impostor, calumniator, knave and heretic . . . ' (12th Letter, p. 135). Molière complained to the King that he had been called 'a devil clothed in flesh and dressed as a man, a libertine, a godless man deserving of exemplary torture' (*Premier Placet*, *O.C.*, I, p. 890).[10]

   The family's failure to counter Tartuffe's moves reflects what Molière, Pascal, Valeriano Magni and many others saw as the helplessness of honest people attempting to oppose the advance of the Jesuits. The family's failure is all the more striking for the fact that Tartuffe's dishonesty is so transparent. Molière appears to suggest that the ordinary weapons of honest men and women are powerless against the ruthless methods of even quite clumsy impostors, when they choose to present themselves as envoys specially elect of God. At every turn, the family underestimates the effectiveness of Tartuffe's preplanned series of manoeuvres. While they are still convinced that they have only to undeceive Orgon to put matters right, Tartuffe has already armed himself with enough material to blackmail Orgon, has procured legal ownership of the house and, under the cover of crooked casuistry, is attempting to seduce his wife. Molière creates the impression that this attractive French family, symbol of the wider family of all true Frenchmen, is attacked on every side, unable to foresee or forestall the numerous hidden traps and pitfalls prepared for it by an enemy deploying the full range of Jesuitical skills and stratagems.

11. The perspective of the *honnête homme*

Cléante is a crucial figure in this society undermined by sophistry and credulity: he illustrates, through both the soundness of his arguments and the modesty of his behaviour, how a good and honest man should behave. In the words of the author of the *Lettre sur la comédie de l'Imposteur*, Cléante recognizes 'the middle way, in which alone justice, reason and truth are to be found' (*O.C.*, I, pp. 1165–6). Cléante claims nothing more than to be able to distinguish between the true and the false (ll. 351–4) but, as Cicero says, this is precisely the purpose of good dialectic, the art of 'sound discussion and of distinguishing the true from the false' (*De Oratore*, II, 157).

Cléante's sound dialectic is deployed most fully in the scene where he first discusses Tartuffe with Orgon (I, 5). His argument is an expression of the commonplace view of anti-Jesuit writers that Jesuits displayed excessive vindictiveness in their treatment of opponents. He dwells on the difference between the truly devout and the hypocritical. Of the devout, he says:

> These are no braggarts of virtue; you will not find in them this unbearable display of pomp and ceremony, and their devotion is human and approachable; they do not censure our every action: they find too much arrogance in such corrections; and leaving proud words to others, it is through their deeds alone that they reprove our behaviour. (ll. 388–94)

He also shows to what extent Orgon, under Tartuffe's influence, has lost touch with both the theory and practice of Christianity: he has ceased to love and respect his family and friends; he has become arrogantly censorious of others, and unhealthily obsessed with the external signs and gestures of religion. He has replaced Christian humility and love with vindictive religiosity.

Cléante is 'the truly good man' whom Molière introduced into the play, as he says in the *Préface*, to provide a contrast with the hypocrite (*O.C.*, I, p. 884). Some critics have observed that Cléante is not an ardent apologist for Christianity, and cite his reticence as evidence that Molière, in whom they see a covert libertine, was indifferent or éven hostile to the Christian faith. This argument does not stand up to close examination. The authority of the Church and its dogma are not under attack in *Le Tartuffe*, so why should Molière appoint someone to defend them? It is appropriate for a satirist and comic poet to satirize hypocrisy, but it would have been considered most inappropriate for him to defend Christian doctrine on stage. More importantly, we have seen that Cléante argues that it is the Christian's deeds, not his words, which speak most clearly. Molière illustrates this point by portraying Cléante not as a man who talks about Christianity but as a man who does his best to behave in a Christian way.

It is part of the satirical thrust of the play that those who never stop talking about God and Heaven are often the very people who practise their faith least. The writer of the *Lettre sur la comédie de l'Imposteur* argues that Cléante is introduced early in the play so that the audience may see an example of 'true devotion' before seeing the hypocrite; the antidote to the poison of hypocrisy, he suggests, is taken before the spectator can be exposed to risk from the poison itself (*O.C.*, I, p. 1150). Cléante's behaviour is seen to be open, honest, tolerant and modest. He confronts the hostility, folly, dishonesty and treachery he meets in this play with neither anger nor complacent self-righteousness. He argues with Orgon and Tartuffe firmly but with control. When he rebuts Tartuffe's sophistry at the beginning of Act IV, his straight, pellucid and common-sense dialectic shows up the crookedness of Tartuffe's reasoning, but he avoids attacking Tartuffe himself. Tartuffe soon has recourse to the trick used by Pascal's Jesuit Father when arguments run dry: he recollects suddenly that he has urgent business elsewhere (ll. 1266–8; end of 4th Letter, pp. 40–41).

Cléante's patience with Orgon, though severely tested by the latter's absurd errors of judgement, never deserts him. When Tartuffe's hypocrisy is exposed, Cléante does not yield, as Dorine does, to the temptation of reminding Orgon what a fool he has made of himself (ll. 1695–6, 1815–20). He restrains Orgon when, shocked by Tartuffe's wickedness, he swears undying hatred for all men of God. At this point, Molière gives Cléante a long speech in which he commends moderation and underlines again that it is vital to distinguish between impostors and true men of God; to push his point home, he suggests that if Orgon cannot avoid straying from the mean, he should rather fall into the extreme of trusting the occasional hypocrite than into the opposite extreme of turning against all devout men (ll. 1607–

28). Again, as Tartuffe is led off to jail and Orgon prepares to speed him on his way with a curse, Cléante intervenes to urge Orgon to hope rather that Tartuffe might mend his ways (ll. 1947–54). The writer of the *Lettre sur la comédie de l'Imposteur* underlines the symbolic importance of Cléante's forgiving attitude: forgiveness of one's enemies, he argues, 'the most sublime of evangelic virtues', is the perfect note on which to end the play, which is nothing else but 'a most Christian instruction on the nature of true devotion' (*O.C.*, I, pp. 1168–9).

## 12. The King's intervention

The same anonymous writer expressed his enthusiasm for the whole dénouement of *Le Tartuffe*; according to him, this feature of the play, the most puzzling to modern directors and theatre-goers, was the best part of the whole comedy:

> It seems to me that, if in the rest of the play the author has equalled all the ancients and surpassed all the moderns, one can say that in this dénouement he has surpassed himself, as nothing could be greater, more magnificent and more wonderful, and yet more natural, more happy and more appropriate ... (*O.C.*, I, p. 1168)

Some of the anonymous author's admiration for the dénouement might be attributed to his wish to please the King by endorsing Molière's portrait of him as the most just and clear-sighted of monarchs; justice and lucidity, this writer argues, are the very qualities which best characterize Louis XIV. In stressing the appropriateness of the ending, however, the author is making the point that the action of the play and the dénouement are well matched. It is a most unconventional dénouement – even fictitious kings did not appear on stage in New Comedy and farce. To present an officer of a reigning monarch who, with full authority from his master, intervenes directly to change the course of events and ensure a happy ending, is an extraordinary procedure. It is unlikely that Molière made use of the King's name without first seeking his permission. If, however, *Le Tartuffe* is a political play translated into a domestic context, an unconventional ending involving a political solution is appropriate. The ending is a reminder to the audience of the wider meaning of the play.

There is evidence that Louis XIV did support *Le Tartuffe* from its inception, encouraging and applauding the play when first performed, in its earliest three-act version, before him and the court at Versailles in 1664, and that even when yielding to pressure to ban further public performances, he did not withdraw his personal support from Molière or the play. Brossette, writing more than thirty years later, reports that, according to Boileau, Molière read the first three acts of *Le Tartuffe* to the King before the first performance (*G.E.*, IV, p. 273). A more immediate and reliable source of evidence is Molière's own *Placets* and *Préface* to the play. In his first *Placet*, addressed to the King in August 1664, Molière expressed his gratitude to Louis XIV for the trouble he had taken to explain why he had thought it appropriate to ban a comedy in which he, personally, could find nothing to censure. Molière added, in the same *Placet*, that his play had also enjoyed the approval of the papal legate, Cardinal Chigi, and of most of the bishops of France (*O.C.*, I, p. 890). In the following year, 1665, Louis displayed his support for Molière and his players in a most public manner by naming them *La Troupe du Roi* and increasing their royal pension. When the play was banned again, in 1667, while the King was with his army in Flanders, Molière wrote his second *Placet* to the King; in it, he makes it clear that this modified version of his satire, renamed *L'Imposteur*, had also been performed with Louis's approval (*O.C.*, I, p. 892). In the *Préface* of 1669, after the King had revoked all bans on the performance of *Le Tartuffe*, Molière, reviewing the troubled history of his play, recalled that it had always enjoyed the approval of the King, the Queen, the royal Princes and the King's Ministers (*O.C.*, I, pp. 883–4).

If *Le Tartuffe* was intended as a satire on Jesuit casuistry and on Jesuit ambitions and their strategies for achieving them, it is clear that the King was pleased to let the Jesuits smart under the satirist's scourge. Perhaps, after a period of hostile relations between France and the papacy following the alleged insult to the French Ambassador to the papal court in 1662 – a period which must have posed considerable problems for Jesuits close to the King and also bound by their fourth vow of special loyalty to the Pope – Louis wished to issue a transparent yet indirect reminder to the Jesuits that, in France at least, their first loyalty must be to their King and to the French Church?[11]

Perhaps, too, without wishing to quarrel openly with the Jesuits, Louis wished to signal to the many anti-Jesuit factions at court and in France generally that he was firmly in control of his own policies, determined to defend French interests and perfectly able to see through any self-interested plans which the Jesuits at court might propose to him? If so, the King's decision to ban the play in 1664 might well have been a political compromise in which he chose to conciliate the Jesuits by banning the play publicly, while reassuring their opponents by making it clear that he had no objection to private performances and readings. *Le Tartuffe* was performed privately – in the presence of the King and the court - for Monsieur, the King's brother, in 1664, and for *le grand* Condé in 1664, 1665, and twice in 1668; those who missed these performances would have been able to listen to one of the many readings of the play which Molière gave in private *salons* (*G.E.*, IV, pp. 270, 287–94). *Le Tartuffe*, like Pascal's *Lettres provinciales*, enjoyed the success which came from uniting behind it those who wished to see the Jesuits ridiculed, those, in still greater numbers, who were curious to see a play which had stirred up such a ferment of controversy; and those who relished lively and entertaining satire.

It is hardly surprising that *Le Tartuffe*, a play of such gripping topicality, should have proved so popular with contemporary audiences. What is more remarkable is its continuing success. By stripping the complex political and religious issues behind the play of all inessential details, by understanding the forces he observed at work in the wider society of France and portraying them simply and directly in a coherent and believable domestic comedy, Molière constructed a comic poem which has easily outlived the events and controversies on which it was based. Modern audiences may lose something from sharing none of the partisan feelings which so excited or enraged contemporaries, but they continue to derive pleasure from the poet's telling comic portraits of a hypocrite and a gullible fool, and their effects on family life.

# 15
# *Dom Juan* and 'the hidden God'

## 1. Science, scepticism and faith

If *Le Tartuffe* is a reflection of Molière's informed interest in some of the major religious and political issues of his time, *Dom Juan* shows that he was equally familiar with some of the theological and philosophical questions which dominated debate upon such important topics as belief in God, libertinism, reason and superstition.

*Dom Juan* was written in 1665, in the midst of one of the great periods of change in Western thought. With the continuing advances of the scientific revolution, humanity was reassessing itself and its place in creation. A spreading acceptance of the Copernican system which had moved the centre of the universe away from man and the earth, proposing a new heliocentric order, recent experiments on the vacuum, and a changing perception of the human body which followed from the anatomical dissections of Vesalius and others and from the gradual spread of Harvey's views on the circulation of the blood were all part of the long, slow process of the breaking up of the Aristotelian cosmology and metaphysics on which scholastic science, taught in all schools and universities, was based. These changes had a profound effect upon attitudes to faith and reason.

To see what Molière and his educated contemporaries were likely to have understood by Dom Juan's atheism, Sganarelle's superstition, Done Elvire's conversion and the functions of the supernatural in the play, and to follow the seemingly tangled, episodic progress of its central action, *Dom Juan* must be set against the background of seventeenth-century arguments on the roles of faith and reason in a changing world.

Renaissance and seventeenth-century thinkers responded in a variety of ways to a world in which so many established and accepted 'truths' were being exposed as errors. Most pedagogues and theologians, teaching Thomist science and philosophy, the

Aristotelian system Christianized by Thomas Aquinas which they themselves had painstakingly committed to memory, clung to scholastic orthodoxy in the face of change. They feared both the loss of professional standing and, more seriously, the threat to the Church's authority which might follow from admitting that the Church's teaching of scholastic science was in error; if Thomist science were to prove unsound, Thomist theology might be undermined too. This was the fear of the Jesuit Noël in his quarrel with Pascal on the question of the vacuum (see above, Chapter 11, 4). Scholastic scientists and theologians believed that the unity and order of creation were natural proofs of the existence of God, and they sought to keep intact the Aristotelian cosmology which showed how everything fitted into a single harmonious picture.

Other Roman Catholics, holding to an older orthodoxy according to which natural proofs of God were visible only to those who, through the gift of grace, had been given the eyes to see them, distrusted Thomist attempts to prove God through natural reason. This is one of the issues raised in Montaigne's 'Apologie de Raimond Sebond', where he questions some of the views Sebond expressed in his *Theologia naturalis* (1487).[1] Montaigne used the full armoury of sceptical argument to cast doubt on the belief that men, by applying reason and the senses to the study of the created world, could find conclusive proofs of God. Human reason, according to Montaigne, was much too weak a pillar on which to rest something so important as the authority of the Church; he believed that scepticism, properly applied, offered much stronger support. Montaigne and other Catholic sceptics used scepticism to defend the authority of the Church against all those who used reasoned argument to question it, especially against Protestants: all the arguments of mere men, they suggested, stemmed from imperfect human reason, and flaws could be found in the argumentation of both Catholic and Protestant scholars.[2] The Church, however, was instituted by God and invulnerable to attacks mounted by human reason. Mere men should submit to divine authority, which was above and beyond the reach of reason and argument.

In the seventeenth century, Charron, reworking the ideas of Montaigne, and Pascal, building new arguments from the same foundations, made systematic use of scepticism to defend the

Christian faith against libertines. Pascal, in his unfinished apology for the Christian religion, the *Pensées*, reassessed man's position in the created world. He evoked the breaking-up of the old, safe and familiar cosmology in which creation revolved around man and the earth as evidence that man's natural condition was confusion; for Pascal, man was lost between incomprehensible infinities, with no sure ground to stand on; terrified, blind and insecure, he could only contemplate 'the eternal silence of infinite space' and tremble (206). For Pascal, as for Charron, man's incurable confusion is evidence that the Christian God is a hidden God, that Providence, to human eyes, appears blind, and that doubt is natural to man in a state of original sin.

René Pintard, in *Le Libertinage érudit dans la première moitié du XVII⁰ siècle* (2 vols: Paris, 1943), has argued that Charron, far from using scepticism to buttress the authority of the Church, was in fact undermining the Church's authority (pp. 60–61). The question is important to an understanding of Molière's attitudes in *Dom Juan*, as it obviously matters whether Molière was writing in the tradition of a covert libertine or of a Christian sceptic. Pintard's evidence for convicting Charron of libertinism is in fact very thin.[3] He makes a libertine of Charron by taking his statements out of context and treating his secular philosophical discourse as if it were intended as a statement of Christian doctrine. Pintard also judges Charron, along with others whom he suspects of libertinism, against his own narrow conception of what a true seventeenth-century Roman Catholic churchman should be – a respectful, conservative figure who avoids asking difficult questions and can be relied upon to take a strong Thomist line on most issues. Pintard's point of view, despite his considerable erudition and his sober scholarly style, is not far removed from the point of view of such aggressively 'right-thinking' seventeenth-century polemicists as the Jesuit Garasse, one of the first to attack Charron.

I have found nothing in Charron's writings to suggest that he was anything other than a straightforward Christian sceptic in the same mould as his friend and mentor, Montaigne; he was one of many loyal servants of the Roman Catholic Church who defended its authority by the use of sceptical argument. His secular work, *De la sagesse* (Bordeaux, 1601), is for the most part a more systematic, if much less engaging, presentation of the main themes in Montaigne's *Essais*. His credentials as a good churchman were unimpeachable. He was a priest of high reputation with special responsibility for teaching theology, a successful preacher, and author of *Les Trois Vérités* (1593), a polemical work defending the authority of the Roman Catholic Church, and *Discours chrestiens* (1600), a work of theology and devotion.

## 2. The views of a Christian sceptic

The main action of the early stage versions of the Don Juan legend portrayed the crimes of a young nobleman abusing the power and influence which were his by birth and breaking divine and human laws in his reckless pursuit of pleasure; in a melodramatic dénouement, the young nobleman, having refused to heed all warnings that he should mend his ways while he still had time, was punished by divine intervention and lowered into the fires of Hell before the eyes of the audience. The principal themes of the myth are the clash between the good authority of a truly noble father and the insolent disobedience of a lawless son, Don Juan's blasphemous violations of the sacrament of marriage, the wronging of innocent women and the warning to the high-born that though their privileged position may make it easier for them to commit crimes and injustices with impunity in this world, they are answerable to a higher authority in the next.

All these themes are present in seventeenth-century French versions of the play, too. However, in his *Festin de Pierre* (Lyons, 1659), Dorimon gave a decisive twist to the character, adding to his crimes the quite specific crime of being a libertine.[4] Dorimon gave the traditional villain a number of characteristics and opinions designed to show that he belonged to a dangerous new group of sceptical libertines who promoted and practised their godless way of life secretly. He modelled this new version of the figure of Don Juan upon the portrait of the libertine painted by the Jesuit Garasse in his notorious polemical work *Doctrine curieuse des beaux esprits* (2 vols: Paris, 1623).[5] Garasse, in turn, created his colourful portrait of the libertine from a patchwork of views and characteristics allegedly taken from the works and lives of a number of figures who included Machiavelli, Cardano, Pomponazzi, Vanini, Théophile de Viau and Charron. Opponents who answered Garasse's polemic, however, had no doubt that the major source of the views under attack was Charron's *De la sagesse*; the main function of the other figures named was to condemn Charron's ideas by contamination.[6] In the case of Pomponazzi, for example, Garasse admitted freely that he had not wasted his time reading any of his works (p. 1013).

To understand the implications of Dorimon's portrait of Dom Jouan [*sic*] as a libertine, it is necessary first to trace his ancestry back to Charron's portrait of the wise man in *De la sagesse*, the figure caricatured by Garasse. Charron's aim in this work was to coach man in the art of living: 'my book offers instruction in civil life, and forms man for the world, in other words, teaches human wisdom and not divine' (*Préface*, p. 7).[7] Following the hostile response in some quarters to the publication of *De la sagesse*, Charron wrote in defence of his aims in his *Petit Traicté de sagesse*, emphasizing again the secular nature of his treatise: 'none of this is to be applied to things divine, which we must simply believe, receive and adore without undertaking to judge them' (IV, p. 53). He goes further and argues, in terms which prefigure Pascal's arguments, that a training in scepticism is an ideal preparation for receiving the gift of faith:

> Having thoroughly argued and won this point, and made men as it were Academicians and Pyrrhonists [sceptics], one must propose the principles of Christianity, as sent from Heaven, and brought by the Ambassador and perfect confidant of the Godhead, authorized and confirmed in his time by so many miraculous proofs and authentic witnesses.[8] Thus this innocent and pure suspension of judgement and ready openness to everything is a great preparation for true piety. (*Petit Traicté*, IV, p. 54)

To perfect the art of living, Charron advised the wise man to follow four rules: know thyself; keep an open mind; follow nature; and maintain a state of true contentment.[9] In pursuing self-knowledge, the wise man will make constant use of the weapons of the sceptic. He will observe that man is in a state of constant flux; he will not trust his senses; he will remember that reason is the servant of self-love, the passions, imagination, prejudice and habit; that men are in part the products of their place of birth, their environment, social rank, local customs and religions. If he is to liberate wisdom from the tyranny of custom, the wise man should look beyond his parish and seek to become a citizen of the world. If his search for self-knowledge succeeds and he attains the ideal state of Socratic ignorance, the wise man will be freed from the blinding errors of presumption and self-love.

The wise man must be bold in his use of freedom:

> it is a weakness to be surprised by anything; we must stiffen our courage, strengthen our souls, make them tougher and harder so that they may take pleasure in, know, hear and judge all things, however strange they may seem. (*Préface*, p. 15)[10]

Freedom of judgement is man's most precious possession, and the loss of it will involve the loss of reason and of humanity itself. The wise man will not bow before the authority of the ancients, will dismiss the sophistries of pedants with contempt and will follow his reasoning as far as it can take him, untroubled by the knowledge that it will often lead him to conclusions that set him apart from the majority. However, he will keep his conclusions to himself if he fears they may upset others and, in all matters of outward behaviour, will prefer to conform to usage and convention.

Charron's wise man will recognize that man, body and soul, was made by God; he will not seek to deprive the body of its natural pleasures, as this would be a kind of suicide. He will aim, rather, to satisfy his appetites with moderation, maintaining a happy equilibrium between body and soul.

Though doctrinal questions lie outside the limits of human reason and are not discussed in *De la sagesse*, Charron does discuss man's attitudes to religion in general. It is in this domain that he especially attracted censure. Among religions, those come nearest to the truth which portray God as first cause, the source of nature and reason, to be worshipped in one's soul (II, 5, pp. 391–3). He affirms that Christianity is the only true religion and should be followed without question and without resort to quibbling, sectarian strife (II, 5, pp. 396–7).

Most men's religion, however, is little more than superstition; the majority insult God by treating Him in a manner which is in turn obsequious, cringing, overfamiliar and pusillanimous (II, 5, p. 389). Charron shared the Senecan view that nothing harms true religion more than superstition: 'it fears those whom it ought to love; it is an outrage upon those whom it worships.

For what difference is there between denying the gods and dishonouring them?' (*Epistulae morales*, CXXIII, 16). Charron also attacked 'les formalistes' – those who feel that a strict observance of the external forms of worship absolves them from all further Christian duties. His harshest words, however, are reserved for those who believe that any actions are acceptable provided that the end is to advance the cause of religion (II, 5, p. 402). The more vigorous campaigners for counter-reform in the Roman Catholic Church – in particular some Jesuits – might have felt that Charron's criticisms of the 'formalistes' and of zealots ruthlessly pursuing what they considered to be good ends were directed against them. Such a view probably contributed to the Jesuit Garasse's implacable hostility to Charron.

Charron gives a more theological account of the uses of scepticism as an aid to knowing God in the first of his *Discours chrestiens, De la cognoissance de Dieu*.[11] Man's state of 'docte ignorance', that true ignorance which is the fruit of long study and the end of scepticism, is, for Charron, the beginning of knowledge of God. Man, finite and transitory, cannot understand God, who is infinite and eternal. Instead of arguing about God as if they knew all about Him, men should begin their search for Him by recognizing that He is a hidden God. Charron questions the value of the orthodox Thomist teaching of the scholastics who attempt to demonstrate God's existence through metaphysical proofs drawn from observation of the created world. 'Philosophers and theologians teach us various ways of knowing God, but all begin with and arise from the consideration of created things, as one knows the cause from its effects, the maker from his works' (pp. 12–13); but, Charron argues, such proofs are of little use, as 'everything which helps and promotes our knowledge of finite and intermediate things stands in the way of knowledge of an infinite God, in whom all is perfection and sovereignty' (p. 7). For Charron, the gap between the finite and the infinite is so great that contemplation of the one can only blind one to the nature of the other. A dangerous consequence of arguing from the finite to the infinite, according to Charron, is that men are then tempted to base their judgements of God on their own finite experience, blindly re-creating Him in their own image:

Some imagine Him to be serious, severe, morose, overexacting, watching every move, trying to catch people out, difficult to please: this is why they fear Him, distrust Him, tremble and are paralysed. Others, or these same men on another occasion, believe Him to be indulgent, easy, rather slack in His supervision, and so are careless in their treatment of Him. (pp. 32–3)

At the two poles of seekers after God are the wise man who has learned, through the practice of scepticism, to know his own ignorance and the superstitious man who, in his vanity and presumption, speaks of God as if he knew all about Him while, in fact, living in a state of blindness.

## 3. A sceptic as libertine

It is not surprising that Charron's views in *De la sagesse* inspired much hostility; in the *Préface* to the second edition, he invited those who disagreed with him to challenge his arguments openly and vigorously, asking them only to avoid indulging in unworthy and pointless backbiting (p. 18). Twenty-two years after the first publication of *De la sagesse*, Garasse took up Charron's challenge. Other critics of Charron included Mersenne, the friend and correspondent of Descartes who kept in touch with scientists and philosophers from all over Europe, and Cotin, whom Molière was to satirize fifty years later in *Les Femmes savantes*.[12]

The tone of Garasse's attack may be gauged from his repeated and unsubstantiated allegation that Charron was a drunkard, and from his more colourful and enigmatic assertion that he was no more than a Peruvian Toucan (p. 27). His polemical techniques are crude: he presents Charron as one of a crowd of other figures whose names were already tainted (rightly or wrongly) through accusations of heresy; he treats the secular philosophical works of his opponents as if they were intended as works of theology directly concerned with Christian doctrine; he has constant recourse to loud and facile ridicule, so ill-focused that his point of view is often lost in verbiage.

The actual 'curious doctrine' in the title of Garasse's polemic – summarized at the beginning of each of the eight books – is such a distortion of the opinions under attack that it is often difficult to pin down precisely which opinions the polemicist had in mind. Many of them, however, may be seen as caricatures of ideas expressed in *De la sagesse*. For example, while Charron argues that it is each man's duty to cultivate the nature he is born with, Garasse attributes indiscriminately to him, his fellow theorists and the 'beaux esprits' whom they have allegedly corrupted the view that as man's destiny is decided before he is born, he is powerless to alter the course of his life and might just as well indulge his natural passions and whims to the full (*Doctrine curieuse*, pp. 327–468). While Charron recommends appropriate and measured enjoyment of bodily as well as spiritual pleasures, he and his followers are accused of giving themselves up, like Epicurean pigs, to drunkenness and gluttony (pp. 720–56). Charron's suggestion that the wise man should retain independence of judgement – except on matters of faith – while observing external conventions in his public behaviour, is represented by Garasse as an exhortation to be an atheist in your heart, whilst hypocritically observing external ritual (pp. 99–204). Charron's judgement that those capable of following the path to true wisdom are a small elite is reflected in Garasse's recurring jibe that libertines congregate secretly in taverns to foster heretical views (pp. 27–98). Charron's commendation of those religions which see God as the first cause and creator of all things becomes a recommendation to forget the authority and doctrines of the Church and become a deist (pp. 242–326).

Behind the bluster of Garasse's vituperative and garrulous style, it is not difficult to see why he was worried by what he saw as the inevitable implications of Charron's scepticism. If people who did not share Charron's faith, piety and moral sense were to adopt a pose of total scepticism in the face of divine and human law, then there would be little to restrain them in the pursuit of private pleasure and self-gratification. Worse still from the point of view of Garasse, who saw himself as a defender of the faith, such libertines could find the seeds of agnosticism and even atheism in the fearless questioning of accepted ideas which sceptics like Charron felt it their duty to carry out. Equally, Garasse must have been one of many who were worried by Charron's brusque dismissal of the religion of many limited and unimaginative people as superstition. While there is every reason to doubt that Charron was a libertine, it is easy to see how others with no love of the Church came to make use of his arguments to challenge the Church's authority.

## 4. Dorimon's *Festin de Pierre*

It was Dorimon's pious intention in his *Festin de Pierre* to construct in his Dom Jouan a working model of Garasse's sceptical libertine and to set it before the eyes of his audience as an example of the dreadful consequences which must inevitably follow when such godless scepticism is translated into action. The subtitle of Dorimon's play in the 1665 edition, *L'Athée foudroyé* ('The Atheist destroyed'), underlines its moral purpose.

The conviction which, more than any other, informs and directs the behaviour of Dorimon's libertine is his belief that his birth, his temperament, his inclinations, his passions, his actions and his death are predetermined by the rule of destiny which the libertine believes, in Garasse's words, is 'irrevocable, inescapable, unchanging, necessary, eternal and inevitable for all men, whatever they may do' (p. 327). It is this belief in particular, according to Dorimon and Garasse (who devotes the whole of his fourth book to it), which leaves the libertine feeling free to lead a godless and lawless life. Dorimon's Dom Jouan says: 'My destiny is written, from my very cradle, and the place already marked which will be my tomb' (ll. 1823–4). To struggle against fate would be futile; on the contrary, Dom Jouan's belief that everything is decided in advance frees him from all obligations to his parents, king and God (ll. 283–92). As the moment of his death is predetermined, he is free to spend the intervening years pleasing himself (ll. 1757–8); his answer to the ghost who warns him that he must repent and lists his crimes is: 'Enough of that, let's hear no more; I await the fulfilment of my destiny with a resolute soul, unmoved' (ll. 1549–50). In his eyes, he is simply following a course natural to hot-blooded youth (l. 194), indulging a young man's passions (ll. 225–6), fearlessly taking up every challenge and sweeping aside all who stand in the way of his reckless pursuit of pleasure (ll. 1355–61). For him, even his father's despair is not his fault but the work of destiny (ll. 255–7).

Dorimon also gives his libertine some views which are more explicitly sceptical. He questions the foundations of his father's reasoning (ll. 191–2). He tells Briguelle – quite arbitrarily from a dramatic point of view – that he is a citizen of the world: 'your relations are everywhere in the world, in Germany, in Flanders, in France, in England, even in Turkey and Japan', he suddenly announces to his puzzled *valet* (ll. 725–7). Dorimon echoes Garasse's assertion that libertines are deists. Dom Jouan says: 'I wouldn't have much reason if I did not know the Author of all things; I know that His hands are the first causes of the works we see and admire on earth' (ll. 1788–91). But Dom Jouan's God, having set the world in motion, leaves it to itself. God has given Dom Jouan 'a mind, soul, knowledge, strength, reason, courage, intelligence' in order that he might make full use of them, freed from all constraints (ll. 1793–6). Dorimon invests his libertine with what Garasse sees as the hubristic curiosity and freedom of thought of the sceptic: having seen what there is to be seen in this world, Dom Jouan wishes to visit Heaven and Hell, to question God face to face (ll. 1732–44).

The most striking feature of Dorimon's play is his answer to Dom Jouan's sceptical, deterministic and deist position. Against the libertine's morally crippling view of destiny, Dorimon presents through the pilgrim (a new figure in the Don Juan legend) a view of a benevolent, divine Providence. The pilgrim has given his life to God and, trusting in Him, travels the world, penniless and carefree. He offers two 'proofs' of divine Providence: first, wherever he travels, he finds in the natural world – in its mountains, winds, rivers and vegetation – a lively and working illustration of a wise and munificent God; secondly, the pilgrim himself, in the safe hands of God, is free from want, from passion and from unhappiness (ll. 627–68). In offering proofs of God from the natural world, Dorimon is drawing upon the Thomist arguments which Montaigne and Charron found weak and dangerous. The Thomist proofs were taught as a matter of course in schools and faculties of theology. Jesuit rhetoricians frequently exercised their art in florid evocations of enchanting pictures of the natural world designed to demonstrate the bounty of the Creator.[13]

The Don Juan legend, a sharply etched picture of divine Providence at work, showing manifestly evil behaviour justly punished by direct divine intervention, might readily be seen as offering support for the dogmatically clear and anti-sceptical views of such as Garasse. This is certainly the perspective of Dorimon, who blackens his portrait of the villain and underlines the innocence of everyone else. His Dom Jouan commits murder on stage, strikes his father and, off stage, attempts one rape and carries out another. He has no redeeming features. The Governor's daughter is never attracted to him; his noble rival, Dom Philippe, has no respect for him and pursues him as a common criminal. Dorimon's play presents a nostalgic vision of a world in which distinctions between right and wrong were unequivocally clear, a world visibly created by God, with man at its centre, watched over and cherished by his Maker. For Dorimon, Dom Jouan is wholly evil, while the murdered Governor, his daughter, her suitor, Dom Jouan's father and the civil authorities of Seville are wholly innocent; and the pilgrim, who has given his life to God, visibly benefits from his faith, enjoying the copious gifts showered upon him by divine Providence.

## 5. Providence in Molière's *Dom Juan*

In choosing to rework the Don Juan theme Molière, too, was committing himself to the portrayal of a world in which divine Providence had the last word. However, in the events preceding the dénouement Molière paints a picture of human affairs which leaves his audience profoundly confused as to the workings of Providence. Good and evil are everywhere mixed. For Molière, as for Charron and Pascal, God is hidden and His ways are inscrutable. Charron writes in his second *Discours de la providence de Dieu*: 'providence often works secretly . . . and the eyes of the flesh cannot see it'; 'God allows the good to endure much, to wait long, to be trodden underfoot and oppressed most unjustly by the wicked' (*Discours chrestiens*, pp. 197–9). The function of Molière's *Pauvre* – a hermit who, like Dorimon's pilgrim, has devoted his life to God – is to show that divine justice can be invisible to the eye of man; while Dorimon's man of God is free from want, Molière's good hermit lives most of the time on the verge of starvation. The position of Dorimon's pilgrim is secure: in exchange for faith he is showered with gifts. Molière's hermit has nothing but his faith to live for, but he would die of hunger rather than deny his faith in order to earn Dom Juan's *louis d'or* (III, 2).

For Molière as for Charron, man's habitual confusion and presumption further hide the face of God. Men create God in their own image and worship Him from superstition. Sganarelle is Molière's model of the superstitious man, and he matches perfectly Charron's description of this vice: 'it is a sickness of weak, base and cowardly souls' (*De la sagesse*, II, 5, p. 389); 'the superstitious . . . want to describe and depict God, and to talk about Him'; 'they all speak of Him boldly, resolutely, assertively, discuss His nature, His works and name Him at every turn' (*Discours chrestiens*, pp. 30, 34). Sganarelle has just this blend of baseness and self-assurance: 'no one could boast of ever having taught me anything; but with my little sense, my little judgement, I see things better than all the books' (III, 1). He believes in God, but equally in werewolves (I, 1) and, above all, in the 'Moine Bourru' (the Bad-tempered Monk); and indeed, of all Sganarelle's brushes with the supernatural, including God and the Devil, the one which has impressed him most is the ghost of the Monk – 'nothing could be more true than *le Moine Bourru*, I would go to the gallows for him' (III, 1). His faith is superficial and meaningless: he urges the *Pauvre* to blaspheme for money and screams for his wages as Dom Juan is led into Hell. He is easily swayed by Dom Juan's twisted rhetoric (I, 2), readily allows cowardice to override principle (*passim*; but especially IV, 5) and fails to pay his debts (IV, 3).

## 6. Sganarelle's faith in reason

Following in the footsteps of Montaigne, both Charron and Pascal showed reason as a dangerous weapon, at the mercy of imagination, habit, self-love and other influences often hidden from the individual. We have seen how all three of these figures questioned the value of attempts to demonstrate the existence of God through natural reason. Once again, we find Molière sharing their perspective. In order to highlight the inadequacy of natural reason, he makes the fool Sganarelle an apostle of reason. In the opening speech of the play, Sganarelle 'proves' that Aristotle and the whole corpus of traditional moral philosophy are mistaken in thinking that it is the practice of virtue that makes men happy; he demonstrates easily and conclusively (to his own satisfaction) that it is the practice of taking snuff that leads to universal contentment. He is equally confident that, given time and the right conditions, he will prove the existence of God conclusively. Like Dorimon's pilgrim – and the Thomists and more recent rhetoricians demonstrating God's goodness through *peintures parlantes* – Sganarelle sets himself the task of proving God from nature. God is knowable through His works, above all through His special masterpiece, man, whom He has placed at the centre of all creation. So wondrous, ordered and coherent are the parts that compose man's being that he must be the product of a superior being whom we call God.

Among the many seventeenth-century texts using these familiar arguments, one which contains dialectic particularly close to the bungled reasoning of Sganarelle is Cotin's *Théoclée ou La Vraye Philosophie des principes du monde* (Paris, 1646). Cotin, who had condemned Charron's *De la sagesse* in his *Discours à Théopompe* in 1629 and who was to be the model for Molière's Trissotin in 1672, sees man as the clearest proof of God. Théoclée, the reasoning voice of Cotin in the dialogues, is himself an extraordinary example of divine creativity; he is described in the third dialogue as having a 'mind so enlightened, so powerful and so wonderful that he has almost the stature of a god among us' (p. 42). Men should learn to be grateful for being so miraculously constituted:

> what can we do but render thanks to this divine magnificence which, making of man the masterpiece of the universe, has given to him as sovereign king of the world after God, both heavenly and earthly qualities? (Dialogue I, p. 10)

Cotin supports his argument with descriptions of the marvellous complexities of the human body:

> What sinuosities, what labyrinths in our ears to receive sounds properly and break them up skilfully! What a complex composition, what ligaments, what arteries, what veins, what muscles, what cartilages! . . . How many proofs that so many different interlocking parts play together at all times and in all places in every kind of animal, and which are so well fitted to one another that they could not have been made by chance? (p. 8)

Sganarelle, too, regards man's physiology as powerful proof of the existence of God:

> Can you see all the inventions of which the machine of man is composed without wondering at the manner in which all that is put together: these nerves, these bones, these veins, these arteries, these

... this lung, this heart, this liver, and all these other ingredients in there and which . . . (III, 1)

and then he runs out of words. Cotin and Sganarelle are stunned by the spectacle of their own extraordinary competence: 'Isn't it miraculous that I'm standing here,' says Sganarelle, 'and that I have something in my head which is thinking a hundred different things at the same time, and which can make my body do whatever it wills?' (III, 1). This kind of argument is sheer presumption for the Christian sceptic. Pascal says: 'Man is but a reed, the weakest creature in nature' and 'Man is merely a subject full of error which is natural to him and which can be effaced only through grace' (*Pensées*, 347, 83). When Sganarelle, whom we know to be a most fallible creature, tries to demonstrate the miraculous control of mind over body, his limbs fail to obey him and he falls; we join with Dom Juan in recognizing that Sganarelle's reasoning is flawed: 'Now your reasoning has broken its nose!' Sganarelle's failure to know himself and his own limitations has led to the result predicted by Charron: '"No one attempts to descend inside himself (nemo in sese tentat descendere)", with the result that we fall on our noses a thousand times' (*Sagesse*, I, p. 22).[14]

Sganarelle's proofs of God from man and nature do not work. At a time when the unified cosmology of Aristotle was breaking up into different sciences with no clear single philosophy to link them together, Christian sceptics were struck not by the power of the human understanding but by its manifest limitations; equally, sceptics saw in the natural world not an image of order and coherence but evidence of inscrutability and opacity. Pascal perceived in the universe neither harmony nor Plato's music of the spheres, but a frightening silence.

In contrast, Sganarelle and Cotin believe that no obstacles can resist the power of reason for long. Human reason, says Cotin in his *Avant-propos* to *Théoclée*, will rise like the sun, dissipate the clouds of doubt and clear away all false opinions. Molière parodies such faith in scholastic argument – which, in Descartes's words, 'provides a means of speaking plausibly of all things' – through Sganarelle who, knowing nothing of reason, sees himself as unbeatable in argument.[15] Outraged by Dom Juan's hypocrisy, he resolves to crush him under a landslide of logic:

SGANARELLE: Do anything you like to me; beat me, rain blows upon me, kill me if you wish: I must get this off my chest and, as a loyal *valet*, tell you what I have to. Know, sir, that the pitcher goes to the water so much that it will at last break; and as that author I don't know says so well, man is in this world like the bird upon the branch; the branch is attached to the tree; he who is attached to the tree follows right precepts; right precepts are better than fine words; fine words are spoken at court; . . . the old love riches; riches make people rich; the rich are not poor; the poor know necessity, necessity knows no law; a man who lives without law lives like a dumb beast; and, in consequence, you will be damned with all the devils.

DOM JUAN: What fine reasoning!

SGANARELLE: After that, if you don't give up your ways, so much the worse for you. (V, 2)

Such 'reasoning' is laughable first because its purpose is to win battles of words and not to seek the truth. Secondly, reason is, according to the sceptics, 'ployable à tous sens': 'can be bent to any purpose' (*Pensées*, 274). Molière gives an excellent example of skilful argument serving a wrong purpose earlier in the play, when Dom Juan outlines his philosophy of life, detailing the 'logical' considerations which have led him to conclude that only a life of womanizing could satisfy the demands of reason. Significantly, Sganarelle listens speechless to his master's rhetoric, impressed in spite of himself, convinced that his master is wrong but unable to spot the flaws in his reasoning (I, 2). In arguments where verisimilitude, fluency and rhetorical skills take precedence over a slow and patient pursuit of truth, it is not the man who defends the truth who wins but the one who displays the greater mastery of rhetoric. Even when used with skill and judgement, according to the Christian sceptics, reason cannot encompass proofs of God. On the lips of a facile rationalist like Sganarelle, reason is presented as a laughably inadequate weapon for combating the atheism of an intelligent man like Dom Juan.

## 7. An uncertain world

Sganarelle is perhaps Molière's most eloquent exemplar of the human condition in *Dom Juan*, but other figures in the play also contribute to his portrait of a world of shifting appearances,

constant flux, uncertain values and inexplicable inconsistencies –
the world of Heraclitus, Montaigne, Charron and Pascal. Molière
demonstrates (in Charron's words) that 'man is marvellously
diverse and changeable', can never be wholly good or even
wholly bad – 'there is no evil without good, no good without
evil in man; all is mixed, nothing pure in our hands' (*De la
sagesse*, I, 38, p. 199; 37, p. 186). The peasants who suffer from
Dom Juan's cruelty in the second act are not portrayed as
innocent pastoral figures. Pierrot and Lucas, who are having fun
throwing clods of earth at each other when Pierrot spots Dom
Juan's party in the sea, almost leave them to drown while they
quarrel and lay bets on whether or not Pierrot's eyes are
deceiving him. Pierrot's love for Charlotte is genuine enough
and an audience might well be touched by his fears that it is not
fully reciprocated, but his love is also selfish, morose and demand-
ing; he would rather see her dead than married to anyone else.
Charlotte, too, is a mixture of good and bad: she is properly
distrustful of Dom Juan's promises, but it is not long before she
begins to feel proud at the prospect of becoming a great lady,
and she slips only too readily into showing gracious condescension to her peasant lover, promising him that once she is
married, she will always buy her butter and cheese from him.

The aristocratic Dom Alonse, blindly bent on avenging the
wrong done to his sister, Done Elvire, compromises the justice
of his cause by allowing Dom Juan no credit for risking his life
to rescue his brother from his attackers (III, 4). Even the good
and noble Dom Louis, Dom Juan's wronged father, is not
blameless; he confesses himself guilty of having plagued Heaven
with selfish prayers for a son instead of leaving such things in
God's hands (IV, 4). Done Elvire, who becomes a saintly figure
in the course of the play, is, at the beginning, guilty of having
broken her convent vows in order to marry Dom Juan (I, 3).

Dom Juan himself is a clear illustration of the sceptical view
that (again in Charron's words) 'our actions often contradict one
another so strangely that it seems impossible that they could
have emanated from the same source' (I, 38, p. 200). He displays
the aristocratic charm as well as the cruelty of 'un grand seigneur
méchant homme': 'a great lord and wicked man' (I, 1). He is
often amusing and always quick-witted in his dealings with
Sganarelle, Monsieur Dimanche and the peasant girls, courageous

and generous in his first encounter with Dom Carlos, and lucid in his condemnation of medicine and pretentious funeral architecture. At other moments he is sadistic towards Elvire, insolent with his father, contemptible in his hypocrisy, laughable for the hubristic vanity which makes him feel that he can challenge God, and absurdly inflexible in his refusal to acknowledge the evidence of the supernatural to which he is exposed in the course of the play.[16]

## 8. Signs in the midst of confusion

Molière uses the whole action of *Dom Juan*, with its apparently loose episodic structure, to illustrate the lack of logic and order the sceptic finds in human affairs. The plot unfolds in a series of apparently random picaresque adventures: Dom Juan meets an enraged Done Elvire, whom he has just married and abandoned; organizes the abduction of his next intended victim; is shipwrecked in a storm and rescued by peasants; quickly turns his attention to the seduction of two peasant girls, to both of whom he promises marriage; abandons them, discusses his beliefs with Sganarelle, encounters in succession a saintly hermit, Done Elvire's brothers, the statue of a *Commandeur* whom he had killed on some earlier occasion, a merchant to whom he owes money, his father, Done Elvire again and the statue for a second time; he then becomes a member of a cabal of hypocrites, convinces his father that his life has changed, arranges a duel with Dom Carlos, which will never take place, and receives a last warning from a spectre, before the statue appears for the third time and leads him down into Hell.

This sequence of events is not linked – like those in *L'École des femmes* or *Le Misanthrope*, for example – into a tight central action, but reflects the arbitrariness with which events often succeed one another in day-to-day life. However, the episodes are linked into a unified central action of a different kind. The links are forged by the supernatural, divine presence in the Don Juan story. By making use of the Don Juan legend, the playwright is able to lift the veil which hides the work of Providence and give his audience a glimpse of a higher order behind the chaos of human affairs. Hence the action of Molière's play espouses two contrasting movements: the first is vacillating and arbitrary, as befits the uneven progress of the lives of men and women, while the second, marked by Dom Juan's continuous refusal to heed repeated divine warnings, follows his headlong rush towards damnation.

Dom Juan is not seen as the victim of an unrelenting fate – he is given repeated chances to amend his behaviour; Molière shows that it is his wilful closing of his ears and hardening of his heart which lead to his final punishment. The audience is expected to feel that his punishment is fully deserved. First, his actions and words condemn him – his cruelty to Done Elvire, his selfish indifference to his father's feelings, his contempt for human laws, his sacrilegious invasion of a convent and his blasphemous disregard for the sacrament of marriage. Then, he is further condemned by his blindness to the kind of evidence which, had he paid attention to it, could have halted his plunge into vice. Dom Juan may be right to mock the 'reasoned' arguments of Sganarelle, but he is foolish to remain deaf to the sound reasoning of Dom Carlos, who urges his brother to join with him in regulating their behaviour towards Dom Juan according to 'the pure deliberation of reason' (III, 4). He is wrong, too, to close his ears to the well-argued pleas of his father, when he points out that nobility of birth is nothing if it is not matched by noble behaviour (IV, 4).

Dom Juan is more wrong still to remain unmoved by the eloquent appeal of divinely inspired love, a gift of grace, 'a flame purified of all commerce of the senses, an innocent tenderness, a love detached from everything, which does not act for itself'; Done Elvire, after her repentance, is the voice of true Christian love, an agent traditionally considered much more effective than reason in persuading people to believe in God (IV, 6). One recalls Pascal's insistence that God speaks to the heart more clearly than to reason: 'Dieu sensible au cœur, non à la raison' (*Pensées*, 278).

Finally, having proclaimed his plain rationalist creed – 'I believe that two and two make four, Sganarelle, and four and four make eight' (III, 1) – Dom Juan is revealed as a dogmatic, self-blinding fool who wilfully discounts clear evidence, refusing to believe the miracle which, as Sganarelle says, was sent to convert him (III, 5; IV, 1). As miraculous interventions recur in IV, 8, V, 5 and V, 6, Dom Juan's refusal to give them serious consideration looks more and more stubborn and absurd. He is seen to be a fool for rejecting grace and the miracles out of hand. For fideists and Christian sceptics, these are the strongest proofs of God. Pascal wrote: 'Two foundations, one interior, the other exterior: grace, the miracles; both of them supernatural' (*Pensèes*, 805). In his last speech, before leading Dom Juan into Hell, the statue reminds him that he cannot spurn 'Heaven's grace' with impunity.


## 9. Dom Juan's hypocrisy

In the last act of *Dom Juan*, Molière returns to the subject of religious hypocrisy and renews his satirical attacks on the target of his previous play, *Le Tartuffe*, which he had been obliged to withdraw from the public stage. He reminds us of the great power of this cabal, so powerful that an aristocrat of Dom Juan's standing would find it useful to have its support. This is the same power which, in Molière's view, enabled the *tartuffes* to persuade the King to ban his play mocking them. He attaches other distinctive characteristics which would encourage the public to associate this cabal with the Jesuits. He has Dom Juan make use of casuistry. In I, 3, having broken the sanctity of the convent to marry Done Elvire, he tells her that it is from motives of conscience, divinely inspired, that he has felt obliged to flee the wrath of God by abandoning her as quickly as possible. Later, after his feigned conversion, he makes use of one of the casuistic tricks which permit a man to fight a duel while retaining a purity of intention which leaves him 'innocent' of an action which in fact is both a religious and secular offence. He says to Dom Carlos:

> I shall pass in a little while down that little side road which leads to the big convent; but I tell you that, as far as I am concerned, it is not I who wish to fight: Heaven forbids me to think of it; and if you attack me, we shall see what happens. (V, 3)

This argument is borrowed from Pascal's Seventh *Lettre provinciale* (pp. 71–2).

Molière also mocks the Jesuits' concern with outward appearance, gesture and facial expression. Members of the Society were called upon to obey Loyola's instructions to cultivate a modest and holy demeanour, keeping brow and nose unwrinkled and eyes lowered, training themselves to orchestrate gesture and movement in such a way as to be a source of edification and contentment to all who see them.[17] Dom Juan says:

> It serves no purpose to be aware of their intrigues and to know them for what they are, they still enjoy credit among people; and a bowed head, a mortified sigh and a couple of eye movements redeem before the world anything they may do. (V, 2)

Molière repeats the accusation he first made in *Le Tartuffe* that for those versed in lax casuistry it is no sin to sin in silence. Dom Juan declares that from now on he will pursue his pleasures discreetly. If he is caught out, he will find defenders among all the other members of the same cabal, including those whose intentions are genuinely innocent, but who are too ready to be duped by the others. He will use his new-found base to pillory all his enemies and, under the pretext of defending Heaven, will damn whomsoever he wishes on his own private authority. There is a clear reminder, here, of Molière's first *Placet* addressed to the King in 1664 and his complaint that those whom he had satirized in *Le Tartuffe* were making systematic use of calumny to discredit him. It was a major plank in Pascal's case in the *Lettres provinciales* that the Jesuits frequently resorted to systematic calumny to discredit their opponents (see especially the 15th Letter, pp. 177–90).

Molière was clearly angry at having been bested (temporarily at least) by those who wanted to have *Le Tartuffe* banned. However, the polemical content of *Dom Juan* shows the playwright doing much more than prolong the battle over *Le Tartuffe*. The central figures in the play – one weak, ridiculous and a rich source of laughter, the other dangerous, sometimes amusing and always sinister and disturbing – represent two quite different ways of abusing religion.

Sganarelle, perhaps, bears the richer satirical meaning. Through him Molière paints a picture – rather like Charron's – of the many ordinary people, resembling Sganarelle, who had replaced faith in God with a cowardly and superstitious observance of some of the forms of religion. Such figures cared nothing for the substance of Christianity, neglected faith, humility, love and true piety, and considered that they were fulfilling their Christian duty when they parroted a few well-worn and half-digested metaphysical 'proofs' of God's existence. We laugh at Sganarelle's abject but typically human attitudes, though we feel less inclined to scold him than did a Seneca or a Charron, both of whom rounded on superstitious men as blasphemers against true religion.

In the person of Dom Juan Molière draws his audience's attention to a much more dangerous abuse. Through him, Molière hints at the harm that can be done when a rich, powerful and godless man finds that he can pursue his crimes with impunity if he once agrees to wear the cloak of religion. Molière's Dom Juan is one of those hardened sinners described by Pascal in the *Lettres provinciales*, 'who sin without regret, who sin with joy and who make a boast of it'; the letter-writer then goes on to say to his Jesuit interlocutor: 'And who could know more about such people than you? It isn't as if you did not confess some of the people I am talking about; for it is among those of high rank that one tends to meet this kind of person' (4th Letter, p. 34). Where Pascal was suggesting – indirectly but unequivocally – that lax casuistry and what he considered to be dangerously naïve views on grace could encourage the lawless rich to pursue their criminal careers in a spirit of cheerful abandon, Molière was showing such a career in action.

For Molière, the true atheist and libertine, enemy of both God and men, was not the honest sceptic, struggling to see clearly in a confusing world. He was much more likely to be a powerful, unprincipled and ruthless aristocrat, operating within a well-established cabal or religious group, manipulating good men and wicked men alike in his lawless pursuit of self-gratification.

## 10. Molière's personal standpoint

There is not enough evidence in either *Le Tartuffe* or *Dom Juan* to show with any certainty what Molière's personal religious convictions were. Neither play was intended to serve as a confession of faith. However, the two plays contain no evidence that Molière was a libertine. *Le Tartuffe* was not an attack on the Church or on Christianity in general. Most of those who satirized the Jesuits in France were, like Pascal, ardent churchmen themselves, but so many different groups opposed the Jesuits that it would be idle to try and identify Molière with any one of them in particular.

The evidence in *Dom Juan* is a little more positive. The angle from which the playwright invites spectators to view the world is that of the Christian sceptic. The legend of Don Juan is itself Christian in its structure, and Molière retains the pattern in which the ultimate judge of human behaviour is God. Only if we take Sganarelle to be the representative of a good Christian can we see Molière's presentation of Christianity as subversive. But Sganarelle, on the contrary, is intended as an example of a bad Christian – of the superstitious and credulous figure who was the butt of so much criticism from Christian sceptics. The true Christians in the play are Dom Louis, Dom Carlos and, above all, the saintly Done Elvire after she has repented of her own misdeeds and forgiven Dom Juan.

The obvious parallels with the Christian attitudes behind *Dom Juan* are found, among contemporary texts, in Pascal's *Lettres provinciales* and *Pensées*. The *Pensées*, however, though completed before *Dom Juan* – Pascal died in 1662 – did not begin to appear in print until 1670, five years after the play was first performed, and were written to persuade readers of the rightness of a Christian life. There is no hint of proselytizing zeal in either of Molière's religious plays. His aim was to expose what he saw as the follies and vices of bad religion to honest laughter, not to preach the Christian faith. He shared Montaigne's view that nothing was easier to counterfeit than an appearance of devotion (*Essais*, III, 2, p. 813). It is in Montaigne, once again, although he belonged to an earlier generation, that one finds his closest fellow spirit. Molière, like France's Socrates, wrote as a citizen of the world, with a gift for seeing, beyond the welter of local and contemporary details, the issues which are timeless and speak to people everywhere. Despite his busy involvement in writing, acting and producing plays, he, like Montaigne, viewed the rich and varied human comedy being performed all around him with the lucid detachment of a Christian gentleman.

# 16
## *Molière's Philosophy*

## 1. A portrait of malfunctioning humanity

Molière wrote to please his contemporaries, and we can assume that they found both his humour and the satirical content of his comedies more accessible than we do. However, if we can clear our minds of clutter, set aside our anachronistic preconceptions, resist the temptation to approach his plays armed with inappropriate theories, and put our trust instead in our own eyes and ears, in our own direct responses to his comic world, and in our own judgement of what is (or should be) happening on stage, we can still see in his comedies a fresh, immediate and compelling picture of human affairs.

Molière had no fixed comic formula for pleasing audiences. He cultivated the flexibility of the *honnête homme*, varying his comic register and techniques from play to play. At times, he sought simply to amuse his public and was happy to do so within existing conventions. In his early one-act farces, for example, he showed an easy and fluent mastery of the stereotyped characterization, earthy dialogue and ritualized stage business which were the hallmarks of the French farcical tradition. When he portrayed the rarer, more stylized world of New Comedy, with its timeless young lovers and grasping fathers, in such plays as *L'Étourdi* and *Les Fourberies de Scapin*, he viewed their adventures, like Plautus and Terence before him, with amused indulgence, exploiting their tangled relationships and their harmless fears, hopes and peevish rages to produce lively, fast-moving, elegant and good-humoured comedy.

In his best-known plays, however, Molière combined and transformed the worlds of farce and New Comedy, adding to them a much richer vein of satire and a new depth of characterization. He turned comedy into a medium capable of presenting a much wider range of human follies and vices. He took his material from the world around him, abandoning the world of

comic fantasy in which a benign Providence ensured that everyone in the play, whatever their behaviour, would be happy in
the end. Though he still amused his audiences with the antics of
young lovers and servants outwitting parents and masters, he
entertained them, above all, by putting before them the comic
spectacle of contemporary men and women in the grip of
swollen self-love, vanity and greed, deceiving themselves and
attempting to deceive one another as each pursues his or her
own narrow ends.

It is not the ready wit of Molière's characters which amuses
us. Unlike the mercurial word-spinners of Shakespeare and
Congreve, his characters rarely make witty or amusing remarks.
A wit stands outside the human comedy and comments on its
ironies and inconsistencies. Molière's characters are locked inside
it, and their function is to illustrate the strange and comic
progress of men and women as they go about their daily
business. He makes us laugh by revealing the mechanisms which
govern human minds and behaviour. While still writing to
please, he appeals less to our ears, but makes great demands of
our understanding and judgement.

By his change of focus from a romantic world where all turns
out well to a world ruled by self-love, Molière raised the status
of stage comedy, making it equal in depth and range to tragedy.
He could introduce into his comic world the petty vanities of
foppish aristocrats, the hypochondria, bilious jealousy and self-
absorption of monomaniacs and melancholics, the calculated
villainy of a Tartuffe and the hedonistic sadism of a Dom Juan.
It is the very ubiquity of such follies and vices that makes his
pictures of contemporary life so accessible to other ages. More
importantly, by choosing not to follow the comic convention of
making vice harmless in order to preserve an atmosphere of
carefree celebration, Molière could parade his rich array of vices
and follies complete with their appropriate accompaniment of
destructive effects, distortions, grimaces, cruelties and injustices.
On Molière's stage folly and vice are vigorous, powerful, almost
irresistible and always incurable. At the same time, because they
are so active, they produce gripping drama, in which fools and
villains clash with one another and with those who show good
sense in a succession of unforgettable encounters. Molière's villains and fools have the uncomfortable fascination of monsters.

We disapprove of them and find them ridiculous, yet we also feel in some small degree attracted to them; we admire their sheer energy and are grateful to them for inspiring so much pleasurable laughter. Molière's is a much larger, more varied and more exciting comic world than those of farce and New Comedy.

Inevitably, Molière's account of a world teeming with flawed characters has a moral dimension. The sight of so much going wrong was – and still is – a reminder to audiences that follies and vices are among the major obstacles to human happiness. It also reminds us, if we are not blinded by self-love, that what we are seeing on stage is a picture of what we are or might easily become. Molière's portrait of the human condition encourages us to feel that a high degree of lucidity and alertness is necessary if we are to have any hope of keeping in check the irrational forces which are always ready to take over our lives.

Molière's priority, however, was always to amuse and please his audiences rather than educate them. He learned quickly that the way to please contemporaries was to hold up a mirror which, through the revealing distortions of caricature, could give them a clearer image of their real selves than they were likely to encounter in the confusing world of day-to-day life outside the theatre. The more telling his portraits, the more they amused. One might also add: the more they amused, the more they informed.

## 2. A shared vision

If Molière's view of the human condition was moral, it was not moralizing. As an *honnête homme* he was much too urbane to use the stage as a pulpit. He offered no prescriptions for social reform, but varied his responses to people and things according to their different characters. He was resigned to the existence of folly and vice, and quite aware that even the soundest and most elegant and amusing of satires were unlikely to have much effect on the balance of folly and sense, of good and evil, in the world. His plays were not a medium for self-expression, but a response to things; the freshness of his vision comes from the things ridiculed, from the inexhaustibly diverse spectacle of folly and vice. He did not seek to impose a private or idiosyncratic interpretation upon events; on the contrary, his expectation in portraying the actions of fools and villains was that all honest men and women, of his own and future generations, would find them equally absurd, and for more or less the same reasons. His aim was to paint with such clarity and immediacy that anyone with a good pair of eyes would share his vision. The perspective of Molière, the views of his *raisonneurs* and the responses of the honest men and women in his audiences are similar – not because all share a single philosophy, but because all respond with the same lucidity and recognition to the spectacle of folly and vice on stage.

As readers and as spectators, however, we should take care to see and interpret Molière's dialogues and encounters in their proper context. We cannot discover Molière's philosophy by pooling the arguments of his *raisonneurs*. The *raisonneurs* themselves lay no claim to special wisdom; their only talent is to have a good uncluttered view of the things around them. Cléante expresses the modesty of their point of view when he answers Orgon's mocking description of him as a revered and learned doctor: 'No, my brother, I am not a revered doctor, and the world's wisdom is not lodged in me. But, in a word, I do know, whatever my knowledge, how to tell the difference between the true and the false' (*Le Tartuffe*, ll. 351–4). Cléante is not claiming that he can distinguish between the true and the false in every domain – a problem which continues to exercise logicians – merely that in the situation in which he finds himself, he can tell the difference between a good Christian and a particularly nasty hypocrite. No abstruse learning or complex reasoning is required for him to make such a judgement; the servant Dorine and most of Orgon's family see Tartuffe's hypocrisy just as clearly as Cléante does. We, too, in the audience, share his clear-sightedness. We are united with the comic poet and the sensible people on stage in our judgement of the crooked behaviour of the villains and fools.

The quality of clear-sightedness, of judgement or reason, is not fixed, but moves permanently as it takes account of changing circumstances. It focuses on one situation at a time, and its common-sense observations, when removed from the situation which inspired them and treated as general observations, easily become nonsense. When Ariste in *L'École des maris*, for example, says that we should always be guided by majority opinion (l. 41), neither he nor Molière is suggesting that we should, in all cases, embrace the morality of the crowd; taken in context, his words mean that in morally indifferent questions such as dress, the reasonable man will follow current conventions. When the sensible Chrysalde assures Arnolphe that even being cuckolded has its pleasures, no reasonable spectator imagines that the comic poet or Chrysalde is advising him to seek happiness through cuckoldry; Chrysalde is pushed into making this odd assertion by the behaviour of a man whose values have been destroyed and whose life is being wrecked by the absurd conviction that happiness consists in not being cuckolded (ll. 1288–305). When we laugh at the neophyte Christian Orgon's assertion that he could see his whole family drop dead without a flicker of emotion, it seems odd and out of context to read into this passage a conscious anti-Christian mockery of the biblical source for Orgon's words: Christ's advice to his followers, in Luke 14: 26, that they should learn to hate their own families and even themselves for his sake. Surely, we laugh because we are seeing a gullible fool sacrificing his family, not to God, but to a hypocrite who is plotting to steal his money and his wife (ll. 276–9). Equally, when Cléante admires those Christian men whose devotion is human and approachable, he is not arguing that religion should be based on purely human values; he is using the argument for the specific purpose of contrasting Christian gentleness with the vindictive rage of hypocrites who use religion as a stick with which to beat their enemies (ll. 351–407).

Molière's comedies retain their freshness precisely because they are not weighed down by the burden of a prescriptive philosophy. Had he offered, through the combined wisdom of his *raisonneurs*, an authoritative set of precepts and rules for behaviour, he would have displayed the very folly which he was keenest to ridicule: the presumption of those assorted pedants, doctors, monomaniacs, melancholics and hypocrites who sought to impose their unwieldy, self-aggrandizing moral systems upon people and events. In their different ways, Molière's would-be learned women, his *précieuses*, such tyrants as Arnolphe, Orgon, Alceste and even the libertine Dom Juan, as well as his pedants and doctors, are shown to be guilty of facing life with fixed rules and unshakeable convictions which prove hopelessly and comically inadequate in the face of constantly changing reality. Molière shared with Montaigne, Charron, La Mothe Le Vayer and Pascal the sceptic's doubts about all fixed philosophical and moral systems.[1]

## 3. A philosophy of judgement

To say, however, that Molière pokes fun at fixed philosophies is not to deny him a philosophy of his own. As Pascal wrote, 'to mock philosophy is in truth to philosophize'; he adds, in the same *pensée*, 'la vraie morale se moque de la morale', which might be paraphrased as 'a true concern with human behaviour cares little for the systems of moral philosophy' (4). Once again, both Pascal and Molière share the humanist perspectives of Montaigne, who had written: 'An ancient who was reproached with professing philosophy, while judging it of little account, answered that that was to philosophize truly' (*Essais*, II, 12, p. 511). Like Pascal and Montaigne, Molière was deeply concerned with one of the central issues of moral philosophy: the problem of how to acquire and practise good judgement. His plays, like Montaigne's *Essais* and Pascal's *Pensées*, are an examination of the whole apparatus of understanding, discernment and choice as they operate in a living and constantly changing world – a world which in their case, as the scientific revolution gathered momentum, was changing at a frightening pace.

The medium of drama is ideal for the poet and philosopher who sees life as a continual exercising of judgement. The comic poet can choose a subject, a representative set of characters, a situation which confronts them with some typical problems, and then show how some characters stumble from one misjudgement to another while others, making sound judgements, progress towards at least a moderate degree of happiness. To represent the relationships between character, behaviour and happiness, Molière equipped himself with a thorough knowledge of moral philosophy. His work reflects an easy mastery of the workings of classical ethics and a thorough knowledge of the writings of the French humanists, Rabelais and, especially, Montaigne. He combined with this bookish knowledge the habit of close and detailed observation of his own contemporaries. It was Molière's confident and erudite presentation of the complexities of human nature which so impressed Boileau when he saw *L'École des femmes*.

Molière shows how the social world – the world of relationships between people – works. It is crucial to the spectator's pleasure and enjoyment that he or she should endorse Molière's account of human behaviour; in every situation he or she is drawn into Molière's moral world and becomes involved in assessing how well – or, more often, how badly – each character judges their own and other people's words and actions.

Audiences share in the endless struggle between lucidity and self-deception, but for them this struggle is a joy and a relaxation because Molière uses the tricks of the stage to accompany every wrong judgement with a gesture, a facial expression, a tone of voice or a farcical routine which shows it up as ridiculous and so lacking in reason. We are invited, when watching or reading a Molière comedy, to let our understanding be guided by laughter. Every time we laugh or smile, we are making a judgement, and our enjoyment espouses the inner movement of the play and its underlying dialectic. Our pleasure, understanding and moral responses are indissolubly linked.

# Chronology

1622    Birth, in Paris, of Jean-Baptiste Poquelin (later Molière) into a family of successful *tapissiers* (tapestry-makers). His father will buy the office of *tapissier et valet ordinaire du roi* in 1631; it becomes Molière's in 1660.
        15 January: Molière baptized.
        The dates and details of his education are uncertain. In the *Préface* to the first edition of his works, probably written by La Grange (1682), he is said to have studied at the Jesuit Collège de Clermont and to have distinguished himself in the humanities (probably his third year) and then in philosophy (his last two [?] years). The Jesuits gave their pupils a thorough grounding in Latin grammar and literature (but not Greek), in rhetoric and in scholastic philosophy. Most sons of reasonably well-off families, including Descartes and Corneille, were educated by the Jesuits.

1640    Leaves school to become a barrister and abandons the profession after about six months.

1643    Receives part of his succession from his father, and joins Madeleine Béjart and others to set up the Illustre Théâtre.

1645    The Illustre Théâtre runs into debt and Molière is briefly imprisoned. He leaves Paris to begin touring the provinces, and spends the next thirteen years performing to provincial audiences, predominantly in the Languedoc and in Lyons.

1653    Molière's company becomes 'la troupe de Monseigneur le prince de Conti'.

1655    Probable date of the first performance of *L'Étourdi* (77 known performances from Easter 1659, when La Grange began to keep his *Registre*, to the playwright's death).[1] This is the first record of Molière's troupe performing a play written by him. Molière, it is assumed, played Mascarille, as in later revivals of the play. He was to manage his troupe's finances, write its most successful plays, direct the productions themselves, and play the leading comic roles until the day he died.

1657    The prince de Conti withdraws permission for Molière's troupe to use his name.

1658    Molière and his company settle in Paris and become 'la troupe de Monsieur', the King's brother. Molière performs Corneille's *Nicomède* and a one-act farce, *Le Docteur amoureux* (now lost), before Louis XIV. The King installs the troupe in the Petit-Bourbon theatre, which Molière shares with the Italian actors. He revives *L'Étourdi* and *Dépit amoureux* (77 performances) for Paris audiences; both plays are squarely in the tradition of New Comedy.

1659    *Les Précieuses ridicules* (71 performances). A one-act farce, but also his first real satire of contemporary life.

1660    *Sganarelle ou le Cocu imaginaire* (143 performances). A one-act farce in verse with elements of New Comedy; this was Molière's most consistently successful play in his lifetime.

1661    Following the demolition of the Petit-Bourbon theatre on 11 October 1660, Molière's troupe has nowhere to perform until the reopening of the renovated Palais-Royal theatre on 20 January 1661.
        *Dom Garcie de Navarre* (13 performances). Molière called this five-act play a comedy, but it was in reality a tragicomedy; it was to be his only play written in a higher, almost tragic, register; it soon flopped.
        *L'École des maris* (126 performances). A three-act play which opens with comedy of ideas; its main action is a lively intrigue typical of New Comedy.
        *Les Fâcheux* (121 performances). His first *comédie-ballet* performed before the King at Vaux-le-Vicomte, Fouquet's château, just three weeks before the arrest of the *Surintendant des Finances*.

1662    23 January: Molière marries Armande Béjart.
        *L'École des femmes* (102 performances). The first of Molière's five-act masterpieces. It stirs up a storm of protest and censure from rivals and from precious cabals, and confirms Molière's reputation as a French Terence in the eyes of more substantial critics and writers such as Boileau and Rapin.

1663    *La Critique de l'École des femmes* (43 performances). *L'Impromptu de Versailles* (29 performances). Two one-act plays written to answer his critics. They are among the richest sources of Molière's own views on comedy.

1664    *Le Mariage forcé* (42 performances). A *comédie-ballet* in one act. The King and some of his courtiers dance in the performance given in the Queen Mother's apartments at the Louvre. The young King will often take a dancing role in court ballets.
        Molière's son Louis is born (he will live for only ten months);

the King is godfather to the child, a mark of Molière's high
standing at court.

*La Princesse d'Élide* (34 performances). A five-act *comédie-ballet*,
music by Lulli, performed as part of *Les plaisirs d l'Île enchantée*,
a celebration at Versailles lasting several days. This event served
almost as an official throwing-open of the doors of Versailles to
the wider world of the court; at this stage it is still a small
château.

*Le Tartuffe* (94 performances). A version in three acts (the first
three according to La Grange) is performed before the King and
the whole court on 12 May, only four days after *La Princesse
d'Élide*, as part of the festivities at Versailles. Further public
performances are banned. Molière continues, however, to give
private readings and performances, and is assured by the King
that he himself sees nothing to censure in the play.

1665    *Dom Juan* (15 performances). Three polemical texts, 'Observations sur une comédie de Molière intitulée *Le Festin de Pierre*',
accusing Molière of atheism and immorality, and two defences
of Molière, a 'Réponse aux observations . . . ' and the much
more persuasive 'Lettre sur les observations . . . ', appear soon
after the play. Molière rests *Dom Juan* for Easter and is never to
revive it.

4 August: birth of Molière's daughter, who will survive him.

14 August: Louis gives a pension of £7,000 to Molière's troupe
and renames it 'la Troupe du Roi'.

*L'Amour médecin* (67 performances). A *comédie-ballet* in three
acts, with music by Lulli.

29 December: Molière seriously ill for six weeks; he is to suffer
recurrences of illness, probably tuberculosis, for the remainder
of his life.

1666    *Le Misanthrope* (62 performances).

*Le Médecin malgré lui* (62 performances)

1667    Molière collaborates with Benserade, Lulli and others, compos-
ing *Mélicerte*, *La Pastorale comique* (one performance each) and
*Le Sicilien ou l'Amour peintre* (21 performances); all three are
incorporated in turn into the *Ballet des Muses*, a royal entertainment at Saint-Germain.

5 August: *L'Imposteur*. A revised five-act version of *Le Tartuffe*
is performed once only and then banned.

8 August: Molière sends his *Second Placet* to the King at the
siege of Lille to ask for his protection and for permission to
perform *L'Imposteur*.

20 August: *Lettre sur la comédie de l'Imposteur*. The anonymous

writer of this letter has a thorough knowledge of the as yet unprinted text of *L'Imposteur*. He outlines a theory of comedy which sheds light on Molière's uses of laughter and the ridiculous.

1668　*Amphitryon* (55 performances). A machine-play adapted from Plautus's play of the same name.

*George Dandin* (43 performances). First performed as part of a lavish pastoral entertainment, with music by Lulli, for the King and court at Versailles.

*L'Avare* (49 performances). An adaptation of Plautus's *Aulularia*.

1669　Following *la Paix de l'Eglise*, in which Louis XIV made peace with the Pope and – for the time being, at least – with the Jansenists, Molière is given permission to perform *Le Tartuffe*. He gives 44 consecutive performances, taking record receipts. The *Préface* to *Le Tartuffe* and the two earlier *Placets* contain discussions on the nature and functions of comedy and satire.

*Monsieur de Pourceaugnac* (50 performances). *Comédie-ballet* in three acts, with music by Lulli.

1670　*Élomire hypocondre*, a personal attack on Molière.

*Les Amants magnifiques*. A *comédie-ballet*, performed 5 times for the court at Saint-Germain.

*Le Bourgeois Gentilhomme* (49 performances). A *comédie-ballet* in five acts, with music by Lulli.

1671　*Psyché* (82 performances). A *tragi-comédie et ballet* and a machine-play, written in collaboration with Corneille and Quinault.

*Les Fourberies de Scapin* (18 performances). Comedy in three acts adapted from Terence's *Phormio*.

*La Comtesse d'Escarbagnas* (19 performances). A one-act farce written to be performed as part of a ballet.

1672　*Les Femmes savantes* (25 performances).

Lulli founds a royal academy of music and persuades the King to give him absolute rights over all music to be performed both at court and in the theatres of Paris. Molière, displaced from the King's favour by Lulli, is subjected to severe restrictions in the number of dancers and musicians he may employ in his performances.

1 October: Baptism of Molière's second son, who lives for only ten days.

1673　*Le Malade imaginaire* (4 performances). A *comédie-ballet* in three acts with music by Marc-Antoine Charpentier.

17 February: Molière, playing the hypochondriac, falls ill during the fourth performance of the play and dies an hour later.

21 February: after an appeal to the King and then to the Archbishop of Paris, his widow receives permission to bury him at Saint-Eustache.

# Notes

## Preface

1. R. Bray, *Molière, homme de théâtre* (Paris, 1954) gives the clearest account of a Molière whose genius is purely theatrical; for him, Molière's satire was essentially benign, good-humoured and of little consequence (pp. 360–62).
2. See *L'Impromptu de Versailles*, Sc. 4, in Molière, *Œuvres complétes* (2 vols), ed. G. Couton (Paris, 1971), I, pp. 687–8. This edition will be referred to throughout as *O.C.*
3. John Dennis (1657–1734). See *The Critical Works of John Dennis*, ed. E. N. Hooker (2 vols) (Baltimore, 1939, 1943), II, pp. 249–50.
4. This critical revolution began and was pursued with most vigour in Italy. The best account of it is in B. Weinberg, *A History of Literary Criticism in the Italian Renaissance* (2 vols) (Chicago, 1961). As pagination in the two volumes is continuous – I, pp. 1–634 and II, pp. 635–1184 – references to this work will give page numbers only.
5. Passages in Greek and Latin are usually quoted in the translations of the Loeb Classical Library. For Renaissance Latin and Italian texts, I use existing translations when these are readily available. Translations of other texts and all texts in French are my own.
6. Translated by Betty Radice (Penguin Classics, 1971), p. 148.

## CHAPTER ONE: Character

1. For a detailed study of theories of comedy before the Renaissance commentators on Aristotle entered the field, see Marvin T. Herrick, *Comic Theory in the Sixteenth Century* (Urbana, 1950), especially pp. 57–79.
2. Cf. Weinberg, pp. 401–2. Weinberg's monumental study of literary criticism in Renaissance Italy offers both a detailed analysis of the Aristotelian commentaries and extensive quotations from Renaissance texts which are not widely available.
3. *Explicatio eorum omnium quae ad Comoediae artificium pertinent* (1548), translated by Herrick and published in an appendix to his study of comic theory, pp. 227–39. This translation is also published in

*Theories of Comedy*, ed. Paul Lauter (New York, 1964), pp. 48–63; the passage quoted appears on p. 54. This useful anthology contains a section on the Italian Renaissance which collects key passages on comedy by Trissino, Robortello, Maggi, Minturno, Castelvetro and Riccoboni.

4. See Herrick, p. 132. Herrick's chapter 'The Conception of Comic Character in the Sixteenth Century', pp. 130–75, examines classical and Renaissance concepts of character in detail and in depth.

5. 'A Large Account of the Taste in Poetry, and the Causes of the Degeneracy of It', in *Critical Works*, I, pp. 279–95 (p. 284) (and in Lauter, pp. 215–38 [p. 222]).

6. .Erasmus, especially in the *Colloquies* (1519–33), where he used characters and dialogues to present moral questions, and *Praise of Folly* (1509), chapters 48–54, in which he characterized the various kinds of fool who were disciples of Folly, offered a particularly rich source of comic characters. Charron's *De la sagesse* (Bordeaux, 1601), which ran to many editions, was the most influential work of moral philosophy to be published in France in the first half of the seventeenth century; in it, he attempted to simplify and systematize Montaigne's ideas in order to teach men how to attain wisdom.

## CHAPTER TWO: Plot and Action I

1. See *L'Arte poetica* (1563). The section on comedy is collected in Lauter's anthology, pp. 74–86; the passage quoted is on p. 84.

2. See 'De ridiculis' (1550), in Lauter, pp. 64–73 (p. 69).

3. See *Il teatro comico* (1750), in Lauter, pp. 171–5 (p. 173).

4. See *The Comedies*, translated by Betty Radice (Penguin Classics, 1976), pp. 215–16.

5. According to La Grange, an actor in Molière's troupe, *L'Étourdi* was Molière's first comedy. See *O.C.*, I, p. 47 and note 1.

## CHAPTER THREE: Plot and Action II

1. The attribution to Molière of the early farces, *La Jalousie du Barbouillé* and *Le Médecin volant*, is uncertain. The manuscripts of the two plays are known to have been in the possession of J.B. Rousseau in 1731. Their subsequent history is told by Despois in Molière, *Œuvres* (13 vols), ed. Despois and Ménard, *Les Grands Écrivains de la France* (Paris, 1873–1900), I, pp. 10–14 (The *Grands Écrivains* edition is referred to in future references as *G.E.*) There is strong evidence, however, that the plays were by Molière. As Couton points out (*O.C.*, I, pp. 5–6), troupes of comic actors had

their own stock names for characters who reappeared in different plays: two of these, in Molière's troupe, were Gorgibus, who appears in *La Jalousie*, and Sganarelle, who plays the *valet* and doctor in *Le Médecin volant*. The close parallels between *La Jalousie* and the third act of *George Dandin* and between *Le Médecin volant* and other medical plays, especially *Le Médecin malgré lui*, also suggest that these farces were probably the work of Molière.

2. This kind of sober and amusing discussion of moral issues was unusual on the comic stage. An obvious precedent was the discussions between Demea and Micio in Terence's *Adelphi*, the major source for *L'École des maris*. Molière's comic imagination might also have been fed by the rich collection of short sketches by Erasmus in the *Colloquies*, written to instruct and amuse the reader.

## CHAPTER FOUR: Comedy and the Ridiculous

1. See the *Examen* of *Mélite*, Corneille's first comedy, produced in 1629 or 1630, in Corneille, *Writings on the Theatre* , ed. H.T. Barnwell (Oxford, 1965), pp. 80–83 (p. 80). The *Illusion comique* (1635) is the exception; Matamore, the braggart-soldier based on Plautus's Pyrgopolynices (*Miles gloriosus*), is a ridiculous figure, but he is a product of theatrical convention, not a satirical portrait.

2. Donatus was a Roman grammarian writing about the middle of the fourth century. See Lauter, pp. 27–32 (p. 27).

3. The relevant extract from *Nouvelles nouvelles* is published in Molière, *O.C.*, I, pp. 1015–23. The passages quoted are from p. 1019.

4. The French Renaissance theorist of laughter, Joubert (*Traité du ris*, 1579, pp. 86, 93), shared the view that events which caused real harm might stir compassion but could not inspire laughter. See M.A. Screech and Ruth Calder, 'Some Renaissance attitudes to laughter', in *Humanism in France* (Manchester, 1970), pp. 216–28 (pp. 221–2).

5. See the extract on comedy from *Poetica d'Aristotele vulgarizzata, et sposta* (1570), pp. 87–97 (p. 88).

6. Corneille's defence of *Le Menteur* appears in the dedicatory *Épître* (1645) of *La Suite du Menteur* (*Writings on the Theatre*, pp. 183–6).

7. Dryden's *Preface* is published in Lauter, pp. 194–205. The passages quoted are on pp. 200, 201–2.

8. The *Coislinian Tractate* is published in Lauter, pp. 21–3. Giraldi's remarks were made in his *Ragionamento in difesa di Terentio* (1566); see Weinberg, pp. 288–9.

9. G. Defaux, *Molière, ou les métamorphoses du comique: de la comédie morale au triomphe de la folie* (Lexington, Ky, 1980, pp. 97–127),

presents the considerable body of evidence from Molière's plays and writings on the theatre which shows that he saw the function of comedy as – at least in part – didactic. Defaux, however, concludes from this that Molière was an optimist who believed that it was possible to correct folly and cure vice (pp. 111, 119–21). I see Molière as more of a pessimist: he enjoyed exposing folly and vice, but there is little to suggest that he believed he or any other moralist could do much to put them right.

10. See *Le Tiers Livre*, ed. M.A. Screech (Geneva, 1964), X, 10–25, pp. 80–81.

11. See the chapter on the *Tiers Livre* in M.A. Screech, *Rabelais* (London, 1979), pp. 207–92, especially pp. 235–8, where Panurge's self-love is discussed. See also the useful comparisons of Chrysalde with Pantagruel and Frère Jean in Defaux, pp. 101–4, and of Arnolphe with Panurge in P.H. Nurse, *Molière and The Comic Spirit* (Geneva, 1991), pp. 74–5.

## CHAPTER FIVE: Reason and the Ridiculous

1. 'Des ouvrages de l'esprit', 68, in *Les Caractères*, ed. R. Pignarre (Paris, 1965), p. 100.

2. See P.H. Nurse (*Molière and The Comic Spirit*, pp. 69–76), who shows that Chrysalde's views on cuckoldry reflect a well-defined Stoic and humanist point of view.

3. Published in *O.C.*, I, pp. 1149–80.

4. See L.W.B. Brockliss, *French Higher Education in the Seventeenth and Eighteenth Centuries* (Oxford, 1987), p. 136 and note 79.

5. A useful and more detailed examination of the history of the golden mean and its role in Molière's plays may be found in Defaux, pp. 70–96.

6. Dennis's perceptive remarks on the reasons why the comic theatre in England had flourished in the Restoration could be applied to France in the time of Molière: 'There is among any people a good taste for comedy when a very considerable part of an audience are qualified to judge for themselves, and when they who are not qualified to judge for themselves are influenced by the authority of those who are rightly qualified' ('A Large Account of the Taste in Poetry', I, p. 289).

It was the learning and refined judgement of many of the people in his audiences which made it possible for Molière to compose and perform such profound and well-judged comedies.

CHAPTER SIX: Body and Soul

1. Jocelyn Powell, in 'Making faces: character and physiognomy in *L'École des femmes* and *L'Avare*' (*Seventeenth-Century French Studies*, 9, 1987, pp. 94–112), offers a fascinating account of the relationship between Cartesian physiology of the passions and the art of acting. He compares Descartes's *Passions de l'âme*, Le Brun's *Conférence sur l'expression* (1698) and Molière's practice in his acting.

2. La Bruyère's description here echoes the end of Erasmus's *Praise of Folly*, 67, where, in Platonic Christian terms, ecstasy is described as a foretaste of death: as the body's organs suspend their action, the soul breaks free from the body and lives, for a few moments, a transcendental life. See M.A. Screech, *Ecstasy and the Praise of Folly* (London, 1980), pp. 62–222 (especially pp. 75–83).

3. Jules Brody, *Du style à la pensée: trois études sur les Caractères de La Bruyère* (Lexington, 1980), in the second of the three essays, analyses in some detail the role of mechanistic language in the style and thought of La Bruyère.

4. Powell, pp. 99–106, gives a detailed technical analysis, with extensive quotations from Descartes's *Passions de l'âme*, of how Molière might have translated Arnolphe's passions into facial expressions.

CHAPTER SEVEN: *Honnêteté*

1. Page references are to La Rochefoucauld, *Maximes*, ed. J. Truchet (Paris, 1977). The *Réflexions diverses*, collected and published posthumously, are on pp. 109–47.

2. See C. Favre de Vaugelas, *Remarques sur la langue française* (Paris, 1647), pp. 476–8.

3. The numbers given refer to the order of the *Pensées* in L. Brunschvicg's edition (3 vols) (Paris, 1904). His numbering is followed by many subsequent editors. Editions using different numbering usually provide a concordance.

4. See *Œuvres complètes* (3 vols), ed. C. H. Boudhors (Paris, 1930), I, p. 11.

5. Page references are to the *Essais* (2 vols), ed. P. Villey and V.-L. Saulnier (Paris, 1978). Pagination throughout the two volumes is consecutive. The authoritative translation of the *Essais* – published since my work on the present study – is that by M. A. Screech (London, 1991).

6. See *Œuvres complètes*, ed. A. Adam and F. Escal (Paris, 1966), p. 246. In the same *Stances* Boileau hailed Molière as the equal of Terence, the highest of compliments in an age which valued the elegance, refinement and moral wisdom of Terence above the

vigour of Aristophanes and the verve and wit of Plautus. Later, in *L'Art poétique*, written between 1669 and 1674, Boileau alluded again to the learning behind Molière's portraits, calling them 'ses doctes peintures' (Chant III, l. 395, p. 178).

7. Voltaire, in *Le Siècle de Louis XIV* (2 vols), ed. A. Adam (Paris, 1966), II, p. 364, describes Molière as 'ce génie à la fois comique et philosophe, cet homme qui en son genre est si au-dessus de toute l'antiquité' ('this genius who is both comic poet and philospher, this man who in his genre [i.e. comedy] is so far above the whole of antiquity'). The passage from Balzac is from *Illusions perdues*, ed. P. Citron (Paris, 1966), p. 224.

## CHAPTER EIGHT: Judgement

1. Méré's writings are a record of such conversations, and one of his main aims is to suggest ways of perfecting the art of conversation. Many of his reflections were in dialogue form (*Les Conversations*, of which there are six, in *Œuvres complètes*, I, pp. 1–92); he also wrote an essay specifically on conversation: II, pp. 97–132. Questions of judgement and discernment are discussed in all his writings, throughout the three volumes of his collected work.

2. See Dennis, 'A Large Account of the Taste in Poetry', I, p. 292.

3. See G. Mongrédien, *Recueil des textes et des documents du XVII^e siècle relatifs à Molière* (2 vols) (Paris, 1965), II, p. 796.

4. Ruth Calder, in 'Montaigne as satirist', *The Sixteenth-Century Journal*, 17, 2 (1986), pp. 225–35, has shown that Montaigne viewed himself as a Horatian satirist whose first duty was to satirize himself.

5. See M.A. Screech, *Rabelais*, pp. 235–6.

6. Montaigne explains that the true gentleman should prefer to lose at chess because it was unfitting for him to be seen to be too proficient at activities of no importance.

7. M.A. Screech and Ruth Calder, in 'Some Renaissance attitudes to laughter', pp. 218–20, trace the history of the view that laughter is the property of man.

## CHAPTER NINE: Sociability, Reason and Laughter

1. Montaigne, *Essais*, I, 30, 'De la modération', p. 197, quotes the same passage from Romans 12: 3 as Philinte: 'Do not be more wise than you ought, but be wise with sobriety'. Montaigne based his reading of this text on the *Vulgate*, not on the Greek, which is concerned with making a sober estimate of one's own importance.

CHAPTER TEN: Families

1. Montaigne, *Essais*, II, 8, 'De l'affection des pères aux enfans', discusses the problems of paternal avarice. He blames avaricious fathers for driving their sons to crime in order to find the money they need to live on (pp. 387–8). He also criticizes the kind of father who leaves his fortune to a widow who might well outlive his children, so starving them of money for their entire lives (p. 396). Through Cléante and his gambling and dealings with money-lenders, and Harpagon's plan to marry a wife the same age as his children, Molière reminds his audience in passing of some of the problems discussed in more detail by Montaigne.
2. For a more detailed discussion of the structural parallels and juxtapositions within the play, see G.J. Mallinson, *Molière: L'Avare* (London, 1988), pp. 63–71.

CHAPTER ELEVEN: Aristotelian Pendants

1. The scenes in which pedants appear are *La Jalousie du Barbouillé* (date unknown), 2, 6 and 13; *Dépit amoureux* (1656), II, 6; *Le Mariage forcé* (1664), 4; and *Le Bourgeois Gentilhomme* (1670), II, 3 and 4.
2. See Molière, *O.C.* I, pp. 3–7. A.J. Guibert has published a text, *Le Docteur amoureux. Comédie du XVIIᵉ siècle* (Geneva, 1960), which he suggests might be the missing Molière farce of that title; the attribution is doubtful (see Couton in *O.C.*, I, pp. 6–7).
3. M. Lazard, *Le Théâtre en France au XVIᵉ siècle* (Paris, 1980), p. 75, suggests that, although cruel at times, the satirical elements in farce had lost all polemical value.
4. See the notes on the text in Molière, *G.E.*, I, pp. 444–52.
5. The content of the curriculum is analysed in detail in Brockliss. For the importance of Thomism, see especially pp. 208–14.
6. Montaigne's criticisms of scholastic teaching and argument are found particularly in *Essais*, I, 25, 'Du Pedantisme', pp. 133–44; I, 26, 'De l'institution des enfans', pp. 145–77; and III, 8, 'De l'art de conférer', pp. 921–43.
7. *Œuvres et Lettres*, ed. A. Bridoux (Paris, 1953), pp. 125–79, p. 129.
8. Perhaps the most comprehensive attack was made by Gassendi in *Exercitationum paradoxicarum adversus Aristoteleos* (Grenoble, 1624).
9. In the 1682 *Préface* to Molière's works, La Grange made much of Molière's academic success at the Collège de Clermont (*O.C.*, I, pp. 996–1002). Molière's familiarity with some of the technical minutiae of scholastic analysis and terminology is confirmed by

the detailed textual annotation of Despois and Mesnard; see, for example, the notes on Pancrace's dialogue in *Le Mariage forcé*, Sc. 4, in *G.E.* IV, pp. 30–46, especially p. 41, n. 3.

10. See *G.E.*, IV, p. 35, n. 3c.

11. The documents connected with the dispute are published in Pascal, *Œuvres complètes* (2 vols), ed. J. Mesnard (Bruges, 1964, 1970), II. They include: two letters from Noël to Pascal, with Pascal's answer to the first of them (October–November 1647), pp. 509–40; a letter from Pascal to Le Pailleur answering points raised in Noël's second letter and explaining why he had not sent an answer to Noël directly (February 1648), pp. 556–76; and a letter which Pascal's father wrote to Noël, at his son's request, complaining that the rector had sought to discredit Pascal by ridiculing his experiments (April 1648), pp. 586–602.

12. Brockliss, pp. 348–50, discusses other hypotheses advanced by Aristotelians seeking to explain away the space above the column of mercury.

13. In *Œuvres complètes*, pp. 327–30. For Boileau's comments on the *Arrest*, see note, p. 1066.

CHAPTER TWELVE: Medicine

1. See Andrew Wear, 'Aspects of seventeenth-century French medicine', in *Newsletter of the Society for Seventeenth-Century French Studies*, 4, 1982, pp. 118–32, especially pp. 120–24.

2. See *G.E.*, IX, pp. 577–8. Molière wrote a sonnet and a letter to La Mothe Le Vayer, consoling him for the death of his son, published in *O.C.*, II, p. 1184, and *G.E.*, IX, pp. 577–80.

3. Montaigne's views on medicine are contained in *Essais*, II, 37, 'De la ressemblance des enfans aux pères', especially pp. 765–82, and III, 13, 'De l'expérience', pp. 1079, 1087–92.

4. For a discussion of the possible models for Molière's doctors in *L'Amour médecin*, see Despois and Mesnard's introduction and notes in *G.E.*, V, pp. 268–76. The evidence for the use of masks appeared in contemporary letters, quoted by Couton, in *O.C.*, II, pp. 1320–21, note 2.

5. See Wear, p. 118, who, writing as an impartial historian, shares Molière's view, pointing out that 'antimony (the chemical remedy of the 'moderns') could kill just as much as bleeding (the treatment of the 'ancients')'.

6. See Montaigne, p. 780. In another chapter, I, 32, 'Qu'il faut sobrement se mesler de juger des ordonnances divines', Montaigne groups 'alchemists, soothsayers, astrologers, palmists and doctors'

together as charlatans whose claims have no foundation in reality (p. 215).

7. There is a double irony in this stanza. As well as mocking doctors for their vanity, Molière is reminding us that once a man becomes a doctor, he loses his status as a man – a process illustrated earlier in *Le Malade imaginaire* through the portrait of the halfwitted, dehumanized and mechanical figure of Thomas Diafoirus, reciting his memorized compliments and proposing to celebrate his engagement by taking his young mistress out to a dissection.

## CHAPTER THIRTEEN: Preciosity

1. Two of Mlle de Scudéry's novels, *Le Grand Cyrus* (10 vols: 1649–53) and *Clélie* (10 vols: 1654–60), tender and heroic romances in which contemporary figures appear disguised as ancient Persians or Romans, are mentioned in Magdelon's speeches about precious love (Sc. 4).

2. Chrysalde's exact words are:

> Oui, mon corps est moi-même, et j'en veux prendre soin.
> Guenille si l'on veut, ma guenille m'est chère.

3. See Montaigne, *Essais*, III, 13, 'De l'expérience': 'They wish to go outside themselves and escape from being a man. This is madness – instead of acquiring the form of an angel, they acquire the form of a beast; instead of raising themselves higher, they plunge down' (p. 1115). For a full exploration of the theme of body and soul in the *Essais*, see M.A. Screech, *Montaigne and Melancholy* (London, 1983), *passim*, especially pp. 114–19.

4. The *abbé* Charles Cotin (1604–82), writer, poet, polemicist, and a well-known figure in the *salons* of the period, was a frequent target of Boileau in his *Satires* (Molière alludes to this in *Les Femmes savantes*, ll. 1026–40). Cotin answered Boileau with venomous satires of his own, published anonymously and without date: *La Critique désintéressée sur les satires du temps* (1667?) and *La Satire des satires*, in which he attacked Boileau and Molière. He is alleged to have quarrelled with Molière in the mid 1660s (see *G.E.*, IX, p. 13). Among other possible reasons for Cotin's resentment of Molière – his portraits of precious circles, his satire of the Jesuits and their allies in *Le Tartuffe* (1664) – is the playwright's mockery of Cotin's facile rationalism in *Dom Juan* (See below, Chapter 15, 6).

5. On Gilles Ménage (1613–92), another *salon habitué*, who quarrelled with Cotin and others, see *G.E.*, IX, pp. 16–22.

6. See *G.E.*, IX, pp. 22–4.

Molière

CHAPTER FOURTEEN: *Le Tartuffe*

1. Dorine comments upon Monsieur Loyal's appearance and behaviour with a pun: 'Ce Monsieur Loyal porte un air bien déloyal!' (l. 1772). This is an allusion to the stock polemical allegation that the Jesuits treated their host countries, especially France, with ingratitude and disloyalty. The accusation appeared in similar punning terms in a collection of anti-Jesuit rhymes, *L'Ave Maria des Jesuites* (1611), in which Ignatius himself was accused of disloyalty to his own king: 'Ignace a faict leur loy, / Qui desloyal trahit sa patrie et son Roy' (British Library: 860.d.6.). For more parallels between *Le Tartuffe* and seventeenth-century French anti-Jesuit pamphlets, see my article 'Molière, *Le Tartuffe* and anti-Jesuit propaganda', in *Zeitschrift für Religions-und Geistesgeschichte*, 28 (1976), pp. 303–23.
2. Molière made it clear in the *Second Placet* (1667), however, that he had given a general clerical appearance to Tartuffe in the earliest three-act version of the play, and that he had taken care in his later revision of the production to give him the appearance of a man of the world (*O.C.*, I, pp. 891–3). This clerical apparel, taken together with the obvious anti-Jesuit elements in the play, might well have encouraged some to see the first Tartuffe as a Jesuit.

   For a history of the successes of the Jesuits in France in their early years, see H. Fouqueray, *Histoire de la Compagnie de Jésus en France des origines à la suppression* (Paris, 1910–23). Rapin (1621–87) was a prolific author, a leading man of letters and a polished society figure. Bourdaloue (1632–1704) was France's leading preacher in the later years of the century. Petau (1583–1672) was an outstanding Greek and Latin scholar. For an appreciation of Petau's achievements, see M. Fumaroli, *L'Age de l'éloquence* (Geneva, 1980), pp. 392–407.
3. Fumaroli, pp. 233–56, describes the background to what he calls this 'inlassable guerre de pamphlets' between the Jesuits and their opponents (p. 235). He points out, too, that the history of this polemical war has yet to be written (p. 235, note 7).
4. For polemical attacks on Jesuits and Jesuit casuistry before and after the death of Henry IV, see Roland Mousnier, *The Assassination of Henry IV* (London, 1973), originally published as *L'Assassinat d'Henri IV* (Paris, 1964), especially pp. 213–28. One of the conditions on which Henry permitted their return was that a leading French Jesuit would always be available at court to answer directly to the King for the behaviour of the Society's members everywhere in France. The Jesuits quickly turned this condition to their own advantage by establishing an assumption that the senior Jesuit at court would also be confessor to the King. See Fumaroli, pp. 237–40.

5. All page references are to *Les Lettres provinciales*, ed. H. F. Stewart (Manchester, 1920, reprinted 1951).
6. Pascal's list of names was carefully selected to exploit French xenophobia, especially their dislike of the Spanish.
7. It is at this point in the most blasphemous of Tartuffe's speeches that Molière added his celebrated stage direction: 'C'est un scélérat qui parle' ('This is a scoundrel speaking').
8. All page references are to the 2nd edition of *Les Peintures morales* (2 vols: Paris, 1645). For an assessment of Le Moyne's efforts to write spiritually edifying literature in a florid and worldly style, see Richard Maber, 'Spiritualité et mondanité chez le Père Le Moyne', in *Les Jésuites parmi les hommes aux XVIᵉ et XVIIᵉ siècles*, ed. G. and G. Demerson, B. Dompnier and A. Regond (Clermont-Ferrand, 1987), pp. 163–71.
9. This poem was published by L.A. Ménard as *Le Livre abominable* (2 vols: Paris, 1883). The lines quoted appear in I, p. 43. For a full analysis of this text and its historical background, see the unpublished doctoral thesis of Fortunée Marcus, 'A study of the major themes in *L'Innocence persécutée* (*c.* 1665), a manuscript first published in 1883 under the title of *Le Livre abominable*' (University of London, 1985). See also Toni Marcus, '"L'Innocence persécutée" (*c.* 1665): one polemicist's perception of contemporary politics', in *Seventeenth-Century French Studies*, 13 (1991), pp. 71–89.
10. This attack was made by the *curé* of Saint-Barthélemy, Pierre Roullé, in a pamphlet entitled *Le Roi glorieux au monde ou Louis XIV le plus glorieux de tous les rois du monde* (1664). The pages in which Roullé attacks Molière are published in Molière, *O. C.*, I, pp. 1143–4. Roullé was not a Jesuit, but he praised the Jesuits extravagantly in this pamphlet and urged the King to listen to their advice.
11. On Louis XIV's quarrel with the Pope, see Ch. Gérin, *Louis XIV et le Saint-Siège* (2 vols: Paris, 1894); and Ch. de Moüy, *Louis XIV et le Saint-Siège. L'Ambassade du Duc de Créqui, 1662–1665* (2 vols: Paris, 1893). There is another connection between the King, his Ambassador to the Pope and Molière, which dates from the months just before the first performance of *Le Tartuffe*, when Molière was writing the play. When Molière's son Louis was born, the King chose to demonstrate his support for his favourite playwright by agreeing to be godfather to the child. At the baptism on 28 February 1664, the King was represented by the Duc de Créqui. Clearly, Molière was in a good position to follow the progress of the quarrel.

CHAPTER FIFTEEN: *Dom Juan* and 'the hidden God'

1. See M.A. Screech, *Montaigne and Melancholy*, pp. 46–50: Adrien Tournebus told Montaigne that Sebond's book was the 'quintessence of Aquinas' (II, 12, p. 440) (p. 45); in fact it owes at least as much to Raymond Lull (p. 15).
2. See *Montaigne and Melancholy*, especially pp. 3–4. For an account of Renaissance scepticism, see Richard H. Popkin, *The History of Scepticism from Erasmus to Descartes*, revised edition (New York, 1964).
3. P.O. Kristeller, in 'The myth of Renaissance atheism and the French tradition of free thought', *Journal of the History of Philosophy*, 6 (1968), pp. 233–44 (also published as 'Le mythe de l'athéisme de la Renaissance et la tradition française de la libre pensée', *Bibliothèque d'Humanisme et Renaissance*, 37 [1975], pp. 337–48), shows how Pintard and others, hunting for the origins of atheism in the writings of late Renaissance Italian philosophers and the so-called *libertins* of early seventeenth-century France, have misunderstood or distorted the meanings of the original texts from which they quote. See also P.O. Kristeller, 'Between the Italian Renaissance and the French Enlightenment: Gabriel Naudé as an editor', *Renaissance Quarterly*, 32 (1979), pp. 41–72, especially pp. 42–3.
4. Dorimon's text, together with those of De Villiers and Cigognini (no date), is published in Gendarme de Bévotte, *Le Festin de Pierre avant Molière* (Paris, 1907).
5. This edition has been reprinted by Gregg International Publishers (Geneva, 1971).
6. See, for example, François Ogier, *Jugement et censure du livre de la Doctrine curieuse* (Paris, 1623), and Jean Duvergier de Hauranne (better known as Saint-Cyran), *La Somme des fautes et faussetés capitales contenues en la 'Somme théologique' du P. François Garasse* (2 vols: Paris, 1626); both authors accuse Garasse of calumny against Charron. Fumaroli (pp. 329–34) analyses Ogier's *Jugement*, presenting it as one of the earliest masterpieces of classical literary criticism. It is interesting to find Saint-Cyran, one of the founders of the Port-Royal movement, among the first to spring to the defence of Charron and his blend of philosophical scepticism and fideism.
7. All page references to Charron's *De la sagesse* and to his *Petit Traicté de sagesse* (a résumé and a defence of the longer work) are to the 1613 Paris edition, which contains material added by Charron to answer criticisms of the 1601 edition; the *Petit Traicté* follows the main text and has separate pagination.
8. Ambassador was a title normally given to St. Paul. Here, Charron appears to be referring to Christ.

9. Charron gives his own summary of his advice to the wise man in *De la sagesse*, II, 1–4, pp. 312–80.
10. In the British Library copy of the 1613 edition, pp. 14–15 occur twice. The passage quoted appears on the second p. 15.
11. Published in *Discours Chrestiens de la divinité, création, rédemption et octaves du Sainct Sacrement* (Paris, 1604), pp. 1–35.
12. See M. Mersenne, *L'Impiété des déistes, athées et libertins de ce temps* (Paris, 1624); Ch. Cotin, *Discours à Théopompe, sur les forts esprits du temps* (n.p., 1629).
13. Fumaroli describes the Jesuit rhetoric of 'peintures parlantes' on pp. 257–391, 673–85.
14. Charron's quotation is from Persius and occurs in Erasmus's *Adages* and Montaigne's *Essais*. See Ruth Calder, 'Montaigne as satirist', pp. 228–30.
15. *Discours de la méthode* (1637), Part I, p. 129.
16. Robert McBride, *The Sceptical Vision of Molière*, pp. 79–106, draws telling parallels between the sceptical views of La Mothe Le Vayer and those of Molière in *Dom Juan*. He has shown (especially on pp. 95–101) how many of the events in this play were invented and handled in such a way as to present a sceptical vision of the world.
17. See, for example, *Règles de la Compagnie de Jésus* (Paris, 1610), pp. 61–4.

## CHAPTER SIXTEEN: Molière's Philosophy

1. The common ground Molière shared with his contemporary and friend the sceptic La Mothe Le Vayer, both admirers of Montaigne, has been richly explored by R. McBride in *The Sceptical Vision of Molière*, passim.

## CHRONOLOGY

1. All the statistics I give for recorded performances are for this period. Even with the help of La Grange's *Registre*, we cannot be sure of the exact number of times each play was performed. It should be remembered, too, that the numbers for later plays tend to be lower because there was less time for Molière to revive them. *Les Fourberies de Scapin*, for example, performed only 18 times in Molière's lifetime, had another 197 performances between 1673 and 1715 (*O.C.*, II, p. 891). I have used the table compiled by W.D. Howarth, *Molière. A Playwright and his Audience* (Cambridge, 1982), Appendix III, pp. 311–15, where all the known performances by Molière and his troupe, of plays by Molière and by other playwrights, are listed.

# Bibliography

## 1. Texts

The best edition of Molière's complete works remains the *Œuvres*, ed. Despois et Mesnard, *Grands Écrivains de la France* (13 vols) (Paris, 1873–1900).

The best recent edition is the *Œuvres complètes*, ed. G. Couton, *Bibliothèque de la Pléiade* (2 vols) (Paris, 1971).

## 2. Bibliographies and documents

Guibert, A.J., *Bibliographie des œuvres de Molière publiées au XVII^e^ siècle* (Paris, 1961, reprinted with supplements 1977)

Jurgens, M. and Maxfield-Miller, E., *Cent ans de recherches sur Molière, sur sa famille et sur les comédiens de sa troupe* (Paris, 1963)

La Grange, *Le Registre de La Grange, 1659–85* (2 vols), ed. B.E. and G.P. Young (Paris, 1947)

Mongrédien, G., *Recueil des textes et des documents du XVII^e^ siècle relatifs à Molière* (2 vols) (Paris, 1965)

Romero, L., *Molière: traditions in criticism, 1900–1970* (Chapel Hill, NC, 1974)

Saintonge, P., 'Thirty years of Molière studies, 1942–1971', in *Molière and the Commonwealth of Letters*, ed. R. Johnson *et al.* (Jackson, MS, 1975)

Saintonge, P. and R.W. Christ, *Fifty Years of Molière Studies: A Bibliography, 1892–1941* (Baltimore, MD, 1942)

## 3. General

Adam, A., *Histoire de la littérature française au XVII^e^ siècle* (5 vols) (Paris, 1948–56)

Allier. R., *La Cabale des dévots* (Paris, 1902)

Anon., *L'Innocence persécutée* (1665?), a handwritten manuscript in the *Bibliothèque de l'Arsenal*, published by L.-A. Ménard under the title *Le Livre abominable* (Paris, 1883)

Auerbach, E., *Mimesis*, transl. W. Trask (Princeton, NJ, 1953)

Baader, R. (ed.), *Molière* (Darmstadt, 1980)

Bénichou, P., *Morales du grand siècle* (Paris, 1948)

Bergson, H., *Le Rire* (Paris, 1940), first published in *Revue de Paris*, 1899; for an English translation, see *Comedy*, ed. W. Sypher (New York, 1956, republished Baltimore, MD, 1980)

Boileau, N., *Œuvres complètes*, ed. A. Adam and F. Escal (Paris, 1966)

Bray, R., *Molière, homme de théâtre* (Paris, 1954)

Brockliss, L.W.B., *French Higher Education in the Seventeenth and Eighteenth Centuries* (Oxford, 1987)

Brody, J., 'Esthétique et société chez Molière' , in *Dramaturgie et Société*, ed. J. Jacquot (2 vols) (Paris, 1968), I, pp. 307–26, republished in *Molière*, ed. Baader, pp. 201–31

Brody, J., '*Dom Juan* and *Le Misanthrope*, or The Esthetics of individualism', *P.M.L.A.*, 84 (1969), pp. 559–76

Brody, J., *Du style à la pensée: trois études sur les Caractères de La Bruyère* (Lexington, KY, 1980)

Cairncross, J., *Molière, bourgeois et libertin* (Paris, 1963)

Calder, A., 'Molière, *Le Tartuffe* and anti-Jesuit propaganda', *Zeitschrift für Religions-und Geistesgeschichte*, 28 (1976), pp. 303–23

Calder, A., 'Attitudes to belief in Dorimon's *Festin de Pierre* and Molière's *Dom Juan*', *Seventeenth-Century French Studies*, 8 (1986), pp. 101–14

Calder, A., 'Dramaturgie et polémique dans *Le Tartuffe* de Molière', in *Les Jésuites parmi les hommes* (Clermont-Ferrand, 1987), pp. 235–43

Calder, A., 'Molière, Plautus, Terence and Renaissance theories of comedy', *New Comparison*, 3 (1987), pp. 19–32

Calder, A., 'Molière's Aristotelian pedants', *Seventeenth-Century French Studies*, 12 (1990), pp. 65–75

Calder, R., 'Montaigne as satirist', *The Sixteenth-Century Journal*, 17, 2 (1986), pp. 225–35

Castelvetro, L., *Poetica d'Aristotele vulgarizzata, et sposta* (Basle, 1570)

Cave, T., *Recognitions* (Oxford, 1988)

Charron, P., *Les Trois Vérités* (Bordeaux, 1593)

Charron, P., *De la sagesse* (Bordeaux, 1601, revised 1613)

Charron, P., *Discours chrestiens de la divinité, création et rédemption* (Paris, 1604)

Corneille, P., *Writings on the Theatre*, ed. H.T. Barnwell (Oxford, 1965)

Corrigan, R.W. (ed.), *Comedy: Meaning and Form*, 2nd edn (New York, 1981)

Cotin, Ch., *Discours à Théopompe, sur les forts esprits du temps* (n.p., 1629)

Cotin, Ch., *Théoclée ou La Vraye Philosophie des principes du monde* (Paris, 1646)

Defaux, G., *Molière, ou les métamorphoses du comique: de la comédie morale au triomphe de la folie* (Lexington, KY, 1980)

Demerson, G. and G., Dompnier, B., and Regond, A. (eds), *Les Jésuites parmi les hommes aux XVIᵉ et XVIIᵉ siècles* (Clermont-Ferrand, 1987)

Dennis, J., *Critical Works*, ed. E.N. Hooker (2 vols) (Baltimore, MD: I, 1939, II, 1943)

Descartes, R., *Œuvres et Lettres*, ed. A. Bridoux (Paris, 1953)

Descotes, M., *Les Grands Rôles du théâtre de Molière* (Paris, 1960)

Descotes, M., *Molière et sa fortune littéraire* (Bordeaux, 1970)

Duvergier de Hauranne, J. [Saint-Cyran], *La Somme des fautes et faussetés capitales contenues en la 'Somme théologique' du P. François Garasse*(2 vols) (Paris, 1626)

Emelina, J., *Les Valets et les servantes dans le théâtre comique en France de 1610 à 1700* (Grenoble, 1975)

Erasmus, D., *Opera omnia*, ed. J. Leclerc (10 vols) Leiden, 1703–6

Erasmus, D., *Praise of Folly*, transl. B. Radice; intro. and notes A. H. T. Levi (Harmondsworth, 1971)

Erasmus, D., *The Colloquies*, transl. C. R. Thompson (Chicago/London, 1965)

Favre de Vaugelas, C., *Remarques sur la langue française* (Paris, 1647)

Fernandez, R., *La Vie de Molière* (Paris, 1929); reprinted as *Molière ou l'essence du génie comique* (Paris, 1979)

Fouqueray, H., *Histoire de la Compagnie de Jésus en France des origines à la suppression* (Paris, 1910–23)

Fumaroli, M., *L'Age de l'éloquence* (Geneva, 1980)

Garasse, F., *Doctrine curieuse des beaux esprits* (2 vols) (Paris, 1623)

Gassendi, P., *Exercitationum paradoxicarum adversus Aristoteleos* (Grenoble, 1624)

Gendarme de Bévotte, G., *Le Festin de Pierre avant Molière* (Paris, 1907)

Gérin, Ch., *Louis XIV et le Saint-Siège* (2 vols) (Paris, 1894)

Gossman, L., *Men and Masks. A Study of Molière* (Baltimore, MD, 1963)

Gross, N., *From Gesture to Idea: Esthetics and Ethics in Molière's Comedy* (New York, 1982)

Guicharnaud, J., *Molière, une aventure théâtrale* (Paris, 1963)

Guichemerre, R., *La Comédie avant Molière, 1640–1660* (Paris, 1972)

Gutwirth, M., *Molière ou l'invention comique* (Paris, 1966)

Hall, H.G., *Comedy in Context: Essays on Molière* (Jackson, MS, 1984)

Herrick, M.T., *Comic Theory in the Sixteenth Century* (Urbana, IL, 1950)

Howarth, W.D., (ed.), *Comic Drama: The European Heritage* (London, 1978)

Howarth, W.D., *Molière: A Playwright and his Audience* (Cambridge, 1982)

Hubert, J.D., *Molière and the Comedy of Intellect* (Berkeley, CA, 1962)

Hunter, R.L., *The New Comedy of Greece and Rome* (Cambridge, 1985)

Ignatius of Loyola, *Règles de la Compagnie de Jésus* (Paris, 1610)

Janko, R., *Aristotle on Comedy* (London, 1984)

Jarrige, P., *Les Jesuistes mis sur l'eschafaut* (n.p., 1648)

Jasinski, R., *Molière et Le Misanthrope* (Paris, 1951)

Joubert, L., *Traité du ris* (Paris, 1579)

Knutson, H., *Molière: An Archetypal Approach* (Toronto, 1976)

Kristeller, P.O., 'The myth of Renaissance atheism and the French tradition of free thought', *Journal of the History of Philosophy*, 6 (1968), pp. 233–44

Kristeller, P.O., 'Between the Italian Renaissance and the French Enlightenment: Gabriel Naudé as an editor', *Renaissance Quarterly*, 32 (1979), pp. 41–72

La Bruyère, J. de, *Les Caractères*, ed. R. Pignarre (Paris, 1965)

Lancaster, H.C., *A History of French Dramatic Literature in the Seventeenth Century* (9 vols) (Baltimore, MD, 1929–42)

Lanson, G., 'Molière et la farce', *Revue de Paris* (1901), pp. 129–53

La Rochefoucauld, F. de, *Maximes*, ed. J. Truchet (Paris, 1977)

Lauter, P. (ed.), *Theories of Comedy* (New York, 1964)

Lawrence, F.L., *Molière: the Comedy of Unreason* (New Orleans, LA, 1968)

Lazard, M., *Le Théâtre en France au XVIᵉ siècle* (Paris, 1980)

Le Moyne, P., *Peintures morales* (2 vols) (Paris, 1645)

McBride, R., *The Sceptical Vision of Molière* (London, 1977)

McBride, R., *Aspects of Seventeenth-Century French Drama and Thought* (London, 1979)

Maggi, V., 'De ridiculis', in *In Aristotelis librum de poetica communes explanationes* (Venice, 1550)

Mallinson, G.J., *Molière: L'Avare* (London, 1988)

Marcus, F.,'A Study of the major themes in *L'Innocence persécutée* (*c*. 1665), a manuscript first published in 1883 under the title of *Le Livre abominable*' (University of London Ph. D. thesis, 1985)

Marcus, F., '"L'Innocence persécutée" (*c*. 1665): one polemicist's perception of contemporary politics', *Seventeenth-Century French Studies*, 13 (1991), pp. 71–89

Méré, Chevalier de, *Œuvres complètes*, ed. C.H. Boudhors (3 vols) (Paris, 1930)

Meredith, G., 'An Essay on Comedy' (1877), published in *Comedy*, ed. W. Sypher (New York, 1956, republished Baltimore, MD, 1980)

Mersenne, M., *L'Impiété des déistes, athées et libertins de ce temps* (Paris, 1624)

Michaut, G., *La Jeunesse de Molière, Les Débuts de Molière à Paris, Les Luttes de Molière* (Paris, 1922–5)

Minturno, A., *L'Arte poetica* (1563)

Montaigne, M. de, *Essais* (1588), ed. P. Villey and V.-L. Saulnier (2 vols) (Paris, 1965)

Moore, W.G., *Molière: A New Criticism* (Oxford, 1949)

Mousnier, R., *The Assassination of Henry IV* (London, 1973)

Moüy, Ch. de, *Louis XIV et le Saint-Siège. L'Ambassade du Duc de Créqui, 1662–65* (2 vols) (Paris, 1893)

Nurse, P.H., *Molière and the Comic Spirit* (Geneva, 1991)

Ogier, F., *Jugement et censure du livre de la Doctrine curieuse* (Paris, 1623)

Pascal, B., *Pensées*, ed. L. Brunschvicg (3 vols) (Paris, 1904)

Pascal, B., *Les Lettres provinciales*, ed. H.F. Stewart (Manchester, 1920; repr. 1951)

Pascal, B., *Œuvres complètes*, ed. J. Mesnard (2 vols) (Bruges, 1964, 1970) (only the first 2 volumes have been published)

Pintard, R., *Le Libertinage érudit dans la première moitié du XVIIᵉ siècle* (2 vols) (Paris, 1943)

Popkin, R.H., *The History of Scepticism from Erasmus to Descartes* (revised edn, New York, 1964)

Powell, J., 'Making faces: character and physiognomy in *L'École des femmes* and *L'Avare*', *Seventeenth-Century French Studies*, 9 (1987), pp. 94–112

Rabelais, F., *Le Tiers Livre*, ed. M.A. Screech (Geneva, 1964)

Rapin, R., *Réflexions sur la Poétique d'Aristote* (Paris, 1674)

Robortello, F., *In librum Aristotelis de arte poetica explicationes* (Florence, 1548)

Robortello, F., *Explicatio eorum omnium, quae ad comoediae artificium pertinent* (Florence, 1548)

Sainte-Beuve, C.-A., *Port-Royal*, ed. M. Leroy (3 vols) (Paris, 1953–5)

Scherer, J., *La Dramaturgie classique en France* (Paris, 1959)

Scherer, J., *Structures de Tartuffe* (2nd edn.) (Paris, 1974)

Scherer, J., *Sur le Dom Juan de Molière*, (Paris, 1967)

Screech, M.A., *Rabelais* (London, 1979)

Screech, M. A., *Ecstasy and the Praise of Folly* (London, 1980)

Screech, M. A., *Montaigne and Melancholy* (London, 1983)

Screech, M.A. and Calder, R., 'Some Renaissance attitudes to laughter', in *Humanism in France* (Manchester, 1970)

Trissino, G.G., *La Poetica* (2 vols) (Venice, 1529–62)

Voltaire, *Le Siècle de Louis XIV*, ed. A. Adam (Paris, 1966)

Wear, A., 'Aspects of seventeenth-century French medicine', *Newsletter of the Society for Seventeenth-Century French Studies*, 4 (1982), pp. 118–32

Weinberg, B., *A History of Literary Criticism in the Italian Renaissance* (2 vols) (Chicago, 1961)

Zaorowski, J.(?), *Advis secrets de la Société de Jésus* (Paderborne, 1661), a French translation of *Monita secreta* (1612)

# Index